All in the Family

All *in the* *Family*

A Practical Guide to Successful Multigenerational Living

SHARON GRAHAM NIEDERHAUS
and
JOHN L. GRAHAM

TAYLOR TRADE PUBLISHING
Lanham • New York • Boulder • Toronto • Plymouth, UK

Published by Taylor Trade Publishing
An imprint of The Rowman & Littlefield Publishing Group, Inc.
4501 Forbes Boulevard, Suite 200, Lanham, Maryland 20706
www.rowman.com

10 Thornbury Road, Plymouth PL6 7PP, United Kingdom

Distributed by National Book Network

British Library Cataloguing in Publication Information Available

Library of Congress Cataloging-in-Publication Data

Niederhaus, Sharon Graham, 1942–
    All in the family : a practical guide to successful multigenerational living / Sharon Graham Niederhaus and John L. Graham.
        pages   cm
    Includes bibliographical references and index.
    ISBN 978-1-58979-802-1 (pbk. : alk. paper) — ISBN 978-1-58979-803-8 (electronic)
    1. Extended families.   2. Intergenerational relations.   3. Families.   I. Graham, John L.   II. Title.
    HQ519.N537   2013
    306.85'7—dc23

                                                                    2012045021

⊚™ The paper used in this publication meets the minimum requirements of American National Standard for Information Sciences—Permanence of Paper for Printed Library Materials, ANSI/NISO Z39.48-1992.

Printed in the United States of America

Contents

PART IV
The Challenges

P A R T

Seeing Your Future

Dodging the Nursing Home

Age is not a particularly interesting subject. Anyone can get old. All you have to do is live long enough.

—GROUCHO MARX

THIS IS A BOOK about families—in particular, families that are taking inventive approaches to coping with the stresses of our changing society. Our focus in this introductory chapter is on how families manage the deteriorating health of a member. Some families handle things well and some don't. Our first story concerns our own family and the difficult death of our wonderful brother Steve in 1998. He was only forty-five.

Our Family

We became a family of seven back in 1959. That's when our youngest brother, Bill, was born. The firstborn of our folks, John and Charlotte, was Sharon in 1942, then came Mary Ellen in 1943, Johnny in 1947, Steve in 1953, and Bill. Our parents loved all of us. But with each birth, John and Charlotte had to move to a bigger house. Our dad was a lingerie salesman. He covered the western states for Warnaco and he traveled a lot. Mom stayed at home and managed the five of us. She did the homemaking kinds of things wives did in her generation.

3

Dad retired at age sixty-four. He got off the road and onto the golf course. He loved the grandkids and finally had time to spend with them. Mom loved them too, but after five kids of her own, she was a bit iffy about having them around a lot. All this is pretty normal we suppose. In fact, so was our dad's relatively sudden death in December of 1983. So many of his generation have lasted just a year or two past retirement. Mom died just nine months later, also common for her generation. She really missed Dad.

The deaths of our parents were tough on us all. They were very young—sixty-seven and sixty-nine. We miss them so much. But they were relatively healthy before their deaths. The five of us kids had no long parental illnesses to handle. Dad died within a month of his diagnosis of cancer, and Mom died suddenly one August night, just after meeting her new grandson, nicknamed "Jack" for her husband.

Our family travail was the illness, long-term care, and premature death of our brother Steve. In 1970 he experienced a seizure. At the time the doctors could not diagnose his problem. His case became the subject of seminars at both the Stanford and the University of California, San Francisco hospitals. It wasn't epilepsy; they were fairly sure of that. There weren't brain scans and MRIs to help them out back then, just fuzzy X-rays and a series of symptoms. Steve took all this uncertainty pretty well. Our parents worried about him deeply. But Steve had inherited a double dose of our father's sense of humor. He often quoted Groucho Marx, and his own jokes got him through much of the inconvenience of his affliction, whatever it was. Indeed, it's too bad Steve couldn't have made it to old age as Groucho recommended at the beginning of the chapter!

Steve attended the Gemological Institute of America and ultimately became the manager of a very nice jewelry store in Palo Alto. Like our dad he was a great salesman—all his customers adored him. The women in our family all loved having a jeweler in the family. Secretly the guys did too—it saved them money! He vacationed in Kenya and Tahiti and enjoyed the good single life. He learned to live with the seizures, and the prescribed Dilantin handled them pretty well. All the while medical science was improving, and in such an odd way it slowly revealed the seriousness of Steve's illness to him.

Our parents had died not knowing what afflicted Steve, not knowing what was going to torture him beginning in the early 1990s. With the new brain-scanning technologies, the diagnosis became easy—a congenital abnormal vascular malformation or AVM. That's medical talk for bad plumbing in the head. Every once in a while, a vein in his head would spring a leak. The "bleeds" caused immediate stroke-like symptoms. At first they were minor, terrible headaches and such. As the blood was reabsorbed into the tissue, his condition would improve surprisingly fast. But after every bleed and recovery, there was scar tissue that refused to let normal functioning return to that region of his brain.

Steve had good medical insurance and the disability insurance helped. And then in 1991 the surgeons at Stanford Hospital decided to take action. The best doctors in the world offered him an awful choice. With surgery things might improve, but untreated, the course of the disease was going to be a slow deterioration of brain functioning over a period of years. Every bleed would mean more disability. That would mean no more driving, loss of short-term memory, and speech problems. He would have to give up the job he enjoyed so much. Unfortunately, jewelers with short-term memory problems lose stuff like diamonds. Steve bravely went for the surgery, and it nearly killed him.[1]

He spent the last six years of his life at the best assisted-living/skilled-nursing facility we could find in Palo Alto. Steve started out with his own apartment there—he had made an unpredicted good recovery from his first deathbed at Stanford Hospital and was able to walk, talk, and even cook for himself with a great amount of effort. His independence was important to him. During those six years there were a series of medical incidents that took more of his brain away from him. Perhaps not being able to talk was the worst. Not being able to swallow ice cream was bad too—our mom had taught us all to love hot fudge sundaes. The decisions about stomach tubes and such during the medical events and hospital stays were awful for us all.

Sometimes siblings are a lot of trouble. Lucky for the four of us, we all did our part in managing Steve's care. Bill and Sharon lived close by, giving them the burden of the frequent visits. Mary Ellen and John lived in Southern California and helped out in the ways they could, given the distance.

The experience of visiting him in the nursing home left us questioning how the infirm and elderly are cared for in our society. Although the facility where our brother lived had a good reputation, we were appalled by the turnover of personnel. We would no sooner get Steve's caregivers up to speed on his needs when they would leave for other jobs. Certainly, this revolving-door syndrome left him and other patients with inconsistent care and confusion. We thought there must be better, more compassionate ways of doing this.

The four of us had a tough time with Steve's declining health. We literally did not know what we were in for. His bleeds moved faster than our decision making about housing options and such. But we got through it. And we learned from it. We learned that even the best nursing home is a bad place to be. Maybe the assisted-living facilities are okay, but they mean separation from loved ones and the beginning of isolation. Those of you that have had similar experiences with family members know this. One of our purposes here is to keep you out of such places, to give you options, to give you more dignity at the end of your life.

Now we appreciate that some of you have had the good fortune to have never visited a nursing home. We want to change that. Before you read another page in this book, we have a little homework assignment for you. Call up the nicest nursing home in your area and ask for a tour. The easiest way to find one is to go to the website www.ourparents.com, input your zip code, and hit search. You can also narrow your search on the website by price and needs if you like. Contact information is listed as well as consumer evaluations. But nothing will be as informative as your own visit. When you get there, take a look at both the assisted-living apartments and the medical care facilities. Be sure to ask to see their state-produced quality report, sometimes called a "Form 2567 from the U.S. Health Care Financing Administration" or the "state inspection survey." After the tour, you will be more interested in the ideas in this book. So, seriously, close the book and make the call now.

CLOSE THE BOOK AND CALL!

The Current State of Nursing Homes

There's a lot to read these days about nursing homes. You can find more than two thousand books if you punch in "nursing homes" at Amazon.com. Assuming you did your homework as assigned above, you now know more than most of the books can teach you. In particular, you know what things are like at nursing homes in your specific neighborhood. Since your visit was not *unannounced*, we'll guess you didn't run into any of the top ten concerns of nursing home industry regulators as listed by *Consumer Reports* (see exhibit 1.1).

Exhibit 1.1. Common Concerns of Regulators Regarding Nursing Homes

The following list covers state surveyors' required conditions for nursing homes:

1. The facility must store, prepare, distribute, and serve food under sanitary conditions.
2. The facility must ensure that (a) a resident who enters the facility without pressure sores does not develop pressure sores unless the individual's clinical condition demonstrates that they were unavoidable; and (b) a resident having pressure sores receives necessary treatment and services to promote healing, prevent infections, and prevent new sores from developing.
3. The facility must ensure that it is free of medication error rates of 5 percent or greater.
4. The facility must not use verbal, mental, sexual, or physical abuse, corporal punishment, or involuntary seclusion.
5. The facility must provide each resident with sufficient fluid intake to maintain proper hydration and health.
6. The facility must establish and maintain an infection control program designed to provide a safe, sanitary, and comfortable environment, and to help prevent the development and transmission of disease and infection.
7. The facility must ensure that each resident receives adequate supervision and assistance devices to prevent accidents.
8. The facility must promote care for residents in a manner and in an environment that maintains or enhances each resident's dignity and respect in full recognition of his or her individuality.
9. Each resident must receive and the facility must provide the necessary care and services to attain or maintain the highest practicable physical, mental, and psychosocial well-being, in accordance with the comprehensive assessment and plan of case.

10. The facility must provide for an ongoing program of activities designed to meet, in accordance with the comprehensive assessment, the interests and the physical, mental, and psychosocial well-being of each resident.

Source: State Operations Manual Provider Certification, Health Care Financing Administration, as cited in Trudy Lieberman and the Editors of *Consumer Reports, Consumer Reports Complete Guide to Health Services for Seniors* (New York: Three Rivers Press, 2000).

This is a scary list indeed. But it's not our job to criticize elderly care facilities—plenty already do that. Instead, our job here is, first, to keep you out of such places and, second, to help you better enjoy growing older in the close vicinity of your family. So please read on.

Why This Book Is for You

We expect the typical reader of this book to be a member of the postwar baby boom generation, aged fifty to sixty-five or so. Folks already into their sixties and seventies will find immediate use for this book as well. Or perhaps you're one of their kids. We're going to address our comments mostly to the older folks facing retirement during the next ten years or so. But for you sons and daughters of baby boomers, there's much here too.

Our cousin Lee in Nebraska, born in 1940, is fond of describing all the trouble baby boomers have caused America over the years. He should know: his younger brother was born in 1946. According to Lee, first it was bikes. Come Christmas 1951 there was a big bicycle shortage in the country. Then it was classrooms and teachers, including not enough seats in colleges around the country beginning in 1963. By 1965 there weren't enough entry-level jobs to go around. About 1972, as the first baby boomers started families, there weren't enough houses.[2] Baby boomers thinking about retirement drove the late-1990s stock market run-up—there was a shortage of good investments. And, of course, now there is a shortage of retirement and pension funds.[3]

Perhaps the best metric for this problem is to compare the number of births in the United States over three periods. About forty million kids were born in the United States between 1931 and 1945. The postwar baby boom (1946–1960) was fifty-eight million strong—a 45 percent increase! Thereafter, births fell to fifty-five million between 1961 and 1975.

Our cousin Lee was right, America has never done a good job of handling those fifty-eight million kids and the incredible demand of their num-

---

Room for Thought 1.1. The Impact of Demographic Shifts

Lower fertility can be good for economic growth and society. When the number of children a woman can expect to bear in her lifetime falls from high levels of three or more to a stable rate of two, a demographic change surges through the country for at least a generation. Children are scarcer, the elderly are not yet numerous, and the country has a bulge of working-age adults: the "demographic dividend". If a country grabs this one-off chance for productivity gains and investment, economic growth can jump by as much as a third.

However, the fall in fertility is already advanced in most of the world. Over 80% of humanity lives in countries where the fertility rate is either below three and falling, or already two or less. This is thanks not to government limits but to modernisation and individuals' desire for small families. Whenever the state has pushed fertility down, the result has been a blight. China's one-child policy is a violation of rights and a demographic disaster, upsetting the balance between the sexes and between generations. China has a bulge of working adults now, but will bear a heavy burden of retired people after 2050.

Source: "Now We Are Seven Billion," Economist, October 22, 2011, www.economist.com/node/21533364.

Note: We in the United States are about twenty years ahead of the Chinese on this demographic disaster! And the Japanese have been about ten years ahead of us.

---

bers. And now our retirement system, designed for the 1930–1945 cohort, faces the boomer onslaught. Indeed, you can already see some of the key systems beginning to fail. Most recently, baby boomers' pension funds, retirement accounts, and housing values deflated during the so-called Great Recession. Consequently, boomers are en mass keeping their jobs longer and thus adding to the country's unemployment problem as younger workers are in effect locked out. Everybody knows Social Security and Medicare will dissolve circa 2020. The private pension funds were beginning to creak even before the disaster of 2008–2009.

If you think the nursing home you visited today is a place you want to stay out of, wait until you see the 2020 version. Who will build enough of them? Who will staff them? Who will pay for them? And with the new medical technologies, we'll all live longer. Rather than dying from diseases, baby boomers will just wear down and wither away. The demographics make the future easy to see, and our future is different, far different, from the retirement our parents are experiencing right now.

Getting ready for this future is what the rest of this book is about. We predict that the retirement of baby boomers will be accommodated by a fundamental change in American culture. Three-generation households will not be seen as a kind of subsidy for our "irresponsible" kids. Rather, three generations living together again, as they have done everywhere on earth throughout history (except in the United States and Northern European countries in the last fifty years) will be the norm. Investing in our kids will be seen as the new kind of pension fund, one that helps everyone. And the close relationship that has held societies together throughout history, that between grandparent and grandchild, will be renewed.

Our parents could afford the independence of living separately. "I will not be a burden to my kids" has been their mantra. Our baby boom generation will not be able to afford the apparent luxury of such independent living. And perhaps it's really not a luxury at all. As we adapt to the new cultural realities, perhaps we'll actually be happier with our rediscovered freedom to live together again in inventive family living arrangements.

In the following pages, we describe what many inventive Americans with foresight are already doing to bring their families back together again. The bricks of our story are the words of the more than one hundred Americans Sharon interviewed who are now building multigenerational households. To protect their privacy, we have disguised the names and locations of the folks interviewed. But we have remained faithful to the content and context of their comments. These Americans are from all over the country: east, west, north, and south. They are black and white, wealthy and not. They speak English, Spanish, or Chinese as their first language. They work as manicurists and writers, Realtors and finance professors. The youngest is nine and the oldest is ninety-seven. We have also add other new ideas posted on internet commentary sites in response to a variety of media reports on multigenerational living. All give sage advice:

> *Helen (a Realtor in her sixties):* When I work with people that are in their late sixties and early seventies, I try to help them see that they are going to be happier if they can move to their final home while in that age bracket. . . . They are not selling their house when they are under pressure for medical reasons or when they are not making good decisions. They don't have to make quick choices about the things that they have loved for so many years, valuable and sentimental things. Also it helps because folks are more adaptable moving into a new situation and developing new friendships when they are in their early seventies. The longer you wait after seventy-five, the harder it gets. I have seen people in their eighties, they just can't do it. . . . That is why I have explored all these options for myself, so I can make my own choices.

And they bring tears to our eyes:

> *Sarah (a seventeen-year-old, talks about having her granddad across the way):* I took a class sophomore year about American history. I fell in love with it. I remember in my junior year, I was studying fascism and communism for an exam, and Granddad helped me. He launched into a twenty-minute explanation of world history, just clarified a bunch of things, and it was one of those [times] . . . you know, I'll remember in twenty years. When I'm getting married, I'll have a funny story to tell about how my grandpa was helping me out with a test when I was sixteen. . . . It's like having your encyclopedia right across the road, across the grass.

Sarah added in her college application essay, "It is listening to your grandfather quote the page you just read in *Macbeth* last night word for word or that afternoon that you spent playing double solitaire with your grandmother as you watch an AMC movie. It is through such life experiences that I begin to realize that because of my past, I am ready for whatever the future has to bring."

The mortar of our story is our observations about and analyses of this growing trend in America. Three generations living together is on the increase according to all sources, including the most recent U.S. census data. Our goal is to help push this healthy trend along and to help ease the transition from a culture of *independent* retirement to one of *interdependence*. We are convinced the latter will be better for all.

The remainder of the book is organized in a similar way as our previous book, *Together Again*. But, here in *All in the Family* we have updated all the statistics as additional data have become available. We have been able to add new stories about both successful and unsuccessful experiments in multigenerational living as reported in the popular press and web commentaries by hundreds of Americans. We also introduce material on the latest thinking about creative processes that can be applied in family meetings. The emphasis in all this new material is on the inventiveness of families as they adjust to circumstances in the second decade of the twenty-first century. Indeed, the complex mix of cultural and legal constraints; family resources, including both housing and finances; the numbers, ages, and health of extended family members; geographic limitations; personality clashes; and differences in cross-generational values makes family design processes daunting, while at the same time providing exciting opportunities.

For the latest information on multigenerational living, including a teaching syllabus and videos, please go to www.allinthefamilybook.us.

Two Decades of Change for American Families Have Already Begun

Happiness is having a large, loving, caring, close-knit family in another city.

—George Burns

The advantage of growing up with siblings is that you become very good at fractions.

—Robert Brault

All kids are trouble, Edith. And I don't wanna spend my reclining years trying to raise another one.

—Archie Bunker

N THIS TOPIC humor is important to have around for a couple of reasons. First, a little levity will help us all get through the rather serious adjustments we'll be making to our family lives during the next decades. Second, we know that humor is an important tool for stimulating creative thinking. Certainly, the writing on the great television shows on the topic such as *All in the Family*,

My Three Sons, and now *Modern Family* reflects such views. But while we very much appreciate the levity of the Burns, Brault, and Bunker quips above, we must say that the folks we have interviewed for our book hold very different views than theirs. Herein we report the stories of scores of American families that have invented ways to live together that serve the fast-changing needs and constraints of our twenty-first-century society. Their stories are about locating *close by* one another to work together creatively and cooperatively, *rather than just dividing things up*. And in their real-life stories, *grandparents and grandkids get along just fine*.

The burgeoning elderly population with their inevitable infirmities and failing finances[1] and pension systems, the care of children in households where parents work full-time, and the volatility of employment and housing markets are the most obvious challenges facing Americans today. Increasingly, multigenerational living arrangements are being made wherein creativity in the design of structures and interaction patterns are reinvigorating extended family relationships. The purpose of our book is to stimulate your own inventiveness as you work through the particular challenges facing your family in these tough times.

In our book *Together Again*, we reported how more than one hundred Americans from around the country had designed inventive solutions to the housing and care of three generations of family members. *Together Again* received excellent reviews (we include an important scholarly review in appendix B of this book) and wonderful publicity (see examples on our website, www.allinthefamilybook.us). In the six years since *Together Again*'s publication, much has changed, and almost entirely in the ways we predicted back then. The American housing bubble has burst with a world-changing bang. Unemployment has apparently settled in at about 8 percent in the United States. More than fifty-four million Americans (one-sixth of us) are now living in multigenerational housing, and the numbers have been climbing fast. New home builders are beginning to adjust and in 2012 began to experiment with new offerings appropriate for multigenerational living. We have heard from hundreds of other Americans that have generally reported the benefits of three generations living in close proximity. And, finally, our ideas have evolved about the phenomenon that inspired *Together Again*.

Circa 2006 our vision of the future of multigenerational living was accurate if not blurry. We stated that the American housing bubble started to inflate in 2003, and we correctly called its bursting beginning in 2006 (see page 9 of the first edition). Indeed, John had initially predicted such an economic catastrophe back in 1997—pertinent parts of his article are included in appendix A. New U.S. census data have added much credence to our emphasis on multigenerational housing as a key solution to the demographic and economic problems that have unfolded in the last five years. At the foundation of *All in the Family* lie five ideas about how American culture is now changing:

1. The retirement and infirmities of American baby boomers are causing a complete restructuring of government and corporate support for elderly in the United States (think Social Security and other pension funds, Medicare, and medical care in general). This will be a ten-year process of adjustment that will be difficult for individuals and institutions.

2. Our fifty-year national experiment with nuclear families (the ideal of two parents, two-and-a-half kids, and the white picket fence) is ending. The old and faithful interdependence of extended family relationships is reemerging as the cultural norm.

3. New housing will be built that is appropriate for mixed-age neighborhoods and multigenerational family proximity. One-third of the present single-family houses can and will accommodate an accessory apartment or the like.

4. The current growth of "boomerang kids," adult children living with their parents in the midst of the present economic travails, will be seen as a kind of spring training for the long, hard season of the baby-boom retirement years. Millions of Americans are now *re*learning the tricks of balancing proximity and privacy that will be crucial in the next decades.

5. Obstacles to creativity in the design of home structures and interactions such as our unusual American cultural fetish with interpersonal independence and/or local building regulations limiting mixed neighborhoods will fade away during the next decade.

These ideas, developed in detail in the remainder of the book, are summarized below in an updated version of an article John wrote for the *Christian Science Monitor* titled "Solution to US Debt Woes Isn't Economic. It's Social," appearing July 27, 2011:

> The clock is ticking loudly in Washington over the debt ceiling and long-term funding problems like Medicare and Social Security. Economists have blamed America's current economic malaise on (take your pick): overspending, greed, government regulation, government deregulation,

subprime home mortgages, executive incentives, efficient markets theory, the business cycle, the Chinese, Alan Greenspan—the list goes on.

But what if the economists have it completely wrong? Suppose for a minute or 10 that the so-called economic decline is simply a severe symptom of a deeper disease, a cultural shift.

The longest view of the progress of humankind suggests that governments have always been unfaithful to humans. The current example, our crumbling Social Security system, has really only succeeded in dividing families. In 1940, about 18 percent of elderly widows lived alone.[2] By 2000, that number had risen to more than 65 percent. Thankfully, this trend of loneliness appears to be finally reversing circa 2010. (See exhibit 2.1.)

Margaret Mead long ago pointed out that the family is the only institution that persistently supports us. What the economists are calling an economic problem is best understood as a cultural reversion to older living patterns. The reason? Our twentieth-century experiment with nuclear families has failed.

That's the problem. Here's the fix: Many Americans are rediscovering the importance of the extended family.

Exhibit 2.1. Percentage of Widows Sixty-Five and Older Living Alone

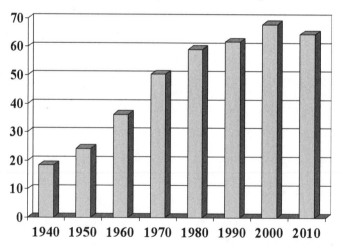

Sources: Kathleen McGarry and Robert F. Schoeni, "Social Security, Economic Growth, and the Rise of Independence of Elderly Widows in the 20th Century," NBER Working Paper No. 6511, April 1998, and U.S. Census Bureau.

Return to the Empty Nest

Consider the phenomenon known as "boomerang kids." Estimates vary, but according to the U.S. Census Bureau, almost one-third of all Americans ages eighteen to thirty-four are now living with their parents. That's more than 21 million young adults. (See exhibit 2.2, which shows the recent upswing of this living arrangement.) Five years ago, popular culture in the form of newspaper headlines, book titles, movie titles (remember that awful 2006 movie *Failure to Launch*?), and a minority of American parents of twentysomethings complained loudly. But when you step back and look at the big picture and the moving picture,[3] it's clear that boomerang kids are just another symptom of the greater cultural change affecting American society as we enter the twenty-first century: that is, the reunification of the extended family.

Exhibit 2.2   **Percentage of Eighteen- to Thirty-Four-Year-Olds Living in Parents' Homes**

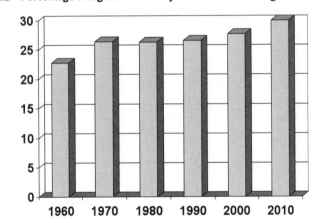

Sources: U.S. Census Bureau.

Grandparents are also moving back in with their children. Three-generation households are on the rise in America, according to the Census Bureau. The Pew Research Center estimates that over 17 percent of the population—over 54 million Americans-lived in multigenerational housing in 2011, up from 28 million in 1980. That number is now over 6 percent of all American households (see the recent growth displayed in exhibit 2.3). The fundamental point is that people are moving back together again because the grand experiment of the World War II generation hasn't worked. Three generations belong together, and not just for financial reasons.

Exhibit 2.3   Percentage of Multigenerational Households

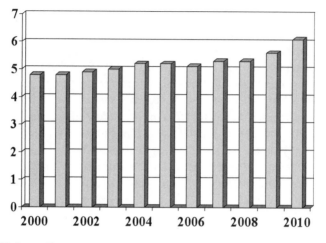

Sources: U.S. Census Bureau.

Fundamentally, humans are psychologically and physiologically designed and have evolved to live this way. We've survived by living in such extended family arrangements. We are happiest in such groups. And, we are now quickly learning that other institutions (companies, unions, governments, religious organizations, etc.) ultimately cannot take care of us. Only our families can and will.

The Housing Debacle—Revisited

The single-family suburban home did work for a time, while mothers stayed at home to raise children and life spans were shorter. However, with the advent of extended life expectancy, and with both parents working, the single-family home for nuclear families is no longer meeting the needs of our changing population.

It's no wonder that the current so-called economic malaise began with housing in 2007. That's about the time the economic system began to realize that the American housing stock is actually worth less because it doesn't fit the coming needs of the marketplace.

America's elderly population is now growing at a moderate rate. But soon into this century, the rate will accelerate. According to census projections, the elderly population will double between now and the year 2040, to over 80 million. By then, as many as 1 in 5 Americans will be elderly. And more than half of them will have at least one disability.

In order to adjust the housing stock of the country to reflect the baby boomers' retirement and the associated growth in multigenerational living arrangements, changes will be required in long-existing and mostly local housing and building codes and associated ordinances. The main battle line in this political fight is over accessory apartments, popularly called "granny flats." Built adjacent to larger houses, they can provide living spaces for adult children or grandparents. They offer both proximity and privacy. Public debate and political battles are being fought, won, and lost around the country over making changes in codes that not only allow for, but actually promote, the construction of accessory apartments in existing neighborhoods and in new developments.

Accessory apartments produce two kinds of complaints. First, physical impacts, such as increased parking and traffic and architectural changes in buildings, are often seen as disruptive to neighborhoods. The second sort relates to social and cultural issues. That is, accessory apartments deviate from the traditional ways of looking at housing, family, and the neighborhood. It stands for a change in the way the single-family house is used, a departure from the conventional meanings connected to residential zoning categories.

While builders and architects do complain about zoning constraints and such, their own practices are often obstacles to housing appropriate for the new century. They talk more about features that will sell to consumers, but won't really serve them. For example, consider a ritzy Newport Beach, California, neighborhood where folks have been sold $2 million homes with granny flats at the tops of stairs. How's granny going to navigate those steep steps?

What America Must Do

Fast-rising life expectancies, the growing costs of elder care, the increasing need for child care, the frustrating lack of affordable housing, and the new disconnectedness—all are producing unfamiliar challenges for families all around America. Fortunately, our aforementioned twentieth-century dalliance with nuclear families and white-picket-fence suburbia is fast winding down. The "social avalanche" of elderly baby boomers will force Americans back to the familiar family form of multigenerational households.

America must spur the comeback of accessory apartments and the flexibility of mixed neighborhoods with respect to size, value, and use. Now that the housing market has crashed, there's some time to reflect on the future and to design communities and homes that will accommodate a fast-graying America in innovative ways.

P A R T

The Benefits

Why Living Together Again Makes Sense

> Never before have so many people lived so far away from the old people they love. And never before have old people lived to be so old.
>
> —MARY PIPHER

 HE DRAMATIC SOCIETAL SHIFTS going on in America are pretty easy to discern. The politicians and pundits remind us almost daily. The dramatic rise in life expectancy, the growing cost of elder care, the increasing need for child care, the frustrating lack of affordable housing, unemployment, and the new disconnectedness are all producing unfamiliar challenges for families across America. But while the problems are easy to see, the solutions are not. The solutions we're advocating here require us to actually look back in time at how families used to live together. And, fortunately, we also have some pioneer stories to share about how many American families are now taking more inventive approaches to living arrangements that allow togetherness and privacy at the same time.

A Brief History of Living Together

We're trying to make this book a multimedia experience for you. We've already sent you on an excursion to your best and nearest nursing home.

After that tough trip we owe you a little fun. Now your assignment is to order from Netflix or somehow download for viewing *The Gods Must Be Crazy*. It's appropriate for the whole family, it is hilarious, and actually it's about the whole family. That is, part of it shows how competition and cooperation are managed in a large extended family of Kalahari Bushmen in South Africa. While the film is a clever comedy, like the Marx brothers comedies our brother Steve enjoyed so much, its insights into human behavior and communication are deep. SO PUT THE BOOK DOWN AND WATCH THE FILM.

Now back to the book. Up until the 1950s in this country, and pretty much all around the rest of the world through today, three (sometimes even four) generations live(d) together in multigenerational families. In prehistoric times these family groupings included all the living descendants in either the male or female line. Each family was practically self-sufficient with men providing the food and women taking care of household duties, children, and elderly parents. The whole family had to cooperate in order to survive. Eventually, families organized themselves into clans consisting of several extended families to share certain ceremonies and traditions. Later these groupings evolved into cooperative tribes for protection. Still later, people began depending on local, state, and national governments for protection, and on persons outside the family for food and education.[1]

The Industrial Revolution caused significant changes in family life. People moved from farms to cities where new factories were being built. In the cities, people no longer worked together in extended family units. Men were required to travel to and from their jobs and had less time to spend with their families. New kinds of jobs called for specific skills. This meant that workers frequently moved away from their local communities and kinship groupings to live near their places of employment. Joint families began to dissipate in favor of nuclear families consisting of married couples and their children. Women still stayed at home to raise the children. However, with the new mobility, multigenerational households began to decline, along with the expectation that children cared for elderly parents in their own homes. Subsequently, assisted living and skilled nursing facilities came into existence as new living arrangements to serve the needs of the infirm elderly.

Housing evolved into single-family structures to accommodate the new and independent family unit. This tradition of single-family dwellings accelerated in the United States after the end of World War II. Since then, America's residential landscape has shifted from city or small-town to suburban living. General prosperity, cheap farmland rendered from new agricultural technologies, easier building techniques, and access to automobiles have all combined to initiate the development of suburban tracts of single-family homes for nuclear families. Americans value these homes for the space, security, status, and privacy they provide.[2] The single-family suburban home worked for a time, while mothers stayed at home to raise children and life spans were shorter. However, with the advent of medical technology and extended life expectancy, and with both parents working, the single-family home for nuclear families is no longer meeting the needs of our changing population.

Despite Botox and Such, Yes, We Are Getting Older

People in the United States are living longer these days than ever before. According to data from the Department of Health and Human Services and the United Nations, average life expectancy is now seventy-eight years. We do better than the Brazilians (seventy-two), the Chinese (seventy-three), and the Russians (sixty-six). We're about the same as the Brits (seventy-nine) and the Germans (seventy-nine), but both the French (eighty-one) and the Japanese (eighty-three) are longer lived than average Americans. Perhaps it's the wine and fish?

The longevity figures are even higher for those who attain the age of sixty-five. In 2007, American men reaching age sixty-five had an average life expectancy of an additional 17.2 years, or living to age 82.2, while women could expect 19.9 more years or living to age 84.9. Medical technology to both prevent and combat disease, along with general knowledge about sanitation, diet, and exercise combine to extend life spans in the twenty-first century.[3]

Having found these data, we thought it might be fun for you to look up how many years you have left, theoretically, that is. So we provide exhibit 3.1, the "Life Table," for your inspection and interest. These data are a little different than the more common "life expectancy" numbers reported above because the latter do not take into account your current age and the overall health of your age cohort. So, if you're sixty now and you're female, you have about twenty-four years to go, *assuming* average health and average luck.

America's elderly population is now growing at a moderate rate. But soon into this century, the rate will accelerate. In fact, by 2050, there will be more people who are elderly (sixty-five or over) than young (fourteen or younger). According to U.S. Census Bureau projections, the elderly population will double between now and the year 2040, to close to over eighty-one million. Perhaps the most noteworthy datum is that eight million of those will be over ninety years old![4] By then, as many as one in five Americans, or 20 percent of the population, could be elderly—see exhibit 3.2.

Exhibit 3.1. Life Table: How Much You Have Left

Age	Males	Females	Age	Males	Females	Age	Males	Females
0	75.4	80.4	34	43.4	47.4	68	15.1	17.6
1	74.9	79.9	35	42.5	46.7	69	14.4	16.1
2	74.0	79.0	36	41.5	45.7	70	13.7	15.5
3	73.0	78.0	37	40.6	44.8	71	13.1	15.3
4	72.0	77.0	38	39.7	43.8	72	12.4	14.6
5	71.0	76.0	39	38.8	42.9	73	11.8	13.9
6	70.0	75.0	40	37.8	41.9	74	11.2	13.2
7	69.1	74.0	41	36.9	41.0	75	10.6	12.6
8	68.1	73.0	42	36.0	40.0	76	10.0	11.9
9	67.1	72.0	43	35.1	39.2	77	9.5	11.3
10	66.1	71.0	44	34.2	38.2	78	8.9	10.6
11	65.1	70.1	45	33.3	37.2	79	8.4	10.0
12	64.1	69.1	46	32.5	36.3	80	7.9	9.4
13	63.1	68.1	47	31.6	35.4	81	7.4	8.9
14	62.1	67.2	48	30.7	34.5	82	6.9	8.3
15	61.1	66.1	49	29.8	33.6	83	6.5	7.8
16	60.2	65.1	50	29.0	32.7	84	6.1	7.3
17	59.2	64.1	51	28.2	31.9	85	5.7	6.8
18	58.3	63.2	52	27.3	30.9	86	5.3	6.3
19	57.3	62.2	53	26.5	30.0	87	4.9	5.9
20	56.4	61.2	54	25.7	29.1	88	4.6	5.5
21	55.5	60.2	55	24.8	28.3	89	4.2	5.1
22	54.5	59.3	56	24.1	27.4	90	3.9	4.7
23	53.6	58.3	57	23.3	26.5	91	3.6	4.4
24	52.7	57.3	58	22.5	25.7	92	3.4	4.0
25	51.8	56.4	59	21.7	24.8	93	3.2	3.8
26	50.8	55.4	60	20.9	24.0	94	2.9	3.5
27	50.0	54.4	61	20.2	23.1	95	2.8	3.3
28	49.0	53.4	62	19.4	22.3	96	2.6	3.1
29	48.1	52.5	63	18.7	21.4	97	2.4	2.9
30	47.1	51.5	64	17.9	20.7	98	2.3	2.7
31	46.2	50.1	65	17.2	19.9	99	2.2	2.5
32	45.3	49.6	66	16.5	19.1	100	2.1	2.4
33	44.3	48.6	67	15.8	18.3			

Source: U.S. Social Security Administration, www.socialsecurity.gov, retrieved 2012.

Indeed, the steep growth between 2010 and 2030 shown in the bar graph in exhibit 3.3 best demonstrates the historically unprecedented problems facing Americans in the next twenty years. Our current systems of Social Security and Medicare simply cannot handle the steep increases between now and 2030.

Exhibit 3.2. The Elderly (65+ Years) Population of the United States (in Millions)

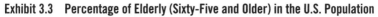

Year	Population
1960	16.6
1970	20.0
1980	25.6
1990	31.1
2000	34.7
2010	40.2
2020	54.8
2030	72.1
2040	81.2
2050	88.5

Source: U.S. Census Bureau, retrieved 2012.

Exhibit 3.3 Percentage of Elderly (Sixty-Five and Older) in the U.S. Population

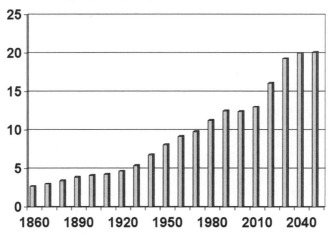

Sources: U.S. Census Bureau.

Room for Thought 3.1.   Extended Family Interdependence in Tough Times

More aging Americans are doing something they never would have imagined: turning to family for financial aid. Some are even asking their children for a place to live. The problem has been building as more Americans 55 and older have lost jobs or run through savings faster than expected. Thirty-nine percent of adults with parents 65 and older reported giving parents financial aid in the past year, according to a September Pew Research Center survey. Some parents may have trouble acknowledging it: 10% of parents 65 and older reported receiving aid.

"I worry about being a burden on my son," says Mary Huss, 60 years old, who moved in with her son in Salinas, Calif., a year ago. Ms. Huss lost her job in 2008 when her non-profit employer lost funding. Unable to find a job and facing diabetes and rheumatoid arthritis, she used up her retirement savings and sold her home. Robert Huss, a data-systems manager for Monterey County, says he expects she will remain permanently.

Source: E. S. Browning, "Money Crunch Reshapes Relationships; 'I Worry About Being a Burden on My Son,'" *Wall Street Journal,* January 1, 2012.

Caring for the Elderly

The rapid increase in the number of elderly people (sixty-five years and older) combined with decreases in financial support for human and health services is already leading to dilemmas and even disasters for some American families regarding care for seniors in the clan. Things will only get worse in the coming years. Caring for the "oldest old" (those eighty-five and older) is and will be particularly burdensome. This is the fastest growing group of elderly and the group with the greatest need for assistance.

Of the current forty million elderly, more than 50 percent now report some sort of disability.[5] You can see the breakdown of these afflictions in exhibit 3.4. For the oldest old (over eighty-five), these percentages can be roughly tripled. At eighty-five virtually all of us can expect to have some sort of disability hampering our activities and requiring some level of assistance—for 45 percent of us it will be some kind of sensory problem (hearing or vision loss, for example), for 85 percent the problem will be physical, and so on. Such projections lead experts such as medical ethicist Daniel Callahan to refer to the fast-approaching "social avalanche" of old age.[6]

Of the current forty million elderly, some 1.4 million need substantial assistance and are living in nursing homes. But, thankfully, the news on this is not all bad. The most recent studies suggest that during the last two decades, the numbers of folks living in nursing homes hasn't grown along with the growth in the elderly population. The best guess is that about half

Exhibit 3.4.   Disabilities of Elderly (65+ Years) circa 2005

	Percentage
With any disability	51.8
Seeing/speaking/hearing	18.6
Walking/using stairs	38.1
Lifting/grasping/sitting/standing, etc.	24.9
Mental	11.4
Self-care	15.6

Source: U.S. Census Bureau, Survey of Income and Program Participation, June–September 2005, retrieved 2012.

a million Americans have dodged the dreary places during the last decades. Three factors seem to account for the decline in the number of seniors living in long-term care facilities:

1. Today's seniors have taken better care of themselves—less smoking, better diets, and more exercise. These positive steps have at least postponed the kinds of disabilities that require nursing home care.
2. More assisted-living options are open to today's seniors. Home health care has increased thanks to changes in Medicare and Medicaid services, and the variety of assistance to seniors has burgeoned as well.
3. And, of course, grandparents are moving in with their children and grandchildren, forming in increasing numbers three-generation households. Indeed, the 2010 census reports that 6.5 million grandparents were living with their grandchildren. And that leads us to the next topic.

Who's Taking Care of the Kids?

Many women, the traditional caregivers, are now working. In fact, 80 percent of married mothers with children are employed outside the home, and women with children under the age of six are the fastest-growing part of the female labor pool.[7] According to a national telephone survey of more than forty-four thousand working parents conducted by the Urban Institute, one in five children ages six to twelve are regularly left without adult supervision after school and before their parents come home from work. Moreover, "older children are more likely to spend their after-school hours home alone rather than in day care, activities at school, or with a relative or babysitter."[8] The good news is that 6.4 percent of children under eighteen are now living with their grandparents—that's up from 5.3 percent in 2000. These demographics not only have implications for who will be available to care for the elderly, but also emphasize the growing need in America for child care.

Markets Go Up, Markets Go Down— Still We Lack Affordable Housing

This is what we wrote in *Together Again* in 2007:

> The panic started in July of 2003. That is, *emotion* began to drive major investment decisions. Interest rates finally began creeping up, halting a three-year decline, and new home buyers attacked the market, believing they couldn't afford *not* to buy *now*. "Next month interest rates will be higher; I've got to get in now," was their rallying cry. Toward the end of 2005, housing prices in America had ballooned to an average price of greater than $275,000. Out in California in many metropolitan areas it was double that. Of course, by winter 2006 housing prices around the country had begun to decline some. As prices declined housing was seemingly becoming "more affordable." But even at lower prices, nobody could afford them! The economy and housing prices continue to be quite uncertain.

Of course, now we know that housing prices peaked as we were writing *Together Again* and very quickly lost some 30 percent of their value, igniting the Great Recession of 2008–2009. Housing remains in the doldrums today, and even with dramatically lower prices remains unaffordable for many. High unemployment and consumer debt levels continue to hamper Americans' ability to buy new housing.

Even before the turn of the millennium, many Americans saw another way to make their real estate more valuable irrespective of the market fluctuations. Houses become more valuable in the most fundamental way if they accommodate more residents. That is, a potential source of more affordable housing is to use the underused space in single-family-home neighborhoods to create accessory apartments and the like. These small dwelling units, also known as in-law units, involve no land acquisition costs and minimal new infrastructure. Estimates are that one-third of American homes can accommodate such flexible options.[9] Homebuilders also recognized and acted on this opportunity circa 2000 when they began adding "nanny flats" to high-end homes in new developments all over the country.

For the past twenty years, housing advocates have been promoting accessory apartments because of their potential benefits to individual home-owners and their municipalities. Accessory apartments are believed to offer homeowners a good investment with a healthy rate of return; furnish hous-ing for family members, including elderly parents and adult children; improve security in the home; and make better use of existing space.

For communities, accessory apartments hold many benefits. They are inexpensive to produce and therefore more affordable. They also use existing infrastructure and better fit today's smaller families. And they generate addi-tional property tax revenues for cities. These units have the flexibility to pro-vide both needed rental housing, especially in today's tight housing markets, as well as multigenerational housing.

Getting Reconnected

The hope was that information technology would provide new ways of being together.[10] Certainly teenagers circa 2012 were using the internet and smart phones for texting, tweeting, and so on in new ways, disrupting classrooms and providing another new medium for which innovation-lagging adults would have to establish new rules. Relatedly, both of us had some years ago been half of U.S. Navy marriages that involved little contact with our spouses for months at a time. But nowadays the internet and tools such as Skype allow even those serving at sea to participate at home to a significantly greater degree. And who can predict how the next "broadening of the band" will affect societal and familial connectedness.

The problem is that no matter how broad the bandwidth, we still miss the humanness of being together. The hugs and kisses, the warmth of sitting next to someone on a couch, the safeness of sleeping in the same house, the aroma of baking cookies—none of these can be shared electronically. Indeed, some are arguing that the technological changes, particularly the new media, are actually exacerbating the disconnectedness in American society.[11]

Phyllis Gilly, John's mother-in-law, tells the story of how air-conditioning changed the way neighborhoods worked in suburban Dallas. Before AC, on hot summer days, the moms sat outside on front porches, gossiped, and watched the kids playing ball in the street and so on. But in the 1960s, air-conditioning moved everyone inside. A generation ago television was the thief of family time. Now the personal computer, the Internet, and smart phones make even greater demands on younger people's attention. Indeed, the continuing explosion of media choice is fast dividing twenty-first-century households into one-screen-per-person units.

We Americans suffer these afflictions worse than any others around the world. Robert Putnam, in his important book *Bowling Alone*, notices:

Compared with the citizens of most other countries, Americans have always lived a nomadic existence. Nearly one in five of us move each year and, having done so, are likely to pick up and move again. As a result, compared to other peoples, Americans have become accustomed to pitching camp quickly and making friends easily. From our frontier and immigrant past we have learned to plunge into new community institutions when we move.[12]

Putnam goes on to explain that the mobility of Americans has actually declined since the 1950s, even if just a little. But we remain the world champions of mobility *and* therefore of familial disconnectedness.

A Pleasant Reality

So far this chapter has mostly been about unpleasant realities. We've written about depressing developments, from disabilities to disconnectedness to debts and death. We do hope you managed to bring a little levity into the discourse with *The Gods Must Be Crazy*. And, of course, our brother Steve's good humor helped. But, overall, our wake-up call so far has been more a dirge than dance. So we want to end this chapter with a happy story about three generations of Americans living together. We do recognize that living with kids, parents, and grandparents all in one house isn't exactly *Mary Poppins*. But the approach we advocate in this book not only can work, *it is working!*

Our story starts with a two-word question: "A toaster?" Now we all know that whenever a male is involved in gift giving, things don't always go as

---

Room for Thought 3.2.   A History of Extended Family Interdependence

Each of our adult children has lived with us when they needed to, and this is an accepted custom in our family for years. In WWII my mother and I lived with my grandparents, aunt, and uncle while my dad was away at the war. I never "went home again" as an adult, but my mom let us know my family was welcome if necessary.

In middle age when the kids grew up, we have had one daughter bring along her ex-boyfriend's cat, another parked her dead old Dodge in the driveway, and our son moved his pregnant fiancée into our sewing room. That is to say, it's not a stress-free situation, but they are your family. When buying various homes it's been with an eye to providing shelter to family members who might need it. When my husband died, the kids all wanted me to come and move in with one of them.

Source: "pandrews" comment on Joyce Wadler, "Caught in the Safety Net," *New York Times*, May 13, 2009.

planned. So when Madeline opened her Christmas present from her son, Jim, his wife, Christine, and their daughter, Katie, the meaning didn't sink in right away. Madeline was wondering why the family was buying another toaster? All four of them had been living together now for three years, and their toaster always worked just fine. Madeline's wrinkled brow betrayed her befuddlement.

Christine noticed first and urged her to open "part two" of the package. Then everything became clear. Inside part two were the blueprints of Madeline's cottage, to be built on their property in the spring. They had all met with builders and looked at different kinds of apartments to get ideas in the weeks before. And Madeline would need a toaster in her new house across the yard since it would have a kitchen of its own. Now we'll let the family members tell the rest of the story in their own words:

Madeline: Jim and Christine moved here in July three years ago and I came out a month later. We had long, long conversations before I came out here. I was living in Florida alone and working. I was then seventy-two years old. They were coming to a strange place. Christine traveled a lot in her work, Jim some. In California they had had excellent day-care facilities for Katie.

Katie was starting first grade. So they discussed with me the cost of me coming out to live with them, hoping that it would be a win-win situation for everybody. So that Katie would have a constant in her life. And they were busy with work and it would be the same person there when she got home from school every day. It would relieve me from having to work—I had injured my back at that time. So it was a big decision for everybody. The key for me is that *I was invited.* At that time I felt like I was in a position where I could give back something and that I was still able to help. So I did live in the house with them for three years, until I moved into my own house.

Christine: That was kind of the plan all along. We tried to recover financially from the move from California first. We had talked about building a place for Madeline on the property. But we didn't want to commit to her, to get her hopes up—in case financially we couldn't. That's why we wanted that acreage so that we would have room to expand.

Jim: When we looked for the house, we looked for a one-story house that had a master suite on one side and bedrooms on the other. That way there would be enough room for it to be comfortable for people. You know, in case someone had to move in with us, like my mother or my dad or her parents, we wanted to provide a facility without having to go up and down stairs. Also, we knew at some point we were going to have to either provide more financial help for my mom or bring her to live with us. It worked for her to come live with us and help with Katie. We were already paying the house payment and utilities, so it wasn't a big issue compared to getting extra help for us from someone else. It allows Christine and me both to work and keep our lifestyle.

Christine: We talked to a lot of people about the idea ahead of time. I think everybody thought we were nuts. Nobody supported us in our decision.

Madeline: I didn't either. Well, you can't really live together in a house, you know, especially three generations.

Christine: I want to say we do better in separate houses. But I think regardless of the input either Jim or I got, we still felt it would be a good win-win situation. I mean I don't know if that would work for every family. Not every daughter-in-law and mother-in-law could do it.

Sharon: Had you heard of others, your parents, participating in similar living arrangements?

Madeline: My grandmother lived with us—same house—the last couple of years before she died. Then later on my grandfather lived with us for a couple of years. They both lived a long time. My grandfather was ninety-three when he died. My grandmother was a very important part of my life.

Christine: We have ground rules. We have two. We talked about one—Madeline was a smoker and both Katie and I are both very allergic to smoke. So that was my biggest issue. She went outside to smoke. That was fine with her. That was a make-or-break deal for me. The other ground rule was that when Jim's dad visited we would have to do something different.

Jim: My mom and dad are divorced. So when my dad would come to visit, my mom would leave so we didn't have them both in the same household.

Madeline: I've been divorced for several years now. But, my former husband has a live-in companion. When I was living in the house with the kids, if he and his companion came for a visit, I left. I either went down to San Diego to visit my son or back to Florida to visit my relatives. He and I had discussed that before I moved in with the kids. That's how we worked things out.

Christine: It sounds like a piddling thing, but we did not want to cut Jim's dad out of our life and make this uncomfortable for anyone. I am somebody who tries to anticipate conflicts and get them resolved before things happen.

Madeline: It never was a conflict.

Sharon: Anything else? For example, do you have a call-first rule? If you want to come see the family, or you want to go see her, do you call her first? Or do you just go and knock on the door?

Christine: Oh, now that she is in her own house, I always call first—maybe 99.9 percent of the time. We never talked about it, it just sort of happened.

Jim: With all the moving, we did have to figure out what furniture to keep. When Mom came we had to figure where to put it and where to keep it.

Madeline: Their house is large enough that when I moved in with them, I had my bedroom, bath, and a sitting room. So you know I was able to bring with me the important pieces and be surrounded with my things. I'm not really big about being attached to things. But, certain things, yes. I had my old things and that worked out.

Jim: Also, she was allowed to pick out all the colors and all the carpet for the new cottage we built. The only things that we picked were the cabinets that would stay in the cottage.

Christine: We picked the permanent fixtures that will be there forever, because eventually that will probably be our office. And then anything else, such as paint, wallpaper, or flooring, Madeline picked all that out.

Madeline: It is eight hundred square feet. The building, the design of it, I like every single bit of it.

Christine: It has one bedroom, a living room, a kitchen, a bath, a lovely roof, and a very large closet off the bedroom which is almost big enough to fit a bed. It also has a covered patio. The cottage is absolutely lovely.

Sharon: How do you handle expenses such as taxes, utilities, phone, that kind of thing?

Jim: The things we pay for are the utilities, because they are tied into our account and the water is off our main meter. And we pay the mortgage, insurance, and property taxes.

Madeline: Yes, they do. I pay for my phone bill.

Sharon: What do you like about your housing situation?

Madeline: Well, I finally have my privacy. Before coming here, I had lived alone for so many years and gotten used to that. I don't think we ever had any issues while I lived with them. But when they had guests over, I was always concerned about how visible I should be. I didn't want to act like I was ignoring their guests, especially if it's people that I knew. But on the other hand, I didn't want to be in the middle of their conversations. So this way I think we each have been able to enjoy our guests more. I also enjoy the fact that they are so close. Katie can run back and forth across the yard, come over and visit me, and tell me what happened that day at school. The dog, we also share the dog.

Jim: The dog stays between both houses. So she can watch it too.

Madeline: The dog spends the weekends with me when they're away. I take care of the dog and the dog takes care of me. It's the best of both worlds. I mean they are right there if I need anything, should I need them.

In February I started walking into the walls, so I went to the doctor and he said I had an ear infection. Then they started testing me and figured out that it was a brain tumor. I had surgery last April and the tumor was benign. But I stayed with them for six weeks before moving back into my own house.

Sharon: Is there anything that you dislike about your current housing arrangement?

Christine: I don't think so. I think what we have now is perfect.

Jim: Actually it has worked out very well for all of us. It took a lot of planning and thinking about what we were going to do. At one point, we went out and looked for a small single-family home to buy for my mom. We looked everywhere and the closest thing we could find in our price range was probably six or seven miles away. We thought that's not convenient, if our daughter is coming home and neither one of us is here. We looked at apartments, but apartments were too expensive. We were trying to find a way to give her private space and keep her close enough. The cottage in back ended up being the most affordable.

The best solution for us was to build on the property, and it was much cheaper than any of the other options. A rented apartment would have just been throwing money away. Whereas, with the improvement to our property, the appraisal value is now double what we paid for the house three years ago. It made the most sense financially and she doesn't have to drive to come see us. She can walk across the yard. It all worked out for the best. We've given her her own space and privacy. We enjoy our privacy and still have a family between us.

Christine: It is important to me for Katie to have easy access to Madeline because she is the only grandparent that lives anywhere close. I want their relationship to grow and develop. The mail sits on our counter until Katie comes home from school every day. I have Katie take it out to Madeline, so that they can visit with each other, even if it is only a two-minute exchange. Madeline does a lot of cooking. She can tell her stories that I don't know. Our perspective is that it has been great to give Katie that other generation's sense of family. I think looking down the road twenty years, eventually Madeline's health won't be as good. It will be a lot easier to have her just out back than to drive ten miles up the road to take out the trash or bring her dinner. It is perfect.

Sharon: Would you recommend your living arrangement to others? Why or why not?

Jim: In these poor economic times, with the cost of housing, I honestly see more and more of it happening. I've had other people at work ask me about the property. Other people in town have said the same thing: "Can I come take a look and see how you did it?" We've been really open to anyone who has thought about doing this. We share what we went through and what we thought about to try to make it easier for them. Then, maybe they don't have to go through the struggles or make a mistake, financially or emotionally. I think the key thing to this is you give the women in the family some privacy. There can be two or three days that we might not see her. We don't see each other every day, but we are only seventy-five feet apart.

Madeline: I am a very fortunate person; I have a beautiful home. I don't know if that would work in every family.

Christine: I think one important thing is that Madeline was able to move out here and get acclimated to the area while she was still able to drive and have the opportunity to meet people and get involved in church. I think it's better to relocate before someone is disabled and can't get out. Do it before it becomes a necessity. If you can swing doing the granny flat or cottage, I think that is a better alternative than a plain house miles away.

Jim: The thing for us is that we already had the property, so it is not like we were going out and buying a second piece of property. We were just doing home improvements. So you know 30 or 40 percent of the cost of buying a house is the land and the rest of it is the building. If you can eliminate that, it becomes a more viable option.

Christine: I don't look at it so much from the cost perspective. I know that Madeline gave up a lot when she moved here with us. When I took her to the grocery store for the first time to stock her kitchen, she bought things that she had never bought in three years. Yes, she did all the grocery shopping in our house. We'd leave her the money, and she'd go do it. I just assumed she was buying what she would like for herself too. I think having two kitchens and two refrigerators allows you more freedom to buy what you want. Madeline is so considerate with not wanting to impose anything on anyone. I think she gave up a lot of herself that we didn't even realize, until she was out on her own in the cottage.

Conclusions

So Madeline has dodged the nursing home. You and/or your parents can too. Indeed, as we have crisscrossed the country, we have found other pleasant realities about how families are moving in together again. Certainly aspects of Madeline, Christine, and Jim's story are unique. For example, an acre of land in their Oregon town is much more affordable than in suburban areas in California or Connecticut. But we have consistently found folks that have similarly seen the substantial advantages, both financial and psychological, of living together again in more flexible housing arrangements. And there are important lessons embedded in their comments about how things work. For example, Katie taking the mail to her grandmother every day accomplishes a number of good things for the family.

In the chapters to follow we describe in some detail how others are adapting to their own special circumstances and how creative ideas make things work better for all. We hope you'll find your own family somewhere in these pages. Our goal is to help you see new ways to best manage the financial, health-care, and child-care challenges that face us all in the next twenty years.

Stories about Caregiving Benefits for the Young and Old

Only a life lived for others is a life worthwhile.

—ALBERT EINSTEIN

 ITH EXTENDED FAMILIES so geographically spread out, and with so many situations where both parents work, who is raising the children and caring for the elderly? Today, child and elder care are frequently neglected. One way to meet both needs is for families to return to pre–World War II living styles where extended families lived in close proximity to one another. Grandparents could help raise their grandchildren. Then, later in life, they would be nearby to receive help with their own care, if needed.

Grandparents Help Out

One Southern California woman has done just that. Susan is divorced and lives in a small residential community. She currently teaches part-time at a university. Several years ago, she came up with an inventive way to age-in-place with a multigenerational living arrangement that utilizes a detached cottage on the same property as her house. Initially, she allowed her daughter and son-in-law to live in the unit while they both worked on their graduate degrees. After they were finished with their degrees, they found local housing to be prohibitively expensive. So Susan agreed to continue to allow them the use of the cottage while they established their careers. A few years later they started their family. At that point, Susan decided she didn't need to live in the big house anymore. It was more space than she needed and she was tired of taking care of it. So she offered the house to her daughter, son-in-law, and grandchild.

Susan subsequently had the cottage remodeled, adding a sunroom, and moved in there herself. She says there is adequate space for her in the smaller place. She is pleased to keep her garden and doesn't have to deal with maintaining the larger house. Her daughter and son-in-law do that. She helps them by babysitting the (now three) grandchildren one and a half days a week. Here's what she said about that child-care arrangement:

Susan: My daughter and I kind of made this deal. I taught on Monday and Wednesday and Friday mornings. So she ended up with a part-time job on Tuesday and Thursday and Friday afternoon. My daughter asked if I could take care of the children on the days that she works. That was the deal we made before the eldest boy was born.

Sharon: You babysit, then, two and a half days a week?

Susan: No, we ended up deciding that I should have a day off on Thursday. It turns out that when my neighbor next door died, her son and his wife moved into her house, and now they run a playschool there. On Thursday morning, I simply walk the twins over at 8:30. They are not picked up again until 4:30. I play golf and do other things on that day.

Sharon: So you're still babysitting one and a half days a week?

Susan: Yes. It's wonderful being able to do that. Also, if I had to drive somewhere else to take care of the children, that would be quite a hardship. I have a friend who has to drive over an hour to babysit her grandson. She doesn't like to come back here the same day, because the traffic is terrible. So, to help out, it means at least one overnight stay for her, in a place that's not her own.

Sharon: If you want to take a vacation, how do you manage child care for the grandchildren?

Susan: Well, I just let my daughter know in advance, and she works it out. Sometimes she just takes off the days that she would usually be working. The oldest is now in school until 2:30. What she's done more recently, now that the twins are older, is send them to preschool on Tuesdays and Thursdays. By the way, the preschool will pick them up. I'd never even heard of that before. Apparently it's become more common, because so many mothers are working. That's an enormous convenience for everyone.

Certainly, Susan's grandchildren have the benefit of daily interaction with their grandmother, and, of course, the parents have a built-in babysitter. Later in life, she will be in close proximity to receive help with her own care, should she need it. In fact, she already has. Here are her comments about her recent hip surgery:

Susan: One other thing I thought of as a benefit to the housing arrangement is them taking care of me, when I'm hospitalized. Of course, just having had hip replacement surgery, I am very aware of that. I just got out of the hospital five weeks ago. I needed a lot of care, and they saw to it that I got to and from the hospital. That would have been very hard to do if I lived alone. In fact, the hospital would not have let me come home if there had not been someone there to help me out. Because they live right here with me, they didn't have to drive a long way or fly out from somewhere to help me out.

Close proximity also allows our sister, Mary Ellen, to help out with her grandchildren. Not long ago, Mary Ellen moved to Texas to a small house just blocks away from her daughter, son-in-law, and two granddaughters. Because she lives nearby, she is able to help out in a number of ways. Mary Ellen is an artist and has a flexible work schedule. Not only does she frequently pick them up after school, but she also assists them with homework. She told us about a science project that she worked on with her granddaughter, Danielle.

Mary Ellen: Danielle's parents were out of town, and I was babysitting. The project involved comparing the evaporation rates of both clear and colored water over a seventy-two-hour period. The assignment was to determine if one would evaporate faster than the other. Initially, we labeled six glass jars that were the same size and filled three with clear water and the other three with colored water. We placed one pair outdoors, one pair in the kitchen, and one pair in the bathroom. Then, every twelve hours we measured with a ruler how much the liquids had evaporated. I helped Danielle design charts and graphs for the project. We determined that, in fact, the evaporation rates are the same for both clear and colored water. She got an A on the project!

Mary Ellen will often use the computer to go online with the girls to assist them with their homework. Also, she helps Michelle with spelling and told us that a while ago she taught her how to play gin rummy and dominoes.

Mary Ellen: I think both dominoes and gin rummy are great games for helping Michelle learn her numbers, especially since I allow her to keep score for both of us. She is so good with numbers. My only frustration is that she consistently beats me!

Surely, Mary Ellen can feel better when she puts her great artistic talent to work with them. She enjoys giving art lessons to Danielle, Michelle, and their friends. They've done a number of T-shirt projects together to commemorate various holidays. In turn, Mary Ellen talks about how Danielle has helped her in her professional life.

Mary Ellen: When I have a painting that needs to be framed, I often take Danielle with me to the frame shop. In teaching her how to do framing, she actually helps me pick and choose the large frames for my paintings. Now, we're talking about hundreds of dollars worth of stuff. She is very good at making the right selections. Where else could she learn about these materials? Certainly public schools don't do this, especially with all of the cutbacks in the arts programs. Yesterday, I had to go to the framers by myself, since Danielle was away at camp. I really missed her good advice.

Speaking of artwork, we all love Mary Ellen's paintings of our brother Steve's pet rabbits. Several years ago, she saw a family photo of Steve as a boy with his rabbits in a box. It inspired her to use it as a theme for a painting (see figure 4.1). We also like the painting because it captures the theme of our book. You can see the three generations of rabbits living together with both the proximity and privacy that we recommend!

Additionally, Mary Ellen babysits the girls when their parents go on business trips or vacations by themselves. She also watches their dog for them if they all go away. One of her favorite activities with the girls has been teaching them how to prepare food. For example, she showed Danielle how to make her own tuna sandwich with pickles and mayonnaise. She also has introduced the electric mixer to them while making walnut pancakes. Her daughter has said to her, "Mom, you're out there building memories with the girls." Indeed, she is.

Exhibit 4.1   "Urban for Rent"

Source: Mary Ellen Wehrli, www.maryellenwehrli.com.

On the flip side, Mary Ellen also received help from them recently, when she suffered a back injury. Her daughter helped her with grocery shopping, cooked meals for her, and drove her to appointments with the doctor and physical therapist. In turn, her granddaughter Danielle helped decorate her Christmas tree and vacuumed her house before Mary Ellen's bunko game night with her friends. It turned out that one of the adults wasn't able to make it, and Danielle not only filled in as a substitute player, but she also won!

Do Susan and Mary Ellen's types of intergenerational living arrangements portend a trend for the future? Indeed, these women may be ahead of their time and may even be signaling a paradigm shift in the way some families are housed in the future.

Not only did we ask grandmothers about ways they help out with babysitting their grandchildren, but we also asked a young couple about their child-care arrangements with her parents. Carol and Greg live on one side of a duplex with their one-year-old son, and her parents live on the other side. They all live together in a residential community in Northern California. Both she and her husband work full-time, Carol as an administrator for a university and Greg as a supply manager for a computer firm. Coincidentally, they were both raised during parts of their childhood in the same households with their respective grandparents. Carol and Greg regard these experiences as having been very positive for them and are delighted to be repeating the life-cycle pattern with their child. Here's what they had to say about ways her parents help them with their one-year-old son.

Sharon: Do your parents help you with babysitting?

Carol: Yes. They actually help us most of the time. My dad watches our son, Ryan, in the morning. My mom works half a day. So after she comes home at noon, she looks after him in the afternoon. We do have a sitter one day a week to give them a day off.

Sharon: What happens if they want to travel or go on a little weekend trip?

Greg: We are usually the ones going on a weekend trip. They don't go out that much and don't seem to mind babysitting for us when we want to go out ourselves.

Sharon: How fortunate for you. What else do you like about your living arrangement?

Carol: Overall, it's just nice having them here. I think for me, it's a sense of security. There's always somebody here when we've had emergencies. For instance, when one of the cats scratched my face at about 10:00 one night, I had to go to the hospital and get five stitches. Ryan was asleep and only six months old at the time. It was just so nice that we could run next door for help and just let our baby sleep.

Certainly, they help us out with Ryan every day, and we are incredibly lucky to have that. I think he's incredibly lucky to have that too. He has such a good relationship with all four of us. It is a wonderful situation. Like I've told you, it started out as kind of an economic necessity for us to live here, but now it's something that we're planning to continue in the future. We want to buy a bigger place where we can continue to live together, because it's nice. It works, and I think we all enjoy it.

Greg: In fact, the benefits for Ryan developmentally are fantastic, because he does have more people. There is no such thing as too much love, and he does have it all day long. He has someone around him who is completely devoted to him. After a few hours, he has somebody new to look after him, someone who has energy. Because you can get exhausted being with a small child, after a while you can pass him off to the next person. His grandparents are always excited to see him. They're ready to read him five books and take him to the park or do something else with him.

Sharon: So he gets lots of positive energy rather than a tired parent.

Carol: I don't know how single parents do it.

Sharon: Anything else you'd like to add?

Greg: Yes. Generally speaking, I think that the way Americans are so geographically dispersed is not healthy for relationships among family members. I think our own housing arrangement is a good way to bridge a lot of that, assuming that the parties can actually get along and make it succeed. Traditionally, people have lived in multigenerational households, and it has worked with a tremendous amount of support inherent in that. Nowadays, people have lost out by moving so far apart from each other.

Carol: I agree. I think it's just healthier for society overall to live like we do. Certainly, it's nice for us now raising a child. I think that twenty, thirty, or forty years from now, we'll help my parents be able to maintain their independence and continue to live in their home. We want them to have the life that they want to live, before they have to go into a nursing home, if they ever have to. So many people end up in that kind of a situation, just because they don't have a support network to help them. I think that's wrong. I really think that families should be taking care of each other and helping each other out.

Down the line, Ryan could have a place where he could come back. He could potentially have my parents' home after they pass on. It just makes sense to me. It seems healthier and more natural, rather than just everybody doing their own thing. I think it stems from American overconsumption. It's like everybody has to have a house with a spare bedroom, a living room separate from the family room, and all of this extra stuff that you don't even use. And everybody has to have their own separate house. I think it just keeps people further apart from each other, and families further apart. I don't think that's a good thing.

Siblings Help Out

Not only are grandparents helping out by babysitting their grandchildren, but more and more siblings are starting to help each other with child care.

In one instance two sisters and a brother, all married with children, decided to relocate together in Denver. They live in separate homes within blocks of each other and constantly look after each other's children. Their mother called her adult son one day to see how he was doing. He said, "I'm sorry, Mom, I can't talk right now." He was babysitting for both of his sisters while they went skiing together that day.

In another case, two sisters, who now live in the Chicago suburbs, had debated whether to stay at home with their children or continue to work. Jean Korelitz describes how they solved their dilemma together in an article she wrote for *Real Simple* magazine, coincidentally titled "All in the Family." Initially, the sisters and their spouses lived half a mile apart in downtown Chicago and shared a nanny for their children while they both worked. Subsequently, one of them moved to the suburbs and the other followed, buying the house across the street. One of the sisters wanted to stay home with her children, while the other wanted to continue working outside the home at a job she loves.

The sisters came up with an arrangement whereby one works and pays the other enough to be able to stay home and babysit all their children. Ini-

---

Room for Thought 4.1. Siblings Collaborate

Last year, Kanessa Tixe's dad had just finished building a three-family house when he lost his superintendent job in February. He wasn't sure how to make the $5,000-a-month mortgage on the new house in Queens, N.Y.

So Tixe and her siblings decided to help out in an unusual way: They moved in. In December, her father moved into the first floor; her stepsister and husband moved into the second floor; and her stepbrother and Tixe took the third floor. The entire family has become roommates, banding together to pay rent and help their dad with the mortgage until he finds long-term tenants.

"We're still living there now. Times are rough," says Tixe, 26, a publicist. "It's been very beneficial that we're all together. My stepbrother and I have a wonderful relationship now. We eat together for dinner, and I've become closer to my dad, too. This is an important time for family to help, the way the housing market is going. Our story is a testament to how families should come together to help with a mortgage."

The weak economy—which has brought surging foreclosures, sinking property values, vanishing home equity and mounting job losses—is playing a major role in family dynamics, pulling relatives under the same roof to pool their resources and aid relatives who've lost their homes.

Source: Stephanie Armour, "More Families Move in Together during Housing Crisis," *USA Today*, February 3, 2009.

tially, the spouses expressed concerns about the two families retaining their separate identities. However, they talked things over and agreed, "This isn't about you or me. This is about what's good for our families." One of the sisters said, "And it's good for our kids to grow up across the street from each other." The other sister commented, "I don't think I would still be working if I didn't know my kids were loved all day. All of our lives are better because of what we have."[1]

A sister and brother living in Los Angeles would certainly agree about the proximity benefit. Kathleen, an architect, and her husband bought a home for themselves and their two small children. Soon after, her brother and his wife bought the house next door. They also have two small children. They are also both married to French-speaking spouses and now share a French nanny for child care since all four parents work. Kathleen describes their arrangement:

Sharon: Why did your brother and his family decide to live next door to you?

Kathleen: After my younger brother had his second child, he and his wife started looking for a house to buy in our area. It just so happened that the house right next door to us came up for sale a year ago, and they bought it. My dad and I helped them remodel it. Now I'm working on the gardens. I do both landscape design and architecture.

Sharon: Aren't they lucky to have your help!

Kathleen: Yes, and everybody who hears this story thinks that we're nuts. They ask, "What's it like living so close to your brother? Doesn't it get kind of weird?" Well, we just love it. His older daughter and my younger son are eleven months apart and have been like brother and sister. They've been together every single day. Generally, the way we keep our sanity is just always helping each other out. We're always picking up someone's children or helping run errands or babysitting. My sister-in-law also works, and my husband and brother are at the same firm. If she has to work longer hours or go out of town for work or even go to the market, she lets me know. Both of us have schedules that are somewhat flexible, so we could take over for the other person.

Also, we share the same nanny, who has an apartment very near where we live. She started working for us after my sister-in-law decided to go back to work after her second child was born. We were now living next door to each other, and I just said to her, "Listen, we should go and find somebody that we both really like, who is French-speaking and can help my mother." The nanny works for me two days a week, and, on those two days, the nieces are with my mother. She works for my sister-in-law two days a week, and on those days my boys go with my mom. Then, one day a week, the nanny will have all four kids. Our kids are all at the same school, so it works out really well. It helps my mom a lot, too, because it allows her to have her own life.

Sharon: How do you pay for the nanny?

Kathleen: We each pay the nanny on an hourly basis. It probably would be more cost-effective if we put her on a salary. My sister-in-law ends up having to pay more, because the three days a week that the nanny is with her girls, the youngest is not in school yet, so she has to pay her during those hours.

Sharon: Then your kids are in school part of the time too?

Kathleen: Yes. For us the nanny comes from 3:00 in the afternoon until 6:00 p.m. For my sister-in-law, it's really like from 7:30 or 8:00 in the morning until 6:00 in the evening. That can vary depending on her schedule, because her schedule can be kind of erratic.

Sharon: So if she's babysitting all the kids at once, do you pay the hours that your kids are with her, and then, your sister-in-law pays the hours that her kids are with her?

Kathleen: Exactly.

Sharon: Since they're right next door, do you have ground rules for making contact?

Kathleen: You know, it's funny because we don't really have anything explicit. I think both my sister-in-law and I are respectful of each other. So we'll always call or yell over the fence when the children come over to play. We're actually going to knock down a little section of block wall in the rear of both of our properties and put in a gate so the children can pass back and forth without having to go out front.

Sharon: Do you have any friends doing what you're doing?

Kathleen: Nobody. Most people look at me sorta like, "There's got to be a catch to all of this. Like, it's not got to be that great." It just works out so well for us. I mean, I take my niece to school every day, because she's in school with my son. We're just starting up this new thing now where we switch weeks babysitting so that each of us can go out.

Sharon: So you get like a "date night"?

Kathleen: Exactly. I'm watching her kids one night, and then the next week she'll watch our kids.

Sharon: If you were telling someone what you liked about your housing situation, what would you say?

Kathleen: I like the convenience of having family so close. I also like the fact that my children really will know their aunts, uncles, and cousins. Also, I have two nieces that are just like daughters, who I see every single day. It really helps that we have similar backgrounds and speak both English and French.

Sharon: Sounds like you would recommend your living arrangement to others?

Kathleen: Oh, definitely. But only if people get along. I've got a very loving relationship with my brother, so I really like having him around. The fact that he is living next door to me is wonderful. My brother is also the godfather of my children. All the families get along. For us, while growing up, we were really close to both sets of grandparents, and my mother's brother, and my cousins. I really like the fact that my children have a real sense of who their family is.

Adult Children Help Out

From accounts about grandparents and siblings taking care of children, we now go to stories about adult children providing care for their close-by parents and grandparents. The folks we interviewed reported mostly positive experiences. However, caring for elderly parents can cause stress on families and their children, and sometimes it can be unbearable. The books and articles on the travails abound. Two recent headlines from the *Wall Street Journal* summarize the issues: "When Caring for Aging Relatives Stirs Emotions You Wish You Didn't Have" and "A Painful Source of Marital Strife: When an Elderly Parent Moves In." While we recognize these potentially unpleasant aspects of helping out elderly parents, this is generally not what we heard from the folks we talked to.

Room for Thought 4.2.   An Adult Child Pitches In

Dr. Arthur Kornhaber, founder and president of the Foundation for Grandparenting, agrees. "We have got more great-grandparents than ever before," he says, "and with increasing longevity, folks are having to find a balance between helping the older and younger generations."

For Nancy Wilcox, 59, that has meant quitting her job to provide round-the-clock care for her 92-year-old father-in-law, who suffers from early to mid-stage Alzheimer's and has had surgery to treat rectal cancer, and her 91-year-old mother-in-law, who suffers from macular degeneration, an eye condition. "This is what the Lord would have us do," Wilcox says.

Caring for her in-laws has become a full-time job, but Wilcox says she still has plenty of contact with her son, daughter-in-law, and infant grandson, who live only a few miles away. "I'm ready to do whatever they need me to do," she says.

In fact, Wilcox believes that moving her in-laws into her home has brought all four generations of her family closer together. "It's made it much easier for the rest of the family to see Mom and Dad," she explains. "And it's made it easier on us—we used to drive down to their place to do their laundry and take them grocery shopping, banking, or whatever."

Source: Jack Beaudoin, "The Four-Generation Family," *Grandparents.com*, accessed January 11, 2012.

A case comes to mind where a married couple owns some acreage in California, near the Napa Valley. Jane writes children's books, and Bob operates a family winemaking business on the property. They also have a family compound there. Both sets of parents have had separate houses on their property for the past thirty years. Today, Jane's and Bob's mothers are both widowed. Jane's mother is an active ninety-seven year old who still drives and lives alone in her small house nearby. Bob's mother is eighty-three, has developed Alzheimer's disease, and now lives with them. They talk about what it's like to have both of their mothers in such close proximity.

Sharon: What prompted you to build houses for both sets of parents here?

Jane: We moved here in 1975. A year later my mother and stepfather moved up. We looked for a house for them with the idea of finding one nearby, but not too close. We thought we would like to be more independent. We looked in other cities that were within a half-hour drive from us. Then we decided that it would be better just to build the house here on our property. There is a road right below our house, and there was a plot of land there that was perfect. We built the house for them with their input. It has one level with a garage underneath. It is built on a hill, so it has a basement and a garage inside. Her house is on top with a wide deck and looks out toward the trees.

As the years have gone by, we've realized that this really has been the best situation. When we were gone on vacation, my mother would keep an eye on the house and look after our animals. We've always had dogs. When we were away, they could go down to my mother's house and stay there. It was good for her, because she felt safer having a dog there, rather than being alone in the house.

Sharon: Did she also help out with the children?

Jane: Oh, yes. John was in the third grade, Kristin in the sixth, and Megan in the seventh when we moved up here in 1975. So she was able to watch them. At that time, we were taking our children with us on vacation. But if we were gone without them, the children could stay with their grandparents. If we were gone, they could pick them up from school. So there were a lot of advantages. The children had a close bonding with both sets of grandparents.

When Bob's parents retired, they came up here to live. We had a small house on the far corner of our property that we were able to tear down. They ended up purchasing a mobile home and had a garage and deck added to it. It has three bedrooms, a kitchen, a dining room, and two bathrooms. Then, after about ten years, his father died of lung cancer. After he died, Bob's mother became very depressed. She just didn't do much and had health problems. She started sitting in her chair and smoking, and that was it. Eventually, with her lack of mobility, she just couldn't walk very far and now needs a wheelchair to go anyplace.

We would have somebody come and stay with her. One time her grandson and his wife and their two little girls came to live with her. But she would not give up smoking. Since they did not want to live in a smoky environment, they moved out. At that time, we did not realize that she was in the beginning stages of Alzheimer's.

Sharon: Bob, what prompted you to move your mother to your house?

Bob: She was really getting to the point where she couldn't live alone, mainly because of her medication. We moved her in here with us and added on to our house. We ended up putting her in our bedroom downstairs and built a new bedroom for ourselves upstairs. At first, she was not happy with the move, but now she seems to accept it.

Jane: After a short time, she became more interested in things. We have a business down below. It's a winery, and our son is now manager of it. Our other son also works there. So we have the two of them going in and out of our house all the time. They talk to her, and so does our bookkeeper, who works downstairs. Occasionally, our bookkeeper's sister comes to stay with Bob's mother while we are gone. They both smoke, like to talk, and get along very well.

Sharon: Any problems with her living here with you?

Bob: She still smokes and is not going to stop now. We put a giant fan right over her chair in the kitchen corner, so it can suck the smoke out of here. She knows this is the only place in our house she can smoke, and she cooperates with us on that one.

Sharon: How do you manage taking care of her in your home?

Bob: You have to have a wife like Jane. I don't know if I could handle it if she could not. I don't do as much of the caregiving as she does. It is easy for me to be busy with other things in my life, even though Jane is very busy herself. I do get all of my mother's pills ready every Sunday and take her places. What I have found is that this works as long as the husband and wife work together to make it work.

Sharon: So it is really a personality and disposition type of issue too. The kind of people that are both giving and willing to help out are the ones to do it.

Bob: Jane is an angel too. She likes most people. Also, Jane takes care of her own mother. I don't think about it a lot of the time, but she is the one that does. It is rough on her, I think. She doesn't show it, but her mother is pretty demanding. Jane is always there. We get concerned about how her mother is going to hold up in the future. One time, when she had a health problem, Jane went down and stayed with her at her place, because we didn't know what we'd do with her here. We may be faced with full-time caring for both our mothers.

Sharon (to Jane): How do you handle communication issues with your mother-in-law?

Jane: We try to make her life comfortable and enjoyable. With Alzheimer's, she forgets things. For instance, she always pulls the ice tray out of the refrigerator and never remembers to put it back. For me to tell her every day to put the ice tray away is not going to make anything any different, so we laugh about it. I just avoid getting into confrontations with her. I find that, as long as we maintain a fairly happy relationship, I can get her to get dressed every day, and I can get her to take a shower every third day.

Also, she likes drinking Dr. Pepper. She doesn't get hungry, but she will go to the refrigerator to get a Dr. Pepper. I'll say, "Paula, you can't have a Dr. Pepper until you have something to eat." She will usually say, "Why?" Then I will say, "Because you need to take your pills." So she will go ahead and have her breakfast and pills, and then ask, "Can I have a Dr. Pepper now?" When it first happened, I remember looking at her and starting to laugh. I said, "Do you mean to tell me that, if I told you no, that you wouldn't have it now?" She looked at me and said, "No, I would have it." She is a very good-natured person. There just has to be laughter there.

Sharon: So you are using Dr. Pepper as a negotiating tool to get her to cooperate. What you are using is humor and a positive lifestyle to keep the peace.

Jane: Instead of telling her what to do, I have learned to ask her, "When would you like to take your shower? Now, or at a different time?" Then, she will look at the clock and say a time. If it's a good time, then I will agree with it. If it's not such a good time, then I will come up with a compromise time. We're kind of bartering to do it. But that is the most difficult issue, because she does not like to take a shower.

Sharon: Also, by posing questions like that, you're allowing her to have control of her life. It's a clever way of doing it.

Jane: There is a conflict, though, in having both my mother and mother-in-law to deal with. Now, because my mother-in-law is in the house, I am not spending as much time with my mother. So my mother gets her feelings hurt. It's easier to be with my mother-in-law, because she's not very demanding. For example, I do the things I have to do in order for her to go to the doctor. I need to get her into the shower, make sure her clothes are clean, and curl her hair with the curling iron. With my mother I do not have to do all that. Instead, my mother needs me to spend time with her. I work this out by sometimes going over to her place or talking to her on the phone, practically every day. If I am home, I might go down before dinner and play cards with her for a while. It doesn't have to be long, but it has to be some kind of contact.

Sharon: What do you like about your housing situation?

Jane: It's so nice to have them right here. It's so much better than having to drive half an hour to go and pick them up. You know how they are doing. You know how they are eating and caring for themselves. With my mother-in-law and her medications, there is no way that she could live by herself. I know that some of my friends have caretakers who stay with their parents, and that works out very well for them.

Sharon: What do you dislike about living so near your mothers?

Jane: If we're going to be gone for a time, we have to make arrangements for someone to look after Bob's mother. His brother lives less than an hour away. When we are going to be gone on the weekend, he will have my mother-in-law come over and stay with them. He is really very good about that. We can leave for a few hours to go shopping or out to dinner, and she is fine. But, if we are going to be gone overnight, we can't leave her by herself. That is when Bob's brother comes over, unless my son and his wife come and stay in our house.

We want to interrupt the dialogue here for a moment just to emphasize a key point. A major difficulty folks have often mentioned in our interviews is the problem of finding help for disabled parents when they are traveling either for business or a vacation. Hopefully, siblings, other relatives, or friends can help out in the way Bob's brother does with his mother as above.

Sharon: So you have an advantage being in close proximity to both of your mothers. Do you recommend your living arrangement to others? Why or why not?

Jane: I would, because I think it is just important to keep the family together. You know, we are used to doing this. Why would you not do it? Now sometimes parents themselves don't want to live with their adult children. My grandmother was ninety-nine when she died, and she didn't move in with my mother until about three years before she died. She was perfectly capable of taking care of herself. With my own mother now, she does not want to move in with any of the younger ones. She likes her independence. I think it is a matter of what has to be done health-wise for the parent.

I belong to a bridge group and some of the members are my mother's friends. Some of them are at the point where they are either moving in with their daughter or son or going into an apartment. Most of them are going into senior apartment complexes by choice. They do not want to move in with the family. I have another friend whose mother asked if she could move in with her family, and my friend said absolutely not. She said the relationship was so strained, and she knew it would not be a good thing. Actually, her mother only lives a few blocks away. They hired a caregiver to come in and stay with her.

Sharon: So what would you change, if you could change anything at this time?

Bob: Well, you accept what is your debt. I don't think I would try to change it. You know, they took care of us. It is kind of our turn. Every Christmas I'm part of a group that delivers Christmas trees to convalescent homes. I wouldn't wish a convalescent home on anybody. I keep thinking of the times where my mother will need a lot more help than we can provide. Then what will happen? So we are trying to avoid that.

Bob and Jane certainly are doing an admirable job of helping out their elderly mothers. Along with everything else they do for them, Jane mentioned they also include their mothers at neighborhood gatherings and sometimes take them to Rotary Club meetings. Certainly, a key aspect of elder care is providing social activities. A woman we interviewed in South Carolina built an apartment attached to her house for her mother to live in. Joan had this to say about how she keeps her mother socially active:

Joan: It's so important in this type of living arrangement that whoever is living with you doesn't feel like it's only the family they are interacting with. They need to have other outlets. My mother fortunately has some very close friends. We make sure that they get together at least once during the week, and then again on the weekend. They will just gather at one of their houses, have coffee and dessert, and talk. My mother now goes to a senior center in the afternoons and it's something she looks forward to. She has a place to go where there are other people who enjoy seeing her and appreciate her, other than her family.

Grandchildren Help Out

Usually, it's the adult children who provide help to their parents, if needed. However, if you think those in today's so-called sandwich generation have a lot of stress, consider the possibility of the children of baby boomers taking care of not only their own children and their parents, but their over-eighty-five grandparents as well. Ellen Graham describes such a scenario happening right now in an article she wrote for the *Wall Street Journal* titled "Two Generations: One Nursing Home." A man with teenagers is responsible not only for coordinating his sixty-six-year-old disabled mother's stay at a nursing home, but also that of his eighty-six-year-old grandmother.[2] In fact, according to a recent study, "8 percent of informal caregivers for the elderly are adult grandchildren—a number many experts believe is bound to grow."[3]

To cite an instance, five years ago, a woman who lives in Connecticut with her husband and three small children bought the house next door for her grandmother. Dana, the granddaughter, is currently a full-time mom and community volunteer. She had been raised by her grandmother after her own mother died when she was three. She talks about both the benefits and hardships she has experienced having her grandmother so close:

Dana: Before my grandmother moved next door to us, she had been living with my aunt for many years. But my aunt worked full-time, so my grandmother was home alone from 6:00 a.m. until 7:00 p.m. every night. My aunt did everything she possibly could to entertain, spend time with, and provide comfort to my grandmother. However, you can't leave somebody when they are a senior citizen at home alone every day. Emotionally, she just couldn't handle it.

When we moved out here from New York City, my grandmother was only one town away. So every other week, I would go and get her and she would spend the week with us. Unfortunately, it would take me two days to get her out of her emotional funk. By the time I got her cheered up and comfortable being around other people, it was almost time to take her home. It was also hard, because she was living in my house all day long. Today, she is eighty-seven years old. Then, she was younger, but I think anyone in their mid-eighties would have trouble adjusting to living with a young family full-time. It was very difficult for all of us.

Fortunately, we were able to buy the house next door for her. I wanted my grandmother here. I did not want her to live in the depression she was living in anymore. I couldn't physically do the every-other-week thing on top of having two babies and having her in my house twenty-four hours a day, along with a husband who travels. It's hard. She's not even my mother, she's my grandmother. I appreciate the financial level that we have. I'm lucky we can give her a place of her own.

Sharon: Even though she is your grandmother, she is like your mother?

Dana: Yes. My grandmother has four children, including my father, who lives in Maine, my aunt Peggy, who lives in Oregon, my uncle Don, who lives in California, and my aunt Jean, who currently has moved nearby. She is the one my grandmother lived with, who works full-time. They all were doing everything that they could to comfort this woman and make her part of the family, but they all worked full-time. It would have been so hard for them to have her live with them.

Sharon: What do you like about your housing situation?

Dana: I like that she's not here twenty-four hours a day. I have my own space, so I do have the luxury to breathe. However, she is here for breakfast, lunch, and dinner every day. I think it's important that she eats with us, because I think for a senior citizen the loneliest time of the day is mealtime, especially dinner.

Sharon: Does your grandmother have any medical issues?

Dana: Yes. The hardest thing that we are dealing with now is her arthritis. Otherwise, she is as healthy as a horse. Arthritis is relatively new to her, and she doesn't know how to deal with the pain. Therefore, her daily demeanor is negative. She doesn't have a life that's very fulfilling. Certainly, I can do things for her, but I think it is very important for her mental health that she do things for herself. She won't unless I force her. I make her go to the senior center. I push her to go out to lunch with her friends, particularly the one across the street who still drives.

Sharon: How do you deal with her negativity?

Dana: I ignore it most of the time. I'll say to her, "Grandma, how are you today?" She'll typically respond, "Oh, it hurts." I'll ask, "What hurts?" She'll reply, "My arthritis hurts." I'll ask, "Did you take your Tylenol?" She'll say, "Yes, I took it." Then, I'll change the subject with a comment like, "So how about those Red Sox!" So I do ignore it.

Sharon: You are very gracious with a difficult person.

Dana: She is difficult, but she's not difficult all the time. She is very grateful for where she lives. She does know that life could be worse. I deliver Meals on Wheels with her once a month because I want her to see how life could be worse for her. When she returns home, she'll call and say, "I know how lucky I am."

Sharon: So it's an activity for her, and she gets to do volunteer work. Would you recommend your living arrangement to others?

Dana: Absolutely. Once again, it's an ideal way to live. To have that type of multigenerational living arrangement that close to you, and yet still have a little distance, is the perfect world. I love having my children grow up with her. Despite her difficult personality, they still have a feeling of responsibility toward their family. And I also think it's going to build their character one day. Not necessarily right now. Jimmy is eight and Blaire is six. But Sam is two and he loves her. He runs back and forth. She loves him. They play ball. They watch baseball. When I need my kids out of the house to get something ready, I send them to Grandma's.

Sharon: So she does help you then?

Dana: As much as she can. I usually have to send Jimmy, too, but she tries. She is most helpful with babysitting while I'm at my night meetings. After I put my children to bed, I'll leave her in the house with them, along with my telephone number, and go to my meetings. She can watch television. If anybody gets up or wakes up or if there is a problem, she'll call me immediately. We live in a very small town, so it's very easy for me to get home.

Also, she helps me with my volunteer work. I have her stuffing envelopes. I want her to feel useful. I want her to feel ownership. I want her to feel part of this world. I try and give her chores, almost like I give my children chores, because I want her to feel a part of this family.

Sharon: What are her chores?

Dana: She is responsible for emptying the dishwasher every day. It's a simple chore, but it's her chore. It's her contribution to our family. It takes me three seconds to empty the dishwasher and it takes her forty-five minutes. But that's not the point. The point is that's her contribution to the family. It also takes away some of her feeling so guilty about accepting so much financial help.

Sharon: She feels like she is working for her room and board.

Dana: Yes. Every time she babysits she feels like she is working for her room and board because she always says to me, "Well, it kind of helps take care of the heating bill." I say, "It absolutely does."

Sharon: Anything else you'd like to add?

Dana: I try not to talk too much about my grandmother with my girlfriends. It's a very difficult situation, and no one wants to be around somebody who is always talking negatively. But the one stock phrase I always use with them is "No matter what I do in my life, this is my guaranteed ticket to heaven." I could do anything else in the world wrong, but, because I've taken such good care of this woman, she is my guaranteed entry into heaven. I live by that. I'm glad I'm doing it, have no regrets, and would do it all over again.

Conclusions

In most cases, people profess to be happy with their caregiving arrangements. Certainly, there are hardships involved, but also we've heard many stories about benefits. Both Susan and Mary Ellen are examples of grandparents who are both helping out and in turn receiving help when they need it. Carol and Greg talked about how wonderful their lives are to have her parents help them care for their one-year-old. Kathleen told about how convenient it is to have her brother and his family living next door to exchange babysitting. Both Jane and Bob are pleased to have their elderly mothers nearby to look after. Joan shared how and why she keeps her mother socially active. Dana talked about benefits being exchanged as she cares for her grandmother. Coming up in our next chapter are stories about the benefits of "grand" relationships.

Stories about Grand Relationships

The closest friends I have made all through life have been people who also grew up close to a loved and loving grandmother or grandfather.

—MARGARET MEAD

OR US, "grandparents" meant Grandma and Grandpa, who lived far away in Nebraska, and Grannie, who lived a few towns away in California. We have wonderful memories of Grandma reading to us and baking bread, as well as Grandpa taking us fishing and working in his garden. We can still smell the sweet peas growing there. As for Grannie, she was all smiles when she saw us and always wanted to hear about what we were doing. Not only was she an avid listener, but we also remember her gardening, sewing, and raising birds and dogs. Moreover, while babysitting, she introduced us to dancing, music, and hot fudge sundaes. Although our grandparents were positive influences in our lives, surely they would have made even more of an impact had they lived in closer proximity to us.

Definition of "Grandparent"

Looking at the word *grandparent*, we wondered how the word came into the English language. Our thesaurus indicates a number of synonyms for *grand*, including *great, exalted, illustrious, magnificent,* and *important.* Equivalent words for *parent* include *source, ancestor, forefather,* and, of course, *father* and *mother.* Perhaps the *grand* part of the word *grandparent* evolved because, by the time you get to be a grandparent, you know the job. Because of the experience you've had raising your own children, you truly are in a position to be a "grand" parent the second time around.

Neale Walsch in his book *Conversations with God* would certainly agree. He says that the mother and father are the wrong people to raise children:

> It's a miracle that so many of them do as good a job as they do. No one is more ill-equipped to raise children than young parents. And no one knows this, by the way, better than young parents. Most parents come to the job of parenting with very little life experience. They're hardly finished being parented themselves. They're still looking for answers, still searching for clues.[1]

That could be why multigenerational households in the United States have been so successful in the past and are now making a comeback.

Role of Grandparents

"What are grandparents for, and what do they mean?" These two questions were asked recently by a five-year-old grandchild in a conversation with her grandmother. The child's queries raise the subject of grandparents' changing role in today's family structure. With the unprecedented increase in life expectancy, more people are experiencing the role of grandparenthood and, increasingly, great-grandparenthood. Women now have the chance of being grandparents for 50 percent of their lives. And over 75 percent of grandchildren can expect to have at least one grandparent alive when they are thirty. Certainly, the prevalence of grandparents who have adult grandchildren is historically unique.[2]

The meanings and roles of being a grandparent are directly influenced by a number of social factors, including geographic proximity, divorce, reconfigured families, and employed, middle-aged grandmothers. Today, grandparents range in age from late thirties to over one hundred years old, with grandchildren extending from newborns to retirees. Consequently, there are multiple roles and meanings for grandparents, depending on the bonds established in these multigenerational and continually changing relationships. Initially, the bonds between grandparents and grandchildren are fostered by the parents, but over time direct and voluntary interaction occurs.

Typically, all sides gain from the relationships: Parents of young children may receive help with child care from grandparents. The grandchildren obtain the gifts of time, unconditional love, and attention from their grandparents. In turn, grandparents get emotional satisfaction from frequent interaction with their grandchildren and from the responsibilities in helping them. Their role also "serves as a symbol of continuity and stability in family rituals and values."[3] Moreover, grandparents can give grandchildren an appreciation of the past and a sense of history with their stories. Surely, this type of interaction could be more easily facilitated if grandparents lived nearby or with their adult children and grandchildren.

A young father who lives with his wife and two children next door to his mother-in-law in Connecticut would agree with the benefits of proximity. When asked what he liked about his living arrangement, Jeff said, "The best part about it is that my children get a chance to be with their grandmother a lot. They get a sense of 'it's not all about them, and it's not all about the moment.' I think our society right now is a sound-bite world. With a

---

Room for Thought 5.1.   The First Grandmother

In January 2009, the nation got a new First Grandmother, and like 5.7 million of the nation's 70 million grandparents, Marian Robinson, 71, may begin sharing a home (a very roomy white one) with her grandchildren. Michelle Obama's mother was the primary babysitter for the family's two daughters—Malia, 10, and Sasha, 7—throughout the presidential campaign. Now, Robinson is preparing to leave her Chicago home and move to Washington, D.C., with the First Family-to-be. The Obamas have not yet confirmed whether Robinson will actually live in the White House, but it's been rumored that she will.

Grandparents move in with their children and grandchildren for a variety of reasons— to save money, to provide child care, or simply to avoid having a long-distance relationship with grandchildren. Lieberman says grandparents need to consider how they feel about the circumstances that bring them to their child's home. "Some grandparents are angry that their children have burdened them with raising another family at this time in their life, whereas other grandparents become possessive of the grandchildren and want to take over the parental role themselves," she says. "A three-generation household is a minefield of emotions. If everyone tries to be open, honest and loving, it can be an enriched environment. But at the first sign of trouble, seek professional help before conflicts are buried and allowed to fester."

Source: Rebecca Webber, "Could You Live with Your Grandchildren?," *Grandparents.com*, accessed January 11, 2012.

grandmother here, they get an idea that there's a lot of other people out there and a lot of people that lived before them."

Grandchildren See Benefits

We found evidence of mutuality across all the interviews we did with grandchildren. In one instance, a nine-year-old talked about how fortunate she is to have her grandmother living in a cottage in the backyard. They live in a small town in Georgia, and both her parents travel with their work. Julie said, "If my mom is going away, and my dad is going away the same day, then I'll spend the night at my grandma's. That way, I don't have to deal with a babysitter." When asked if she saw anything else as a benefit to being near Grandma, she replied, "Since she's so close, we don't have to wait until a vacation to see her." Certainly, Julie's comments argue in favor of the proximity dividend.

In another case, a nine-year-old grandson talked about the benefits he receives from both of his grandparents living in a cottage in the backyard. Peter lives in a residential community in Northern California, where his mother is a homemaker and his father is a general contractor. When asked to give examples of what he did with his grandparents, he responded, "After school I go over there and they help me do homework. I have snacks and stuff. We also watch TV and play card games." In addition, he said they worked in the household garden together, growing "flowers, carrots, pumpkins, and squash." Of course, as a result of this interaction, the chances are good that Peter will have his own garden when he grows up.

Further testimony that grandchildren see benefits came from an interview with three teenage sisters. It was their father who, in 1996, approached his in-laws about the idea of buying a place together. In his case, his family with three young children needed more space and wanted a swimming pool. In turn, his wife's parents were tired of taking care of their big house. It made perfect sense to all of them to combine financial resources and buy a place together in a small residential town in Northern California. For several years now the maternal grandparents have lived in a guesthouse behind the swimming pool in the backyard. In separate interviews with the grandparents, the parents, and the grandchildren, I (Sharon) learned that the living arrangement has worked beautifully for all of them.

The granddaughters told wonderful stories about how they have profited by living so close to their grandparents. They talked about getting help with homework, learning about values and family history, being driven places, attending sport events, and receiving advice on shopping. In addition, they mentioned the importance of a strong family connection as a deterrent to negative behavior. They also gave accounts of the downside of being nearby. They talked about noise issues, such as having to be quiet in the hot tub at night, being interrupted when doing homework on the computer in the family room, and having to introduce a boyfriend to four adults, instead of two parents. Here is what they had to say about their "grand" relationships.

Sharon: Have you heard of other people participating in a living arrangement similar to the one you have with your grandparents?

Kristine (age fifteen): I don't have very many friends who have that situation. When I mention it to them, they go, "Oh, that's so cool that your grandparents live with you." Because their grandparents live far away or in another part of the country.

Sharon: What do you like about your housing situation?

Margaret (age thirteen): It's really cool because if you need something like sugar, you can walk over and get some. But, like, if we have any questions that our parents can't answer, they just tell us to go over and ask Grandpa. So we just go and talk to him.

Sharon: Do you have a specific example of a question?

Catherine (age seventeen): Yes. Grandpa knows a lot about our family history. So with him being a lot older, I want to make sure that we get the real story now. I'll ask him, "How did Great Uncle Ralph get here?" I have a little tape recorder that I've used to tape our conversations. He's a great storyteller. I'm just passionate about learning about our family's history and also American history. I don't know if I would be interested in history if it wasn't for him.

Sharon: Anything else you want to add in terms of what you like about your housing situation?

Margaret: Besides getting sugar and food from them, I had a situation once when I was doing my homework and needed help with a math problem. I asked my mom if she could look at it with me. She is not a pro at math like my dad is, but he wasn't home. She said, "Just go ask Grandpa." So I did, and, in no time, we had figured it out.

Kristine: Also, what I like about living with them is they help a lot with driving. I'm still fifteen, so I'm not able to drive yet. Sometimes, my sister drives me places, and so does my mom. But at times, if I'm stuck someplace, or if I need to get somewhere and no one can take me, it's really good to be able to walk over and ask them to drive me places.

Catherine: Over the summer we played a lot of water polo across the bay. I had a game at 3:30 one afternoon, and Grandpa and Nani had driven across the bay and surprised me! I didn't know they were coming. They brought their own chairs. I just remember when I was playing and would score, I'd hear, "Way to go, Cathy!" I'd look up, and there Grandpa would be standing with the college shirt he always wears and his glasses. It was like having another set of parents right there, encouraging you at a sports event. It's really special. A lot of people don't even have their parents there, let alone their grandparents.

Sharon: Anything else you want to add? Have you thought about other ways that it's helped you out in your life, having your grandparents around?

Kristine: Nani is a great shopper. She buys us clothes for Christmas. She is a very wise shopper. If I need any advice on sizes or colors, she is always an expert there to help me.

Catherine: Just being older, I know that I've grown up with values that I've gotten from both my church and my family. I feel like, as a family, we respect older people. I see we are nice kids with great values.

Kristine: It's like the values you learn from the relationship with your grandparents carry into other activities with your friends. Just knowing that helps.

Margaret: I go to my friend's house or we're setting up a play date, but then they say, "I can't, my grandparents are coming." I never think twice about saying, "My grandparents are coming." They are already here, so my friends can come over without feeling like they're butting in on "company."

Kristine: When our grandparents come over for dinner, it's not like having company over, since they're already part of our family. Nani always does the dishes at our house. If she is over here and the dishes are piling up, she'll come into the kitchen, and when she leaves the sink is all clean. I'm sure our mother appreciates that a lot.

Margaret: I think it's a plus for parents, too, because they could never leave the kids home alone once they're in high school. There will never be wild parties thrown or anything like that.

Sharon: Is there anything you dislike about your living arrangement?

Catherine: It was hard sometimes when I would be writing papers or we would be in the family room, and they'd walk in from their domino night. They would interrupt us, wanting to visit. You know, while you're doing homework, you have that surge of energy. Then your grandparents walk in, and it stops.

Kristine: One day, I had a really bad day and I stayed home. Nani asked how my day was going. Truthfully, I was in the mood to just go to my room and not think of anything. But, instead, I found myself having to explain my whole day to her. I wasn't in the mood to tell my grandmother what was going on. But I felt like I needed to tell her, since she was there and asked me to.

Sharon: What would you change about your living arrangement if you could change anything?

Catherine: I don't think I would change anything. It's so fun. We have such a strong family connection and I think it's definitely because we are living with our grandparents.

Sharon: Would you recommend your living arrangement to your friends?

Margaret: Definitely. I think it helps a lot for the parents too. If they are going out of town or they are out for the night, then they don't have to hire a babysitter. If there is an emergency, you just run over there. I think if everyone had a grandparent living with them, there would probably be a lot less problems, because they could have the extra help.

Catherine: One of my closest friends is Alicia. Her grandma doesn't live with them, but will come over every day. She lives in a neighboring city. She is another example of someone with a close relationship to a grandparent. Her parents are married and are close. They have two kids and are just a great, close, functioning family. I would recommend it. Kids would grow up in a more healthy environment.

Grandparents See Benefits

Not only do grandchildren benefit from having grandparents so close, but we also ran into instances of grandparents feeling that they themselves learned lessons from their grandchildren. I (Sharon) have so enjoyed living near my grandchildren and watching them grow and develop. It's like déjà vu with my two granddaughters, reliving the joys I had raising their mom and aunt. When the girls were younger, I spent hours reading aloud to them, just as my grandmother did for me. I'd like to think I played some part in Tori's exceptional love for reading. When I've picked her up from school, she will often read a book on the ten-minute drive home. In fact, her mom tells me she prefers reading books to watching videos and television.

On the other hand, they've certainly taught me things. In fact, recently, Tori showed me her science homework assignment, requiring her to make drawings of several forms of sea life. On the back of each illustration, she listed the creature's favorite foods and interesting facts. Her drawings reminded me of the small-boat cruise my husband and I took with her and her sister through Alaska's Inside Passage. As we were out kayaking and hiking, one of the many highlights was seeing sunflower starfish. Tori's sea-life drawings brought back these happy memories. I happen to love the ocean and sea life and was amazed at how much I learned from my fourth-grade granddaughter that day!

In turn, I've had fun introducing the girls to my favorite French impressionist artists. A couple of years ago I bought a Monet Memo game, consisting of thirty-six pairs of Claude Monet's paintings printed on two-by-two-inch cards. Similar to the card game Concentration, all cards are placed face down. In each round a player turns two cards face up so that all the other players can see them. If a player uncovers two cards with the same picture, he keeps the pair and goes on uncovering two more cards. If they are not identical, they must be turned over face down to their original position. The player with the most pairs of identical cards wins. Sad to say, try as I might, I've never won! Miranda was only five when she beat me the first time—twenty-four to twelve! I facetiously yelled at her, "You're not supposed to beat your grandmother!" Needless to say, three years later, it's still the game she wants to play the most when she comes to Gran's.

We've also enjoyed a card game like Go Fish, featuring a number of French impressionist artists. I found it at a local art museum, where I had taken the girls on a tour of a special exhibit of Salviati Venetian glass. One of my favorite grandparent activities has been taking them to art galleries and museums. I get to enjoy the exhibitions and share my love of art history with them, both at the same time. Who knows? As a result of these exposures to art, one of them might become a professional artist or major in art history in college.

Then, when Miranda was only four years old, she asked me several significant questions within a half-hour time period. The first was, "Gran, how did God make everything?" I mentally gasped, thought quickly, and said, "Well, darling, I don't really know how God made everything. I do know that things are made up of tiny atoms." As I started to launch into a description of the structure of atoms, her older sister, Tori, who was six at the time, interjected, "Oh, Gran, we're studying about atoms in school right now." I was relieved to be enrolled in a Master of Liberal Arts graduate program at Stanford University where, coincidentally, I was taking a class on material science. How else was I going to keep up with the latest generation of elementary school students!

Now *girls* I understand. I have two daughters and two granddaughters. The last time I remember being around little boys a lot was when I was twelve and my brother Steve was born. I became his second mother, but that was almost fifty years ago.

So when my grandson John was born in 1999, I was in for some grandparenting adjustments. Instead of dolls, I was headed for the world of bugs. Honestly, I hadn't paid much attention to bugs before John. They were just there to be ignored, swatted, or eliminated. However, to be popular with him, I soon learned that it was important to acquire bug-locating skills. When we went to the local park playground, an important part of the outing was for me to locate trails of ants and sow bugs. "Oh, John, look what Gran found!" I would shout. We would examine the ants and try to follow them home. We soon graduated from ants to bumblebees. One time we were watching bees at eye level, only a foot away, as they were pollinating some flowers. I recall saying to him, "Look, John, the bees are having lunch." That was my way of explaining nature to him.

He also got me into bird watching. John loved to chase robins on the grass at the park. One time when we were at a duck pond, he suddenly started to laugh out loud. It seems that while he was watching ducks swimming in the water, they would tip over to eat with their tails sticking up. He thought this was so funny. You know, I found myself laughing too. In fact, these days, when I see a snake, I don't recoil in fear like I used to. I find myself wanting to watch and examine it. Thanks to being with my grandson, I feel much closer to nature.

In another example of grandkids teaching grandparents, my friend Diana told me about a recent experience with her grandson at Petroglyphs, a ceramics store where you paint pottery objects and then have them fired. Begrudgingly, she and her husband went—their *darling grandson* wanted them to take him there. To their surprise, they had a good time! In fact, not only were they anxious to see how their creative project turned out, but they have indicated an interest in going back.

My other grandson, Christopher, was born in 2002. His emerging interests are centered around gardening, vehicles, and tool projects, following the pursuits of his dad and grandfather. Two years ago, his great-grandmother and I had fun working together to create a needlepoint alphabet picture for him. Now he likes to read too. I am truly blessed to have such wonderful grandchildren!

In another case, a fitness instructor shares a house with her husband, his daughter, and his daughter's three children. The daughter has a separate apartment downstairs and they live upstairs. Dorrie spoke to us about the advantages she has experienced from this type of living arrangement.

Dorrie: I think some of the benefits of their living with us is that we've gotten closer to the kids than we would have if they were living someplace else. Not having had children myself—you know Denise is my stepdaughter—I was dropped into being a grandmother. So for me it has been certainly more experience with young children than I'd had before. That is advantageous, I do believe, for me. For both of us, I think that having young children

---

Room for Thought 5.2.   Designed for Family Life

And while many observers assume that economy-driven multigenerational living is an emotionally traumatic hardship, that's another myth. The truth? Many grandparents tell us not only that they love having their family back under their roof; they also love being needed again. They say it brings purpose to their days, and meaning to their lives. The physical demand of keeping up with the kids makes them feel younger; outdoor play burns off both calories and tension; and helping with homework provides excellent mental stimulation.

There's a lesson here. We humans are built for family life. In a crisis, or after a disaster, it's always family that gets us through. Children must be fed, dressed, and taken to school, so we rally and we do it with a smile. In fact, studies have found that the more we act like everything is okay, the more we actually believe that everything is going to be okay. Family living forces us to have regular, face-to-face contact, which reduces isolation and wards off depression. The predictable routines of family life reduce stress; the act of nurturing, researchers have found, triggers innate biochemical stress-antidotes.

Source: George Witkin, Ph.D., "When Families Live Together: A Survival Guide," *Grandparents.com*, accessed January 11, 2012.

around helps keep us young and gives us a different perspective on life. You know, we're at a certain point where we wouldn't reach out to that younger generation otherwise. You just kind of get into your routine. I think that is a real advantage for us and helps keep us current in the world and in a more youthful culture.

Indeed, grandchildren can provide their grandparents with opportunities to be curious about nature, to be excited about life, and to be playful. As Michael Prichard says, "You don't stop playing because you grow old; you grow old because you stop playing."

We interviewed another grandmother who lives in a house across the street from her daughter, son-in-law, and two grandsons in a small residential community in Northern California. She tells wonderful stories about the interaction between her pet turtle and her grandsons, as well as a special trip to the zoo.

Sharon: Do you have any special activities that you enjoy doing with your grandsons?

Jean: Well, we have a couple of things. I ended up adopting a turtle a few years ago. He came to visit me, and I ended up saving his life because he was trying to cross the street. I didn't know what I was going to do with him, but I went and got some grass and put him in our backyard. Now he is our pet turtle, and the boys just love to come over and see him. We have named him Ernie. Ernie goes into hibernation in August and the boys know we can't find him from August until around Easter time. So they start asking in February, "Is Ernie back?" They like to come over and feed Ernie dandelions, and it's really fun. It's a very unusual thing. Ernie has been with me now for almost three years.

Sharon: Have you bought any books on turtles?

Jean: Yes. This particular turtle is called a redneck slider. The boys and I didn't know what he ate, so we went to the pet store and got some turtle food, which was terribly expensive. Then by mistake one day, one of my little ones gave him a dandelion and we found out that he loves dandelions. Now we don't need to buy the expensive turtle food. Also, right now, outside my kitchen window, I have a bird in a bird's nest. The oldest boy comes over and checks the bird in the nest every day. So I've got nature close by.

Sharon: Do you take trips to the zoo?

Jean: Yes, we do. My fiancé and I took Martin to the zoo a month ago. We told him that we were going to have a mystery trip. I said, "I'll tell you, if you want, or we'll keep it a surprise." He decided he wanted a surprise. We headed to San Francisco and he immediately fell asleep. When we got there, I woke him up and said, "Okay, Martin, we are at our mystery location. Where do you think we are?" He had to figure out where we were. There was a construction project nearby. "We've come to see them build a house," he said. I replied, "Not exactly." So we got out of the car and I said, "Look at the flags." He said, "Why do they have animals on the flags?" Then, all of a sudden, he realized where we were. He was thrilled! We had a wonderful time at the zoo.

Finally, after hearing a lecture extolling the benefits of three-generation households, Bill sent us an e-mail telling about his own experience. He is a retired physician who lives with his wife in Southern California. Here is what he had to say:

Bill: My wife and I enjoyed a few short years of three-generational living in a two-flat house in Chicago. We occupied the first floor. Our daughter and her husband and our two grandchildren lived above us. We sat around the same dinner table every night. Those were the happiest, richest, and most rewarding years of our lives. Today, those two grandchildren are outperforming all their peers. Both are graduates of Harvard. Our grandson earned a master's degree in computer science at Harvard. He then went to Boalt Hall Law School at UC Berkeley and had his pick of law firms. His little sister is in her third year pursuing a doctoral degree in statistics at UC Berkeley. She was a math major at Harvard. Was three-generational living in their early formative years environment enriching? Yes!

A Granddaughter Looks Back

We interviewed a landscape architect who currently lives with her husband in a small residential town in Southern California. Elizabeth was asked to recall the benefits of her childhood experience living next door to her maternal grandparents on a family farm in central California during the 1940s to 1960s. Her stories demonstrate the lifelong influence grandparents can have, which in her case determined a career choice.

Sharon: Tell me about your childhood housing situation.

Elizabeth: I was born in a small town in the Salinas Valley in an agricultural community where my family lived just at the edge of the town on our family farm. It was a complex of houses. My grandparents had lived there since they were married. My mother married my father just at the end of World War II. My maternal grandfather asked my father to go into the farming business with him. That's when they moved to a house already on the property, next to my grandparents' house. Over time it was enlarged and that became our home. So we were right next door to my grandparents' house. There were several other houses on the property where some of the employees lived and migrant workers would come seasonally. So it was like a compound. I lived there for seventeen years, from the time I was born until I went away to college.

Sharon: How did you benefit from living so close to your grandparents?

Elizabeth: I thought it was wonderful living next door to my grandparents, being able to go back and forth. Their home was like a refuge where I could go to get away from my parents. I could go over anytime, and the door was always open. My grandparents were such good friends to me. My grandfather would see me running out the door in the morning to go to school. If I was running late, he would quickly run out the door to see if I'd like a ride. So he drove me to school almost every morning, even though it was only a few blocks away. My grandmother helped me with all kinds of things. We did a lot of sewing projects together.

Sharon: Did she share your love of landscaping and gardening?

Elizabeth: A little bit. She had a gardener, actually, who lived in another cottage that was out behind her house. He was an old Irish man who came when he was in his sixties. He took care of the chicken coops and grew some vegetables that we didn't grow on the farm. My grandmother loved her geraniums, and we would often sit in her patio together where she planted them. But my grandfather actually loved landscaping and architecture. I was always quite interested in the projects that he was doing, like building little ponds and landscaping different parts of their property. I think watching him while I was growing up influenced my decision to later become a landscape designer.

Sharon: What did you like about your housing situation? You mentioned that you were close to your grandparents. Can you see ways that it helped you out in your life?

Elizabeth: Well, I think my grandparents always gave me a lot of encouragement, along with unconditional love and support. So it was like having two support systems, my parents and my grandparents. It was very stable and nurturing. Also, my mother really had built-in babysitters. I never had a babysitter take care of me while I was growing up because my grandparents were always next door to help out.

A Grandson Looks Back

A corporate executive who currently lives with his wife and two children in a suburb of Atlanta, Georgia, was asked questions about his childhood years. During the 1960s to 1980s, Ted lived in New York City in a flat downstairs from his paternal grandmother. His stories tell about the positive interaction he had with his grandmother, including the emotional support she gave him.

Sharon: Tell me about your housing situation as a boy growing up.

Ted: Well, we had a set of flats in New York. My family, including my mother, father, brothers, and myself, lived downstairs, and my grandmother lived upstairs. I imagine they would be considered condos today. The upstairs unit had one bedroom, and the downstairs had two bedrooms. They had separate entrances and backdoors, fully equipped kitchens, bathrooms, dining rooms, and family rooms. It was a freestanding building.

Sharon: Can you give me some examples of how you benefited from living so near your grandmother?

Ted: As a child, I was completely spoiled by my grandmother. I made sure I took advantage of that as much as possible. For example, if my mother said, "No," then I could run upstairs and ask my grandmother. Of course, that did cause friction between my grandmother and my mother. That continued until I moved when I was seventeen years old. Also, my grandmother was more affectionate than my mother, so I got more nurturing from my grandmother than I ever did from my mother.

Sharon: Other examples?

Ted: I could use her car whenever I wanted to. Also, we had a black-and-white TV, and then Grandma bought a color TV. So I no longer watched TV with my family; I watched TV with Grandma. If my parents weren't going to our weekend home, I could convince my grandmother to go to the weekend home. That meant I could go to the weekend home with her, even if my parents did not want to go. And I enjoyed the different foods she served me, including frogs' legs, rabbit, and sweetbreads. Since she grew up in a small village in France, these were common meals in her house. Of course, nobody cooks those things anymore.

Sharon: Are there other specific ways having your grandmother around helped you out in your life?

Ted: Yeah, it is kind of hard to say, because of my parents' situation. Again, she was the nurturing person in the household. If I had a problem, it was easier to talk to her than my folks. She was a good listener. Because she had lived in Europe on her own and was older, she could give you life experience as feedback. When giving advice, she would tell real-life stories to make a point. She would tell stories about family or friends or situations that someone else had experienced. "This is what this person did and that is how it came out. The moral of the story is . . . and it might end up that way for you."

Sharon: What role did your grandmother play for you?

Ted: She was the most secure and stable person in the household. You could always count on her. My parents were alcoholics, so you really couldn't count on them. When I had problems downstairs, I could always go upstairs. Her role was nurturing, secure, loving. She really played the large part of a stand-in mother for me. I loved her as much as I loved my mother and possibly more. Had she not been there through my developmental years, there is no telling what I would have achieved in school or professionally. I think my behavioral makeup would have been different had she not been present in my life.

Sharon: You have certainly achieved a lot in your lifetime, not only with your professional life, but also here you are in this beautiful home with your lovely wife and two sons. It is apparent that you give your grandmother a lot of credit for the success you are experiencing.

Ted: I have a lot of the security in knowing what good parenting may look like. So I think by her being there, I got to experience what I didn't get through being parented well myself. If you look at families a hundred years ago, they pretty much stayed together, because travel was so much harder. Today, that is not the case, and people are spread all over. I think the family does suffer because of that. The children suffer and I think the grandparents suffer. I believe there is a relationship that is missing for many: a nurturing, stable, and secure relationship that should be encouraged. Children should know their grandparents.

Conclusions

So, in spite of having alcoholic parents, Ted has succeeded in life thanks to the nurturing he received from his grandmother. Elizabeth has developed her career in landscape design in part due to living next door to her grandfather. Bill credited three-generational living in his grandchildren's early formative years for enriching their environment and leading to their academic and career achievements. Jean told stories about enjoying nature with her grandsons who live across the street. I gave examples of how my friend Diana and I have ourselves grown from interacting with our grandchildren. Catherine, Kristine, Margaret, Peter, and Katie all spoke highly of the benefits of their "grand" relationships.

Next, we will be telling the stories of those involved in tackling the practicalities of living together. We will cover when and how to make the decision to live nearby, along with privacy issues. Also, how to find, buy, or build housing will be included. If you want to stay in your own house, we tell the stories of those who have remodeled for privacy and accessibility for seniors. Read on!

P A R T

The Practicalities

C H A T E R

Deciding to Live Together

Inventive Negotiations

Life is what happens to you while you're busy making other plans.
—JOHN LENNON

HEN MY GRANDDAUGHTER TORI was four years old, she said to me (Sharon), "Gran, I love you . . . and, I like you too!" To this day I regard her statement of affection as one of the highlights of my life. *Love* is one thing, but *like* is quite another. For many, *love* can also mean *like*. For others, to love a family member can be considered an obligation, one that doesn't necessarily mean that the person is also liked. In fact, one of the major factors in deciding to live together is whether or not family members like each other. After all, if you like someone, chances are better that you'll get along if you decide to live together.

On the other hand, for some grandparents, living adjacent is not a viable option because they don't want daily interaction with their grandchildren or to be on-call to babysit whenever needed by the parents. Some people simply don't feel comfortable being around crying babies or physically cannot lift them. They prefer not to deal with noisy, active children who might trip them, or with teenagers who play loud music. Nor do they desire to be in close proximity to a son- or daughter-in-law with whom they don't necessarily get along. Ultimately, these people want to preserve their ability to make choices, preferring to retain their privacy and independence by living apart.

Often, making the decision to live together is not easy, but it is most assuredly a crucial decision influencing human happiness. This chapter is about when and how to make such decisions. The following true story illustrates the need to plan ahead.

The ugly headline read, "Car Plows through Market, Killing 9." An eighty-six-year-old man drove his Buick through a crowded farmers' market in Santa Monica, California, injuring fifty-four men, women, and children and killing nine, including a three-year-old girl. The driver, unhurt, reported that his foot may have hit the accelerator instead of the brake. A bystander said of the driver, "He looked very confused when he stepped out of the car. He definitely shouldn't have been behind the wheel. He was definitely not quite with it." The police reported after his arrest that the elderly man had no alcohol or psychiatric medications in his system.[1]

When to Start Talking about Changes

The toughest part of making decisions about living arrangements for the elderly is *when* to start talking about it. For most families it seems such decisions are forced by incidents like that above or perhaps health problems of some sort. Clearly the driver should have been in a living situation that allowed him the freedom *not* to have to get behind the wheel of a car.

Now we appreciate that age itself doesn't define one's driving abilities. Some ninety-year-olds are fully capable of driving safely. And, of course, some twenty-year-olds shouldn't ever be behind the wheel of two tons of steel. Our point is simply that you and your family should not wait until some sort of disaster strikes to begin talking about alternative living arrangements. Indeed, if you're lucky, your family has already begun the planning (see Room for Thought 6.1).

One story illustrates well the advantages of foresight and action:

Bob (a small-business owner in Northern California, talking about his mother-in-law): She was really getting to the point where she couldn't live alone, mainly because of her medication. If she didn't take her medication, there were problems. We finally said, "Look, you can't live alone," and moved her in with us. Initially, she wasn't real happy with it, but now she has adjusted to living with us. We're not worried about her taking her medicine anymore.

Room for Thought 6.1.   Some Are Already Making Plans, Taking Action

Daniel Duncan
Arcata, California
Our society has always valued independence. If it turns out that 9 or 10 percent unemployment is the "new normal" then we will have to adapt to that reality as a society. Maybe having extended families living together, or sharing the property, will also become the "new normal." I am okay with that. My house is bigger than I need, and if downsizing on this small planet needs to start at home, I'll be first on my block to remodel the sucker.

Debbie Deland
Orlando, Florida
We have [a] 4 bedroom house with a 20 something son living-in. Took on a roommate to better utilize house footprint and help someone who would have been homeless. It matters how little we use and how much we restore our ecosystems (water, air, resources, green places) to leave more for our futures. More heads under one roof (healthfully), the more sustainable.

theantibush
Honolulu, Hawaii
My wife and I (she is a medical research doctor and I'm a scientist, and together we pull in a serious 6 figures with no debts of any kind whatsoever, and no kids) moved into her parent's house a year and a half ago, after remodeling their upstairs. The upstairs remodel took considerable time largely due to commuting, so for the basement finishing we decided to move into the basement to get it done ASAP. That worked, and we turned it into an apartment with separate entrance and attached garage. Since the upstairs and basement now had a solid, locked door between them, we decided it safe enough to live here permanently despite her mom's inclination to meddle in and destroy the lives of her children. The door stays locked, and its all fine.

uofcenglish
Wilmette, Illinois
I believe that almost half of households today are headed by one person. It only makes sense for generations to combine. I am divorced for 8 years and alone. My 21 year old daughter still has a room at home. I do not like living alone. I enjoy company. I have built a new (renovated 5 bedroom and five bath home in which there are 4 en suite baths). I designed this home (which is not huge) to provide privacy and comfort for everyone. I

feel that we can be together and still have privacy. Kids move out and parents want them out to "have their own space." My new house has this in one place.

sophia
New York State
My house is retrofitted with a mother-in-law section. I have built on, with the hopes that I can grow old here and have family members move in. At age 52 and with grown children I understand that I can have it two ways. I can choose a house that doesn't get messy, is quiet and I have the place to myself. I could also choose to have a house full of life where I'll have to stay on my toes and deal with the chaos of living. I chose this over silence and peace. From what I hear, it's quiet when you're dead. Solitary confinement lacks personal appeal.

Lisa Stockwell
Santa Rosa, California
The difference I see in my children's generation is that the baby boomer generation tried harder (or at least my friends and I did) to develop relationships with our kids that would allow us to get along as adults. I wish independence for my kids as they find lucrative careers, but I know that if we do need to create a multi-generational family when I am older, it can be a positive and happy situation. (I also have created backup plans with friends who are interested in sharing housing if we don't remarry.) We do have options, and multi-generation housing is not a bad one.

justcurious
Oregon
I think there are other options for shared housing among elderly populations, beyond the extended family. I am making tentative plans to age with a friend of 30 years, sharing a home. We are each divorced and have adult children whom we do not wish to inconvenience. We are excited to plan our elder years with support, dignity, companionship and lots of independence. I'd like to see more trends this direction. It could be vibrant and fun and comforting and economical.

Source: Online comments from the *New York Times*, Room for Debate, "The Whole Family under One Roof?," December 26, 2011.

Based on our studies of the matter, the discussions should begin when the older parent hits age seventy. We suggest waiting until about a month after the actual birthday. At seventy-five, when most people have about ten years to go (see exhibit 3.1 in chapter 3), folks need to be in a place and situation that can accommodate growing disabilities. And starting the talking, research, and experimenting at seventy gives everyone time to comfortably consider all the options and implications.

Charlene (a Washington Realtor, describing the problem of waiting too long): I've been working with my mother-in-law, who because of a medical crisis is now in a facility. Her daughter and son, my husband, helped her with the move. She is now missing several of her things. She did not directly supervise the dispersal of her things. Today, we had to shop for summer clothes because she didn't think to save any. Where is her swan pin? Where is another necklace? It's hard to dispose of a lifetime of things. Imagine yourself having to break up your house and get rid of things you've had all your life. Wouldn't it be nicer to go through things when you're feeling okay, instead of being groggy on meds. Do it while you're young. Be where you want to be before you're seventy.

The American Association of Retired Persons (AARP) provides a wealth of information on the topics we cover in this book. In exhibit 6.1 you will find the association's very useful checklist of signals that indicate it's time to start the dialogue. While it is possible for families to complete assessments on their own using standard checklists, there are also experienced professionals who can help. While checklists and professionals will vary somewhat, exhibit 6.1 provides some basic areas you and your older family members may want to focus on.

Exhibit 6.1. The AARP Answers the Question: "How Do I Help Them Know If They Need Help?"

Physical Health: Have they been diagnosed with any chronic diseases such as diabetes, high blood pressure, arthritis, or emphysema? Or other diseases, such as bowel or bladder problems, heart disease, stroke, or cancer? Do they have vision or hearing problems, excessive weight loss or gain, or difficulty walking? Make a list of health professionals they currently see. Add any recent hospitalizations.

Mental Health: Have they been diagnosed with any psychiatric disorders such as depression, anxiety, or psychosis? Have they been diagnosed with Alzheimer's or another form of dementia? Are they showing signs of confusion, disorientation, or isolation? What about mood swings or forgetfulness? Sadness or loneliness?

Medication Use: What medications are they currently taking? What is the dosage? How often? Include over-the-counter medications. Are they taking their medication as directed?

Daily Living Skills: Are they able to dress, bathe, get up from a chair, use a toilet, climb stairs, use the phone? Do they know how to get help in an emergency? Can they shop, prepare meals, do housework and yard work? Can they safely drive?

Home and Community Safety: How safe is their neighborhood? Does their home have smoke alarms, and can they hear them adequately? Can they avoid telephone and door-to-door fraud? Can they maintain their house?

Support Systems: Do your older loved ones have frequent visitors or see friends? Do they go to a senior center or get out of the house for other social reasons? Do family members live close by? Do they keep handy the names, addresses, and phone numbers of key friends and family members they can call in an emergency?

Appearance and Hygiene: How is their overall appearance? Hair clean? Teeth brushed? Shaved? Do they dress appropriately in clean clothes?

Finances: Can they live on their current income? Can they meet future needs with their current income? Are there any legal documents such as trusts, living wills, and/or durable power of attorney? Do they pay bills on time and make informed financial decisions?

Interests/Lifestyles: Do they engage in their favorite hobbies, read books, watch their favorite TV shows, exercise, play a musical instrument, go to church, keep up with their friends? Are they still engaged in the activities they have always enjoyed?

Source: American Association of Retired People, www.aarp.org, 2004.

There are good assessment tools and professional consultants who can help you and your older loved ones decide when assistance is needed. Some hospitals and clinics offer geriatric assessment centers. Some city or county agencies on aging provide this service. There are also independent geriatric care managers (also called case managers).

How to Start Talking

If you're older than a month over seventy, then your job is pretty easy. You've already read this far in the book, so some of what we are saying must be making some sense to you. All you have to do at this point is begin talking to your kids or your kin about your plans for the next couple of decades. Your conversation might start out something like this: "This book I'm reading tells me that I've got about fifteen more years to go before I kick off. It also says my brain and/or body will begin to fall apart pretty soon.[2]

Room for Thought 6.2.   Humor Is Huge

After her parents separated four years ago, Madi, her 13-year-old sister, Zoee Frakes, and their mom, Kristel, 35, moved into Madi's grandma's house. Her great-grandparents moved in last fall after her great-grandfather, Ken, got sick. "It's like *The Waltons*—and *The Simpsons*—around here," jokes Madi's grandmother, 53-year-old Sandra McKenna. Seven people now live in the four-bedroom Tampa, Fla., home that McKenna once shared with only her husband, Ralph Finkenbrink, 48. "It's jam-packed and loving, and if you didn't have a sense of humor you'd lose your mind," Sandra says.

"Mcmedia" commented on the article that day online:

Living in a multi-generation household presents many challenges. . . . The one thing that gets us through the tough times is an unshakable sense of humor. I remember my entire life looking at the bright side because of the values that my family instilled in me. Is it always as pretty as the picture? Heck no. But, we are committed to making the best life possible for all of us under one roof. I am grateful for my friends, and for my family who continue to encourage me to follow my dreams. Life isn't always perfect but I wouldn't change a thing!

Source: "Happiness Is a Full House," *Parade Magazine*, May 2, 2011.

So here's my (our) plan for the next couple of decades. Please tell me what you think."

Even if you have it all figured out so that your kids don't have to participate or help, just telling them about your plan will accomplish three good things. First, they won't worry about you. Second, they can plan accordingly. And, third, they may actually have some ideas about ways to make things even better for you, for everyone.

Alternatively, if it's your parent that's hitting seventy and a month, then the task is tougher. This is particularly so if you were raised in an autocratic family with Mom and/or Dad giving orders as the bosses. Even if you come from a more democratic family where everyone is heard, you still cannot tell your parents what they should do. So how to start? Here's how some folks got the conversational ball rolling. Sometimes it's easy:

Alice (ninety-seven-year-old widowed doll maker from Northern California): Actually, my son Bob came over and said that I should come to live with them. He used to come to San Jose and visit me and it was a long way to bring the children. So he said, "Don't you think you could sell your house and buy a place near us?" Right away, I said, "Fine." I was lonely there without them. Even though I had lots of friends and belonged to clubs, it's not the same. I'd rather live here.

For some it just seems to dawn on them. At least that's how Janet and Craig described their decision to buy a home together with Janet's parents, Nancy and Rick (midseventies, both retired), in Northern California:

Craig (midforties international finance executive): We've been living here since '96. It actually happened when my in-laws, Nancy and Rick, were looking to downsize from the home they had lived in since in the early sixties. At first, we were actually trying to get Janet's brother and sister-in-law, who were planning to move into a bigger house, to combine with them. They weren't interested at the time, so we said, "Why don't we do it." We can get a lot more house for both of us, and, as long as it gives everybody privacy, it would be a great idea.

Janet (homemaker and mother of three): My folks wanted a smaller house with a swimming pool but found it was expensive to buy one in the same neighborhood. We had a beautiful home, but we didn't have a pool. The kids were young, and we thought that might be kind of a nice thing to have. It just dawned on us that if we combined our resources we could get what they wanted, and we could upgrade too. So we started looking, and then Craig and Mom found this great house with both a pool and 1,200-square-foot cottage in the backyard.

Craig: The layout allows us to have our privacy and at the same time be close enough to go back and forth. Also, if they want to entertain a large group, they'll come over here and use our place and we'll go out to a movie or do something else.

Sharon: What made you decide to participate in three-generation housing?

Craig: Part of the idea is knowing that it would give them a place where they could relax and grow old at the same time and also watch the kids. I remember when I was in grad school, we had a curriculum which was a mix of business language and area studies. The area I concentrated on was Asia. I was always interested in the philosophy of China. You get often three or even four generations under one roof. They do it mostly for economic reasons, but also the family is important to them.

Sharon: So a seed was planted back in the college days?

Craig: Yes. And the other thing is, as we met and were married, the family was always very close, my side of the family and Janet's side of the family. When the opportunity presented itself to merge households, we felt comfortable doing so. The reason we didn't stay in our other home is that it didn't lend itself to the two families living together. In fact, they prefer smaller square footage because they like having less space to have to maintain.

If you're lucky enough to have a cooperative relationship with your siblings, then by all means get together and talk. You'll notice that Janet's brother was involved in arrangements described just above. When we were handling the various problems with our brother Steve's health and care, it was most helpful and reassuring to have other loved ones involved in the decisions and discussions. Indeed, had our parents made it to their seventies in good health, the five of us would have conferred on the best way to approach them. Maybe we would have asked our sister, Mary Ellen, to broach the subject. Or, if you're familiar with the Geller clan on the TV show *Friends*, Ross would probably get the job ahead of Monica, for example. And it may or may not make sense to have everyone gathered at a big family meeting. It may be better to get your parents thinking about these kinds of things with a gentle conversational nudge from the parental favorite. Finally, another approach is simply to deliver a copy of this book as a seventieth birthday present.

After three such nudges or giving them three copies of this book, you're probably pestering. But a key thing is to give your parents *time* to consider these ideas. We all like to ignore the inevitability of our own death. But, really, this is not much of a step beyond insurance policies and wills. It's simply a matter of planning ahead, dealing with the foreseeable future. And setting up your everyday living arrangements is probably more important than all the paperwork preparations put together.

It's always helpful to plan a sticky conversation. Again, the AARP provides some very useful information about conducting the negotiations with your family members (see exhibit 6.2). One of these ways to break the ice might work for you and your family.

Who Should Be Involved

The answer here is simple—everyone. It may mean convening the family from around the country or around the world, but everyone should be

Exhibit 6.2. The AARP Recommends You to . . . Plan the Conversation[1]

Approach the subject indirectly: "I know you're taking lots of pills. How do you keep track of them? Would a pill organizer from the drug store help you?" "John says his dad has given up driving. How would you get around when you can no longer drive?"

Be direct but nonconfrontational: "Mom, I'm worried that you seem to be unsteady on your feet. I'm wondering how I can help protect you from falls." "If you ever get to the point where you can't live alone, Dad, where would you want to live?

Watch for openings: "Uncle Joe, you mentioned having problems with your eyesight. Have you seen the eye doctor lately? Does it seem to affect your driving?" "Gramps, after you said last week that you had trouble turning the handles on the water faucets, I wondered how you were managing with the shower."

Share your own feelings about your parents' changing life: "You've always been so independent, Dad. I imagine it's now hard for you to ask for help. Is it?" Let your parents know they can always ask you for help when they need it. "It's hard to see you give up reading, Mom, now that your eyesight is getting bad. Do you miss it? Would you like to try a book on tape?"

Make a list: Family members are sometimes uncomfortable jumping right into a talk about sensitive topics, such as finances. If so, consider giving them a list of questions or concerns and schedule a time to talk. This lets them think about the kinds of help they may need and prepare for the conversation.

Dealing with resistance: Some resistance to talking about independence is normal. They may put you off with reassuring statements or tell you to mind your own business. But experts advise: (1) Respect your parents' feelings if they make it clear they want to avoid a subject. Try another time. (2) Push the issue if health or safety is at risk, while recognizing your parents' right to be in charge of their own lives. (3) Act firmly, but with compassion, if you decide you cannot avoid intervening: "Dad, we can't ignore this any longer. We have to deal with it."

Facilitators are crucial. Involve other people who your parents respect, such as a minister, lawyer, or a family friend. *It would be ideal to meet at their church, office, or home as a neutral venue. In a location other than your parents' home, it may be easier for all to break out of old parent-child roles and behavior sets. Such facilitators may also be able to help you borrow ideas from other families. Indeed, that is the primary purpose of our book—to provide you with others' inventive ideas and best practices about family arrangements toward stimulating your own thinking.*

Look for community resources that can help a parent remain independent, such as transportation, home health care, meal delivery. Share the options with them.

Hold family meetings where everyone discusses concerns and jointly develops a mutually agreeable plan. Make sure your parents feel a sense of involvement and control over their lives. Listen to their opinions and recognize their right to make decisions. Stay focused on current needs and avoid past resentments. They'll feel more in control if the meeting is in their own home. *But, as we advised above, a neutral location is probably best. Getting to an egalitarian discussion where all are treated as adults may be more difficult at your parents' home. This would be particularly so with a father like Archie Bunker, who said, "Whatever happened to the good old days when kids were scared to death of their parents?"*

Perhaps the best way to start such a meeting is for everyone to describe how they see things ten years out. Then try to invent and agree on a common story about the future. This also serves to enhance everyone's focus on the future.

Don't try to change minds in one such family meeting. Give everyone a chance to ruminate on things overnight or over a few days. We know that the brain works more creatively as it is leaving or entering sleep. Breaks can also provide a chance for all to consult with others or to discuss among themselves such big changes.

Techniques of brainstorming may also be appropriate. The key is having everyone participate, and a facilitator can be particularly helpful in ensuring everyone gets a chance to talk. Humorous, even crazy and impractical, ideas should be encourage and "Yes, but . . ." responses forbidden. Often such crazy ideas lead to wonderfully inventive options.

Sharing food or a glass of wine may also be helpful as long as no one has alcohol problems.

Finally, mark momentum. The first "baby steps" are important and should be noted. Celebrate worthwhile new ideas early and often. When you acknowledge areas of agreement or work together to bridge any of your differences, you establish critical momentum and a track record of success.

Keep it positive: Avoid role reversal. Talking to parents and helping them doesn't mean you are "parenting" them. In your talks, treat each other as equals. Be prepared to let your parents make their own choices, even if you don't agree with them. As long as they are not impaired with Alzheimer's disease or other dementia, your parents have the right to make their own decisions. Growing older does not obviate that right. Even when they make what you think is an unsafe choice, it doesn't necessarily mean that they are no longer capable of living independently. If their choices disturb you, you may need to set your own limits to how involved you can be, so that their decisions don't run your life.

Source: American Association of Retired People, www.aarp.org, 2004.

1. We have added our own advice in italics to the AARP's excellent list. Our comments are based on John's 2013 book with coauthors, *Inventive Negotiations* (see www.InventiveNegotiations .com).

involved in the initial discussions. The invitation list should include the sister you hate and the brother that drives your mother crazy. And the emphasis of this first meeting is to lay out all the alternatives *without discussion.* This is crucial—*without discussion.* Avoiding ruling things out immediately keeps everyone involved and maximizes inventive thinking.

How many possibilities are there? When our father died, our mother might have moved in with any of the five of us, or any of us might have moved in with our mother—she had a big house. Now obviously some of those ten options were clearly impractical. But at the first meeting with everyone present, all options, even the bad ones, should be put on the table.

Norma (seventy) and Roger (seventy-five) have retired in Oregon on a property that includes a main house and two accessory units. They were careful to include everyone concerned in their evolving decision making.

Norma: When our daughter Jane graduated from college in California, she said she liked our area too and was going to look for work up here. So she said, "Why don't we make an apartment out of the back of your house." At that point, all the kids were gone. It was just the two of us here.

Roger: When we bought the house, we planned to have a lot done to it. The five-bedroom area was designed in such a way that it could be separated and made into an apartment with a kitchen and outside entrance. So when Jane said, "Make it into an apartment and I'll be your first tenant," that's exactly what we did. We thought, "We don't need all of this space."

Norma: Jane's been subsequently married and has two daughters. After the kids came, we added another bedroom. Then they approached us and said, "How would it be if we built a house on the property?"

Roger: So that's where it got tricky because, since we couldn't divide the property into two lots, we ended up with joint-tenancy ownership. We knew that this might be a problem in dividing up our estate inheritance-wise, because of the other two siblings. But after discussing it with all the kids, we just decided that we'd give it a try anyway. So they built their house. The local government did require that it be smaller in size than the main house. So they had to go by those parameters.

Where to Talk

Some place neutral, not at the home of anyone in your family, is probably the best choice. In exhibit 6.2 we emphasized the importance of facilitators, and perhaps they might provide a good, neutral venue at a church or in their office or home. It might be at a local restaurant or picnic place. The food will keep everyone there and even the big talkers in the family will have to eat, thus allowing others to contribute to the conversation. This initial discussion with all the family involved should be someplace comfortable and informal and should allow an open-ended time frame.

Needs and Resources

The fundamental assumption about family responsibilities made by mainstream American culture goes something like this: "When kids hit eighteen, they're on their own. Legally they're adults and neither parent nor child owe each other anything."[3] Most folks may be willing to help out with college, but in America kids are nudged out of the nest one way or another after they finish high school. And both sides proclaim their rightful freedom. Parents congratulate themselves for a job well done and kids celebrate their freedom from parental control. *Yes!*

So that makes any decision to live together a negotiation *between equals.* "Ideally, it's a negotiation among equals where everyone's feelings are taken into consideration," agrees Dr. Joshua Coleman, a psychologist specializing in child-adult relationships.[4] Both parents and kids have needs and resources to trade. The decision-making process is really just a matter of determining and agreeing on what will be exchanged, when, and how.

We all have basic needs. Psychologist Abraham Maslow described a hierarchy or pyramid of human needs.

1. At the base are *physiological needs* for food, sleep, and shelter—the things that keep us going physically. If any of those needs is not satisfied, we may experience pain, sickness, and so on. Only if those most basic physiological needs are satisfied do we then begin to worry about the next level of needs, those related to our personal safety.
2. *Safety needs* are more psychological in nature and have to do with feelings of security in a chaotic world.
3. Once physiological and safety needs are satisfied, then we begin to focus on *relationship needs*. Given that we're social animals, acceptance, belongingness, and love are important.

4. Maslow argued that only when the first three levels of needs are satisfied do humans begin to focus on *esteem needs*. These include both self-esteem and the esteem of others.
5. Finally come *self-actualization needs*—simply stated, the need to fulfill one's potential as a human.

Maslow's hierarchy, while useful here, should still be taken with a grain of salt. For example, Mary Pipher, in her excellent book on the elderly, *Another Country*, argues that you can't always neatly categorize human needs. That is, the mind and body are connected:

> Communities keep people healthy. In 1988, James House of the University of Michigan found that the lack of social relationships constituted a major health risk, rivaling cigarette smoking or high blood pressure. Research on Roseto, a village of Italian immigrants with three-generational households, indicated that people lived longer if they stayed in Roseto than if they moved away. This increase in longevity rates wherever there is community is called the Roseto effect.[5]

Still, family members often have the abilities and resources to supply all these needs. Certainly, sharing shelter and food preparation and the financial aspects of both might be part of any exchange. Child care and elder care would also both fall into the category of physiological needs. Or simply sharing the chores around the household also fits the description. All kinds of offers might be made regarding sharing rent, mortgage payments, insurance, washing machines and dryers, and so on. "You cook on Tuesdays and Thursdays, and we'll cook on Mondays and Wednesdays," or "You help out with the grandkids during the next ten years or so, then we and the grandkids will help out when you start to fall apart in your eighties."

Following are three instructive stories about how living together in three generations can satisfy a variety of human needs:

Joan (late thirties, Ph.D. financial consultant): Back in the late 1980s, my mother was living in a home in Charleston. My father had passed away in 1980. So for almost ten years, she was maintaining the house by herself. That worked out fine. However, my husband and I began seeing that it became more difficult for her to maintain the house. She had trouble finding someone to mow the lawn, clean the gutters, and we weren't always able to help out. We did what we could. But to find people to help out was becoming more difficult. We started to project down the road what her long-term housing situation would be. We knew from a financial perspective that she would not be able to afford a long-term care facility.

When we bought this house, it had a garage with an entrance that went out to the side of the property. It was a piece of land that we never knew how to landscape because it was not really that wide. We thought about putting in a pool. But we also thought that it's kind of a natural area to put on an addition where there would be an entrance from the garage into what we called the guesthouse. There would be access to it from the house, but not from the main part of our home. So we began getting some drawings in place of what it would look like. I had also talked to a few Realtors who told me this was a positive thing to do when you go to resell the home.

From my perspective, my mother was still driving. She was mobile. She was involved in the senior center. It was an extra set of eyes that I felt was around the home environment during the day. Even though we had a caregiver for my daughter, if that person wasn't able to come or was coming an hour late, there was just another person around. We did it for that reason, for my daughter to have a relationship with her grandmother.

Eleanor (a successful Northern California interior designer in her early sixties describing how her mother helps out): Yes, she still drives, but slowly. She also takes care of our kitty when we are gone. She watches over our house. It gives her a sense of responsibility. I think that is very important. She feels useful. I think the real fear of getting older and being alone is wondering, "Why am I still here? What am I good for?" Because she lives with us, she'll come down and see that I've got the laundry piled up and offer to help with it. She'll do dishes for me. Also, if I'm going to be out on an appointment and my husband is coming home, I can leave stuff out for dinner, and she will put it together for him. If I have to travel for business where I'm gone for several days or a week, she may fix his dinner every night. He'll call her when he is on his way home and say, "Mom, I'm on my way home. What's for dinner tonight?" She will cook what he wants. It's not easy for her. It's very difficult for her to move around and do things, but she has a sense of accomplishment by helping out.

Don (a recently retired air traffic controller in California talking about the arrangement he and his wife have with their daughter and her family living with them next door in their duplex): It's really very mellow. The only problem is we are all running out of room. I mean, the kids want to move because they want their own house. There is no way they can afford one here. They want to go back east, and we are going to go with them. You are talking about shared income now. In other words, we need to have some flexibility in how we do it. There are a lot of things we have to look at from a financial end before we make the move.

Sharon: So when you move, you are planning to do a joint venture with your daughter and her husband again, so you'll share the funding of the house?

Don: Right. Depending on the price. As necessary. It would be perfect if they could go back there and buy it on their own and we could have a place to live with them. But then finding that along with where we want to live and at the right price, they haven't hit the lottery yet. So we'll be sharing the cost.

Just having someone in the house, next door, or at least within yelling distance adds to one's feelings of safety, whether we're talking about high-security gated communities or dangerous inner-city neighborhoods.

Beyond the physiological and safety support close extended family members can supply when they live near one another are the companionship needs. The mutual satisfaction of these depends completely on the mutual enjoyment of one another's company—*liking* one another. For most American families this means sharing entertainment experiences—television, movies, sporting events, and such.

Elisa and Neal explained to us how this "liking" stuff works, and how it's fun. They're both in their midthirties. She's a stockbroker and he's an accountant in Cleveland.

Sharon: So what made you decide to live with Elisa's parents in this apartment above their garage? Whose idea was it?

Elisa: I've always known that we could move in here. So it was just one of our options. I like being close to my family. It's a good way to get started financially and get a house fast too.

Neal: We looked at other choices and in the end we realized it was the best, especially since we wanted to get a home soon. If we had to pay money to rent a place, it would prolong our [in]ability to get our own house. It's nice being rent free.

Over half of the people we interviewed said that their families have been involved in multigenerational living arrangements before. So a history of extended-family living can be an indicator of those who later decide to live together again.

Sharon: Had you heard of others, your parents, participating in a similar living arrangement?

Elisa: My parents lived with my grandma for a few months.

Neal: I know my parents lived with my mom's brother and his wife for a while. It was a rough situation because they were all in the same house. It wasn't a separate thing like we have. So when my mom heard that I was thinking about doing this, she said to just be aware that it's a large family we would be living with. She recalls having to deal with her brother, who had a lot of kids, and they didn't have a separate type of entrance or kitchen like we have. So she was a little concerned. I let her know that it was a completely separate home that we were going to be in, a separate living area. She said, "That sounds like a good deal."

And if things work out best, living with extended family members should also add to one's satisfaction of both esteem and self-actualization needs. For example, among the benefits of helping with elderly parents might be the esteem-building gratefulness of those parents and your siblings, or the self-actualization of helping and supporting family members. Mary Pipher says about assuming responsibility for the care of those we love, "It is not just a burden, but a joy to help those we love. It is a chance to stay connected, to return love, and to grow ourselves."[6]

Exchanging Information

Once families have creatively listed all the potential living arrangements, the next step is to trade information about what needs and resources might be associated with each arrangement. Frankness and realistic estimates of what folks have to offer one another are key. Write all of these considerations down on paper and let everyone involved review them. List the advantages and disadvantages of each living arrangement being considered. Once all the information is on the table, literally, then it's time to make a choice.

We must also add one caveat here about information exchange. Depending on how communicative family members are, it may be important to augment their descriptions of their needs with observations of their limitations and so on. Accompanying loved ones on doctor's appointments or shopping trips may be more than just helpful, but also informative. Observing meal preparation or gardening activities at home are other examples of learning about needs by just "being there." It may also be quite useful to compare notes with siblings or other close relatives and friends.

Exhibit 6.3 provides a useful checklist of things to consider in making decisions about moving in with elderly parents. Virginia Morris's book provides more details. In chapter 13 we add the notion of "caregiving contracts" to her lists.

Compatible lifestyles are key as described by Colleen, a retired school administrator in Michigan.

Colleen: Because I had decided not to move into my vacation home, I thought I should move in with one of my kids. Well, with the four having such different lifestyles, I knew I could get along best with my daughter. And she had just lost her husband in a car accident and has an eight-year-old son. She suggested we get a place together since she was gone a lot with work and I generally stay around home writing and doing other kinds of things with community groups and such.

Exhibit 6.3.   A Checklist for Caring for Your Aging Parents

Their safety

Your limits

Costs

Location

Loneliness

Future care

Can you get along?

What about the rest of the family?

Do you have the space?

Is your house equipped for this?

How much attention does your parent need?

Do your lifestyles meld?

What are the advantages?

Source: Virginia Morris, *How to Care for Your Aging Parents* (New York: Workman, 1996), 192–96.

If you've started early in this process, at the recommended seventy years plus a month, then you also have time to experiment with different living arrangements. No matter how carefully folks have considered what living together again might be like, some things (good and bad) are simply impossible to anticipate. However, we also want to raise a flag of caution here. Obviously, in most cases it will be impractical to add kitchens or find duplexes during such an experiment. And we know that seemingly trivial privacy considerations can make big differences in how households work. For example, imagine living with your three generations together in a six-thousand-square-foot house versus a small apartment. The physical environment can be a powerful influence on how folks get along. So be careful and note that it will take some imagination to look beyond such temporary environmental obstacles. But the key point here is that more information will be created during such experiments that can better inform ultimate decisions. So try things out if you can.

Following are a series of illustrative stories about trying things out. We'll begin with Dorrie, a fitness counselor, and her husband, Tim, a retired architect. They share a divided house with his daughter in Northern California.

Dorrie: Well a number of years ago, Tim's daughter had three children and was in a difficult marriage living in Fresno. We found that when the children were very young, she would come and visit us on the weekends and bring them with her. Then she would come on vacations and stay and would also spend Thanksgiving with us and the kids. She would stay a little bit longer each time. We knew that things were not good in their relationship. It was a real strain. We could tell that she needed to get away to a safe place, a haven to come to with the kids.

One summer she asked us if she could come and spend an extended vacation during the summer. We said, "Sure." I looked at Tim at that time and said, "You know this extended vacation might indicate that we should start cleaning out the extra bedrooms downstairs." Sure enough, she came really with the intention of just getting away for a while to clear her head and have a little break for the kids. I think underneath there was a definite possibility of a breakup in her marriage, but I don't think she was ready to admit it to herself at the time. But psychologically we started to gear ourselves up for the possibility that by the time school started in the fall, we would have a family of four living with us. That's what happened.

Tim: We are fortunate to have a rather large house with six bedrooms and five bathrooms, designed so that it is totally separate between the two levels.

In fact on the first level, which is where they stay, there is a complete kitchen and family room, along with two bathrooms and three bedrooms. It lends itself very well to having a second family of four people stay with us. In fact, there is even a separate driveway so they can come and go without our even knowing it.

Todd and Lynne, both in their midthirties, own two nursery schools near Denver, Colorado. They also took an incremental approach to living with Todd's parents.

Todd: Actually, my mom and dad moved up here about a year and a half ago. They moved in with us in the beginning until their house, which had renters in it, was vacated. They stayed for three months and it worked out very well. Now they are planning to sell their house, and we are going to build a new house in the back of our property for them too.

Lynne: During the time they were living here with us, it was such a pleasant experience to be able to lead separate lives, but also come together for family meals, as well as share the housework and the kids. That's when we said, "When we build our new house out back, might you consider buying this house from us?" So for a while that was the question. We would be about a hundred yards from each other. Since then, the situation has changed for them. They want to go more to simplicity, to downsize to something more reasonable at their age and be even closer. So we'll sell this house. That is the plan; we will live in our new house, and they will live in, quote, a "guesthouse."

Sharon: So what made you decide to participate in three-generation housing? Was it based on the success experience that you had just having them nearby, or were there other reasons?

Todd: We purchased this land with the intention of being able to take on whatever we needed to do for the family. It was a very good deal. I looked at it and said, "I don't know what their retirement is going to be. They might end up here anyway, so we might as well plan for it." Either set of parents, we don't know who might show up, could be in the future guesthouse. Eventually, when we are old, maybe we will be in the guesthouse, and the kids can take over this house. Also, we never know if my brother might show up one day.

Lynne: It wasn't until they came here and we lived together that the message to us was very loud and clear: "We are here to support you." Once that message sunk in, it was an obvious win-win situation. That's when we really started talking about it, when they moved here.

Without question, our favorite story about trying things out is that of Helen, a real estate agent who in her early sixties began experimenting with housing arrangements during visits with her daughter. Here's Helen's story:

Helen: I've tried out a variety of options. I've tried staying in a hotel, but it was expensive and too far away. Next I rented an RV to park in their front yard, but it was not insulated very well and that didn't work. In the middle of the summer, I asked if any of my daughter's friends had an extra guest bedroom that I could rent within walking distance. That wasn't a comfortable option for her. Then I started looking for houses nearby. So for two years I looked. The house next door came up for sale, and I could see it had a lot of potential for a long-term investment. Also, three months before I bought that house, I had a medical emergency and became acutely aware that I might need somebody to take care of me. I might need to have a place where my daughter could look after me. If I have a rental, I can easily live next door for six months, depending on what I needed. It would be easy for her, and I could be involved with the grandchildren.

What I am doing right now is renting the home out. First, I went and fixed it up. It had two bedrooms and one and a half baths, and I could legally convert it to three bedrooms, two baths, making it more valuable. I added a full bathroom with wheelchair access width and a shower that has a three-inch sill, which I figured I could get over easily. I also put in handrails.

I decided I would rent the house short term. I do know my daughter is committed to staying in Arizona until the kids are out of high school, and that is another seventeen years. Another benefit this gave me was a project to do while I'm there that is not family related, so that I have something I can do on my own and be independent.

So that was the sequence—first the trailer and then the house. Originally, I helped them buy their house with the understanding that it would be large enough that we could put in a mother-in-law unit someplace or there would be an extra bedroom. Once they got in the house, they changed their minds. They loved it, but they decided that they did not want to put in a mother-in-law unit. It would block their view, and they would not have enough play space in the backyard. It was perfectly fine for me to stay in the guest bedroom for a while. Now they have three children so that is not possible.

Now I am back to using the RV, and that is a little bit better for me. What I like best is being able to walk out the door and have privacy when I need it. The other thought I had, when I bought this house, is that there is a large area where my RV could be stored to the right of the house. But I really don't feel good about the RV, so I haven't really found a total answer yet.

Ruling Out Options

Finally, it is very important to recognize that some situations simply do not work out. For example, it is often impossible to overcome conflicts about geographic preferences.[7] Knowing when to say no or when to give up is important. Having carefully considered the options by itself often brings a kind of peace.

A young mother shared a story about the dilemma that she and her husband are facing about how to care for their respective mothers. Both women are difficult personality-wise. Her husband's mother yells at the children and is very demanding. Lorraine's ten-year-old son commented after a visit from his grandmother last summer, "Mom, she is so mean to me." It seems the woman would yell at him a lot for minor things. Lorraine's own mother is very negative and finds something wrong with almost everything.

Her husband is adamant that he does not want his mother, who now lives in Texas, to come and live with them. His mother had intimated she would like to relocate to join them. Lorraine said her husband's brother and his wife moved to a house in Texas, five minutes away from his mother. Shortly thereafter, they moved to a place three hours away, just to get away from his mother.

What should this couple do in these situations? Right now, Lorraine's husband is sending his mother money to help her out. Surely, the number one priority should be their own immediate family, and the mother should absolutely not be allowed to come and live with them. They can continue to send her money and get the other siblings to help out as well. We did not talk about what to do with Lorraine's mother.

In some cases, accessory apartments and close proximity to the grandkids will not be preferred by some. For them, independence, privacy, and separation from noisy kids will be more important than the convenience of proximity. A friend's nanny, Isabel, told us the story about her oldest daughter, Maria, who has just moved back to their home with her four-year-old son. Isabel's daughter and her husband had been living for twelve years with his grandparents in a separate apartment in their home. Her husband worked with his grandfather in a business owned by the grandfather. In exchange, he received a salary and they enjoyed free rent in the apartment in the grandparent's home. Also, they were told, "When we die, everything will be yours."

Room for Thought 6.3. Living Together Is Not for Everyone

Linda
Apache Junction, Arizona
Not every multi-generational home consists of 2500 square feet with lots of bedrooms. Not every "child" living with their parents is a never-launched 20-something. After losing his job in the economic downturn, our son's family (including him, his wife, two children and his wife's mother, two cats, a dog and an aquarium) lived with us for almost two years in our three bedroom, 1600 square foot house. (Full disclosure: We parked our small motor home next to the garage for our bedroom.)

humble view
Canada
Living harmoniously with any mix of others requires skills that you hopefully acquire during childhood. Consideration. Tolerance. Respectful communication. Mutual productivity. Problem solving. If you've cultivated these values all along with your boomerangs, things will probably work out just fine under one roof. Many people prefer to live alone because "I don't have to be nice to everybody"—my elderly father's words.

AngelaM
New York
I grew up with my grandparents living upstairs and although I loved it as a kid, my mother, whose parents they were, hated the arrangement because she was never allowed to leave the role of "child." Even when my mother was already in her 40s, my grandmother still found it necessary to criticize the way my mother chose to clean the windows, among other things. My mother swore she'd never, ever live with any of her children (she had 3) and never did. My own grown children (2) are at this moment home from college. I am very ready to have them go back already. As for my husband and myself, we like the peace and quiet without them. We love them, we support them and love to see them visit. After that, not so much. They have their own lives, their own schedules and we find it much more enjoyable when everybody lives on their own.

Concerned Citizen
Anywheresville, USA
40 years ago, my widowed and sickly grandmother moved in with my parents, in our already snug 1500 square foot, modest colonial in the 'burbs. I was already old enough for her to share how miserable this made her—she had to give up first her dignified little bungalow, then her tiny 1-bedroom apartment—now she was living in our spare room.

She had no privacy and dignity; she was ashamed to need charity and medical help. But she had no choice; she was alone in the world. With only one child, this was her only option outside of a nursing home. The fact that people lived in big multiple-generation households does not translate into "and that's what they wanted and made them happy!" Now, I LOVED having my grandma there, but it wasn't the best thing for HER.

When people have money and options (and their health), overwhelmingly they choose independence, privacy and dignity. People want the ability to close a door . . . have the bathroom to themselves . . . be able to make noise (or enjoy silence) as THEY would have it. Often they want the right to decorate or arrange their space to suit THEMSELVES, not the owner of the house! Everyone in such situations knows who is getting "charity" and who the real homeowner is. The idea that multiple-generation households were happy is a lefty liberal myth.

Barbara Lee
Philadelphia
House-sharing posits a reasonably tolerable existing relationship with one's family. It is less likely to work or be considered in the presence of historical abuse, violence, etc. My grandmother brought her parents to live with her and afterwards vowed never to move in with her daughter (only child) and did not.

Coming back from college, I lived at home for 3 months and it was one of the most miserable experiences of my life. I got the dingy little apartment in the seedy neighborhood, an old car that barely ran, a roommate, and a just-above-minimum-wage job. But it was still better to eat Ramen than to stay in the toxic home environment that was my parents' house. As they aged, I provided the necessary support and care, but having either of them move in with me was simply out of the question.

marge
Colorado
Let me start collecting my pills and sharp objects. I love my kids but I also want them to respect my space as I respect theirs. I also know I don't want to live with any of them in the future and am taking steps to figure out an old age hippie retirement with like-minded people of my own demographic. I want people I can fire and hire at will, especially after watching some of the dismal ends of friends' parents. I have 8–12 more years of my youngest at home and then hope to run away and join the circus (or the commune), join my aging nurse friends as an office assistant, or maybe just join a volunteer group and spend my more active "declining" years teaching and sharing. The only reason I can think of for my living with my kids would be if some of them wanted to support the frustrated artist, baker and cheesemaker I want to become, but I don't see them understanding that eccentricity.

Source: Online comments from the *New York Times*, Room for Debate, "The Whole Family under One Roof?," December 26, 2011.

Unfortunately, the emotional cost of living with them was more than Maria could stand. It seems the grandmother had a key to their apartment. She would find out when they were going to be out, and, without asking, would enter their place to look around. Maria's housekeeping was simply not up to the grandmother's standards. Not only would the grandmother give her a verbal scolding for not being neat, but she would tell the neighbors that Maria was a lousy housekeeper. Moreover, if Maria went bike riding with friends, she would be criticized for "not being a good mother" because "she should be home taking care of her son." Bottom line: Maria could no longer take the grandmother's continual interference in her life.

According to Isabel, Maria's husband is perplexed about what to do. The grandparents have told him that, if he leaves, he "will lose everything, . . . not receive an inheritance from them." Logic suggests that, if he wants to keep his marriage, he needs to find other work and a new place to live. Sometimes *proximity* is not a good thing in living with extended family. Sometimes the best decision is to live somewhere else.

Conclusions

For many of the folks we've interviewed, the decision-making process was relatively simple. The fact that you're reading this book suggests this isn't necessarily the case for you. We've tried to outline a road map you might follow to engage your family in an exploration of all the options for best managing the inevitable decline of the seniors in your family. And, of course, all families are different in size, wealth, geographical constraints, interaction-style, and so forth. That's exactly why we've presented so many different stories here.

The keys are creativity, communication, and getting an early start. As Anne Frank so eloquently put it in her diary, "How wonderful it is that nobody need wait a single moment before starting to improve the world." Perhaps the best place to start is with your own family!

CHAPTER 7

Proximity and Privacy

Living Together in Helpful Ways

The kitchen mediates between power and submission and love and hate and all the other dynamics of living day by day.

—BETTY FUSSELL

In the words of Harry S. Truman: "If it's too hot in the kitchen, stay away from the cook."

—ARCHIE BUNKER

HERE ARE MANY helpful ways to live together and apart at the same time. By far, the two most important considerations are a separate entrance and kitchen. It may be a cliché, but the kitchen really is the *heart of the home* and is traditionally run by the female head of the household. As we learned in some of our interviews, two women trying to manage one kitchen can present serious problems.

In one case, a woman shared the story about her experience living with her mother-in-law. Laura is American and married to a Chinese man from Beijing. He is one of four children—the only son. The prevailing custom in Chinese culture is for the oldest son's parents to move in with him and his family. The young couple recently had a baby, and his widowed mother flew out to California from Beijing to help out. Unfortunately, no time limit was set on her visit. The first problem to surface was that his mother does not speak English, only Mandarin. Not only was Laura unable to communicate with her husband's mother, but also the mother-in-law began to take over her kitchen. Laura began to see all kinds of Asian foods she had never seen before. Without asking, her mother-in-law threw out Laura's cooking pots and replaced them with her own. Along with the pots, she threw out Laura's snack foods, including her cookies. Ouch! When queried about this by her son, she said she thought the cookies were stale. After a few months, mom was asked by her son to return home to Beijing. Laura said that things might have been different if the mother-in-law had her own place with her own kitchen.

In another case, a woman from Pennsylvania told the story about her mother-in-law coming to live with her, her husband, and their two children. Kathy said that she and her husband both worked and needed help with child care. Although the mother-in-law was given a wing of their house to live in, she gradually took over the entire house, including the kitchen. Kathy began to feel like it wasn't her home anymore. She told us that she and her husband almost got a divorce over this conflict. However, they eventually built a cottage in the backyard for the mother-in-law, and things have been fine ever since, especially since she now has her own kitchen.

The importance of privacy was also more generally demonstrated in a recent study of multigenerational living commissioned and reported by *Builder* magazine. Researchers from San Diego–based Marketscape Research and Consulting spent days in people's homes asking questions and observing how folks actually lived in their houses. The following quote well makes our point:

> Not surprisingly, privacy is a major concern. While the families spend a lot of time together in the kitchens and living areas, each member feels a significant need for a place he or she can be alone. As one grandmother who has her own suite put it, "I've been living alone for four years. I wanted privacy; they're here when and if I need help. That part was very important."[1]

And we have Archie Bunker's complaint as well:

Archie: How long have them two been up there?

Edith: An hour and a half.

Archie: [knowing they're having sex; looks angry] In the middle of the day?

Edith: Seems like an awfully long time to be showing her his grades.

These stories illustrate that *proximity* and *privacy* are two key words to think of when you begin the process of deciding what type of housing to use for extended-family living. Once you've made the decision to live together with family members, there are a variety of ways you can do so. Options include houses with accessory apartments, duplexes, town houses next door, two or more condos in the same building, family compounds, or cohousing developments. Certainly, houses next door, behind, or across the street from each other, as well as those a few blocks away, can also work.

Accessory Apartments

Suitable for one or two people, an accessory apartment is a self-contained dwelling, usually installed in the surplus space of a so-called single-family home. It can also be a detached building or a portable unit on the same property. Minimally, it features an outside entrance, a bedroom, a bathroom, and some form of kitchen. In addition, some units may have a living room and an outside patio or deck. At most, an accessory apartment shares an entrance, a yard, and parking with the primary residential unit. It is subordinate to the host home in size and appearance, often invisible from the street. There are many other names for this type of housing, including accessory dwelling unit, granny flat, sonny flat, in-law apartment, guest suite, cottage, lifecycle unit, second unit, studio apartment, bonus unit, *casita*, carriage unit, *ohana*, and efficiency apartment.

The accessory apartment is one of the most versatile types of housing. It can offer homeowners a good investment with a healthy rate of return; furnish housing for family members, especially elderly parents; provide flexible living space for adult children or grandchildren, a nanny, a home office, a tenant, or caregivers of the elderly; and improve security in the home. This flexibility provides a tremendous advantage to household structure. In our society, which values both community and privacy but provides few choices between those two extremes, the accessory apartment allows an extended family to live together and apart at the same time.[2]

One Southern California woman has realized these benefits. Susan is divorced and lives in a small residential community. Several years ago, she came up with a novel way to age-in-place with a multigenerational living arrangement that utilizes a remodeled garage on the same property as her house. At first, she used this accessory apartment as a rental to supplement her income. Then she allowed her daughter and son-in-law to live in the unit while they both worked on their graduate degrees and subsequently established their careers. After they started their family, Susan traded places with them. While she had the apartment remodeled, she lived in the big house with her daughter and family and found it difficult. She said, "When you're sharing a house with four bedrooms, and you're in one of them and the kids are using the others, it's hard. But by the time I moved out to the apartment, it was much better. I'm very separated in the sense that I don't even hear the grandkids crying during the night." Here's a story she shared that underscores the benefits of separate living quarters:

Susan: By the way, I just became aware that my daughter's mother-in-law is expecting her own daughter and husband, and their three little boys, to come and stay with her. They now live in Arizona but are moving out here. She was looking forward to sharing space with them for a couple of weeks, then they were going to either rent or buy a place. She's just discovered that they're not planning to buy a house here until the house in Arizona has been sold. Meantime, all the kids will be living with her and her new husband. She is suddenly much more bothered than I thought she would be. It's going to be awfully crowded in her three-bedroom house. Actually, it's four bedrooms, but her husband uses one of them as an office, and he works at home a lot.

Someone said to me, "Oh, she's all upset, and she's really just going to have what you have." And I said, "Oh, no, not at all. We don't share the same roof. I don't hear them wake up. I can go home to my little place and do exactly what I want, play my music loud at night." It just reminded me of the extent of that difference. I mean, my kids can walk over and visit me. That's lovely. But the separation, even sound-wise, I think is quite important.

In another instance, a childless couple has come up with an inventive way to make use of the downstairs accessory apartment at their beach house in Northern California. They loan it out as free vacation housing for their "extended family" of school teachers. Here's Dan's story of how and why they choose to do so:

Sharon: What led you to offer your unit to school teachers as free vacation housing?

Dan: We have a friend who is a retired local school teacher who lives nearby. We also know another teacher who lives in Los Angeles and stays with us when she comes to visit her brother, who lives in a studio apartment close to us. She typically brings a school teacher friend of hers because our unit is really big enough for two people to stay in comfortably. After we got these three teachers together, they became a circle of friends. Then, among my clients, I have quite a few school teachers, and a lot of them are single. A couple of them are divorced and have children. Since their children would be with their fathers on the weekends, they would have an opportunity to get away. However, they don't have the money to spend on something like that.

One day, I thought, "What a great way to give back to school teachers!" I think they are the most important people on this planet for what they do. And I thought, "I know these people." So we let them come and stay for free. We don't charge them. The only prerequisite for them coming is that they just totally enjoy themselves and not think about anything. They don't need to feel obligated at all to call us or knock on the door. We just want them to think that it's their own private little getaway.

It's been so great because I wanted the downstairs apartment to be used a lot more than it had been. By the way, our retired school teacher friend helps us out with the reservation process. The teachers who want to use our unit will call her to see when it's available. She also opens up the place for the guest teachers, saying, "This is your place for the weekend." We've had a lot of her teacher friends stay here too. The other neat thing is that they've all been so considerate about leaving the place clean.

Sharon: Have you heard of anyone else who has offered free housing to teachers?

Dan: No. But I really hope more people will open up their hearts and do the same thing. My basic philosophy in life is what goes around, comes around.

Sharon: Along with feeling good about making a donation to teachers, do you see any other advantages to having an accessory apartment?

Dan: Definitely. Since we've had the separate unit, when we've had our other friends, not school teachers, come and stay, it is just so wonderful for all of us. When you do stay with people . . . and I think everyone has had this experience . . . you try not to inconvenience your hosts. In turn, the hosts do their best to entertain and take care of you, and you are both being inconvenienced. I think that's another facet to this thing, just the convenience that having separate quarters brings. You can have your own privacy and really enjoy your friends more.

Mobile Homes

Included in the category of accessory apartments are mobile homes, trailers, or manufactured housing. More than twenty million Americans now live in these types of structures.[3] Mobile homes can be useful in many ways. For one, they can serve as places to live when visiting family members. Jack and Mary, a retired couple who live in Arkansas, spend a good deal of their time traveling in their mobile home to visit their four children and grand-children, who reside in Delaware, Michigan, Washington, and Texas. They typically stay with each child for two months at a time. They can either park in the yards of the children or in nearby trailer parks. Their mobile home allows them the freedom to have their own things in their own place. Fur-thermore, when the grandbabies start crying or the teenagers start playing loud music, they have a detached place to which they can escape. This is yet another example of the benefit of separation to get away from noise.

Duplexes

Duplexes are two homes sharing interior structures, such as a wall or a floor and ceiling, in two-story units. The floor plans of these homes may be iden-tical or different, but usually they offer very similar amenities. Owning a duplex allows the same flexibility as an accessory apartment, in that one of the homes can provide housing for family members, a nanny, a tenant, or caregivers of the elderly. In fact, duplexes are gaining popularity as adult chil-dren are opting to live near aging parents. This home style is ideal for pro-viding semiregular care to otherwise independent family members. Duplex homes allow each family to retain complete privacy, while proximity makes shared errands and frequent visits easier. Also, since a duplex has two sepa-rate addresses, there is no need to sort the mail at the end of the day. Utility bills are separate too, making that aspect of living together less complicated. One Northern California woman who co-owns a duplex with her daughter and son-in-law spoke about the advantages of this type of housing. Elena, a high school counselor, has shared a duplex for the past twenty years with them and her grandchildren. Here's what she had to say.

Elena: After my divorce, I was looking for a small place that I could buy. The places where I wanted to live were so expensive, more than I could afford to pay. At the time, my daughter and her husband were living in an apartment, and I suggested that we find something together. I was willing to buy a house with maybe mother-in-law quarters. That way we could combine our resources. Although they didn't have any money, his parents wanted to help out. They are lovely people, by the way, and so is my son-in-law. So we looked and looked. Nothing fit until I found this duplex and fell in love with it. It is not the kind of duplex where the two homes are separated by garages. It is L-shaped with the garage in the front and my doorway around the side. But their entrance is on the opposite side, way behind the garage.

Sharon: So you have the privacy thing then.

Elena: That's right. But they do not have an attached garage like I do. I have a single-car garage and they have a double-one that is separate. Their place is not only bigger, but they also have all this space on the side and behind their house where they can barbecue and entertain. Occasionally, I use it for entertaining too.

Sharon: That's a nice advantage. Are there other ways living together has been helpful to you?

Elena: Oh, there are lots of other benefits. If something breaks, like a plumbing problem with the toilet, my son-in-law is available to fix it. Many times I don't even have to ask him . . . he will offer. Being by myself, I do rely on him. I also remember when he and his parents helped paint the inside of both of our units. Then, one time I had car trouble and they were right there to lend me one of their cars. A while back, I ordered a computer and he put it together for me, and my daughter taught me how to use it. The longer I live here, the more I appreciate their willingness to help out.

Also, I'm here to help them. When we first lived together, if they were going somewhere, I would babysit the cats. I would go over and feed them. Then, later, after they started having children, I would babysit the grandchildren in the evenings. I was right there. They felt good about it too because they didn't have to get anybody to look after the kids. I like to help them with the garden too. Mainly I pull weeds. Another thing my daughter likes about me living next door is she can always help herself to whatever she needs and just leave me a note. Actually, that is neat for both of us, because it works both ways. We have keys to each other's places.

Sharon: So it has been a big help to you having the family so close.

Elena: Yes. I feel connected; I don't feel like I'm living alone.

Sharon: Together and apart at the same time.

Elena: Right. I would recommend it. You have to have an open mind.

Town houses

A town house is one of a group of two- or three-story houses of similar architectural treatment, usually joined by common sidewalls. Two town houses next door to each other can offer many of the same amenities as a duplex. A young Chinese woman who now lives in Los Angeles told us about the benefits of living in the town house next door to her parents and brother. Lan is married, works as a manicurist, and has two small children. A year ago, she and her husband bought their town house and a few months later bought the one next door for her parents and brother. Here's what she had to say about the mutual support and emotional well-being that close proximity has to offer them.

Lan: Having them live so close to us makes it easier for them and easier for my kids too. My parents can enjoy my kids every day, anytime they want. Likewise, my kids feel the same way about their grandparents. They can help me out with my children, and I can help them go to the supermarket and doctor's appointments. I drive them, since they don't drive. Also, my mom has diabetes. I know what she should eat, tell her, and check on her to make sure she knows. Because she doesn't speak English, she never talks to anybody. So if I know something, I'm going to tell her. Since they don't speak English, I'm there more to help them out.

Sharon: Was it your idea to live together, or was it theirs?

Lan: My idea. I'm the one who brought my parents here. I'm responsible for them. I wanted to make sure my parents are happy. If they live far away in China, I'm just nervous. They have retirement income there, but no one to look after them when they get older. I brought my brother to the U.S. to help me look after them. It's better to bring them now, so they can help with my kids.

Sharon: What I'm hearing from you are positives. But do you ever wish they weren't next door?

Lan: No. Someday I would like to buy a bigger home with maybe five or six bedrooms, so my parents could stay in one of them.

Sharon: You could also buy a house that's big enough that you could create a little apartment for them, where they have their own place with an outside entrance and separate kitchen. That way, it's like what you have right now. It's called an accessory apartment. A lot of people are using them now to house older parents.

Lan: You feel good when you can take care of your parents. You always expect your kids to do that, but I don't know about the kids that are born and grow up here. If they see what we are doing now, I think they will do the same thing for us.

Sharon: Children do observe what happens.

Lan: Oh, yes. A lot of people say that my parents are so lucky. When they go to learn English at their school, they meet a lot of other parents there. They invite them to come over. When they are all here, sitting around and talking, they tell my mom how lucky she is to have so much room and a daughter next door too. They love that. They say that they want that too.

Condominiums

A condominium is an apartment house with individually owned units, typically referred to as "condos." The condo owners in the complex share in joint ownership of any common grounds and passageways. They elect a board of directors to manage the operation and maintenance of these co-owned facilities. Families who live in the same condo complex, whether next door or on a different floor, can have many of the same benefits as duplex and town house owners. Beverly, a Southern California Realtor, gave us an example of how this works:

Beverly: Over lunch, a friend who also works in real estate told me about an elderly client who wanted to sell her home and move to a multigenerational condominium complex. She not only wanted one for herself, but also a separate condo in the same building for her divorced sixty-year-old adult son. My friend was sure the son wouldn't be interested in moving from his house to a condo, but she followed up with a phone call to him. Surprisingly to her, he was receptive to the idea. Ultimately, he did sell his home and move into a condo in his mom's building. He said it is working out very well. When he travels on business, Mom will look after things for him, watering the plants and collecting the mail. He doesn't have to worry about maintaining his former house and managing the pool service, the cleaning people, and so on. Also, he is nearby if Mom needs help with something and to check in on her.

Condo Conversions

These days, a lot of apartment buildings are being converted to individually owned condominiums. A friend told us about a widowed grandfather who sold his big house and bought a small apartment building with four separate apartments. He was able to convert them into separate condominiums, one for himself and the three others for adult grandchildren. Over time, he is gifting the units to them so they will own them individually. In turn, they will be there to help him out as he gets older.

Condo conversion is being done more and more as a way for young families to achieve home ownership, as well as to provide affordable housing. Be aware, however, that some municipalities discourage this practice by charging high fees for conversions, and some don't even allow it. Consequently, before exercising this proximity option, be sure to check into the financial and legal details. You also may want to consult an attorney regarding these issues. Also, please see chapter 13.

Family Compounds

A family compound is two or more separate houses on the same property. We spoke to a young woman who lives in Southern California in a family-owned subdivision compound with her husband and four children. Karen is an attorney and real estate broker. Her family developed the property to include three lots adjacent to each other on the same hill. On one lot, there are three structures, including the main house (rented out) and two detached apartments. On the two other lots, there are two additional houses built like duplexes. On all of these properties, in a total of four structures, live two brothers and four sisters with spouses, their mother, and twelve grandchildren. Karen told us about the advantages of having such close proximity with so many members of her family.

Karen: My parents purchased the original fifteen-acre property thirty years ago. My dad, who is now deceased, had the idea that our family members could settle around one another. As the property was sold off and subdivided, different family members purchased the property from my parents. At this point, I co-own a one-acre parcel with my sister. On this property there are three different structures. There is a guesthouse, there is a granny unit, and there is the original house that was built fifty years ago that we rent out. My sister lives in the guesthouse. It is a freestanding unit; she has her own kitchen and shower. My seventy-year-old mother lives in another unit with my forty-five-year-old sister, who has multiple sclerosis. My sister is very homebound and has her own caregiver, since my mother still works full-time, twelve to fifteen hours a day.

Sharon: So are the guesthouse and the granny unit the same thing?

Karen: No, they are not. It's interesting, three structures, but two legal residences. My sister's guesthouse is more like a recreational facility, not a traditional home. So my mother, sister, and brother live in the granny unit, and my other sister, who co-owns the property, lives in the guesthouse.

Sharon: She co-owns the property with you?

Karen: Yes, and I don't even live on the property. We bought it ten years ago and I never moved onto it. We were already in a situation that we were happy with. We live on an adjacent property that my mother also owns. On that one, we have a house that's divided into units. We have the one side. My sister, her husband, and two children live in the other half. They have their own kitchen and bath.

Sharon: Like a duplex in a way?

Karen: Yes, it is. It is something like that. It really is a single residence, but they have their own living area, their own kitchen, and separate entrance. We come through the back and they come through the front. I live in the other part with my husband and our four children. We've lived there for fifteen years now.

Sharon: And the three pieces of property are adjacent to one another?

Karen: They are all touching, all around the edge, on a hill. We all share the same swings, a swimming pool with a Jacuzzi, a trampoline, and even a tree house. The kids run up and down the hill from the three houses. They play with each other practically all day. They are in somebody's house, over next door, or up at Grandma's house. The dream my dad had has come true.

Sharon: What do you like about your housing situation? What do you like about living so close to everyone?

Karen: For me, it's ideal; I love it. I think it's because I love being around my family. I continue to grow as a person in the same environment where I grew up. I have so much freedom. Most of all, I love that the cousins can grow up knowing each other.

Sharon: Would you recommend your living arrangement to others? Why or why not?

Karen: You know, in my family every person is so completely different. Because we are four married and two single siblings, that means a lot of different interests and people at different stages. People are financially in different places; people are religiously in different places. Fortunately, the spouses are very easy to get along with, amazingly so. I think that is why it works. I think, if we can do it, others might be able to also.

We also talked to a friend about how her married sister and adult children live together on a thirty-four-acre farm in Kentucky. Three of the four adult children have separate living quarters in this family-compound living arrangement. A son has built his own place on the property for his wife and their three-year-old child. He was careful to have a legal agreement over ownership of their home drawn up between himself and his parents, who own the farm. A daughter and her husband, who have spent lots of money for fertility treatments in order to have children, have moved into the main house on the property. They plan to live there temporarily in order to recoup some of their expenses for the fertility treatments by not having to pay rent on an apartment. Fortunately, the daughter is now pregnant with her first child. Another daughter who is unmarried with a little girl has moved into a trailer home she placed on the property. As for our friend's sister and her husband, they live in a remodeled cottage on the property. In a variety of ways, this extended family has successfully achieved proximity with privacy.

In yet another case, we spoke with a young man who is planning on joining his three other brothers on a family "colony" compound in Hawaii. One brother owns the property and is inviting each of the three other siblings to build their own homes, all with attached "*ohanas*" or guest units for family and friends. Here's what Mike had to say about how they were planning to manage privacy in their future arrangement:

Mike: We plan to have a central sort of communal area that all the houses will share. It will include a small structure with a meeting place, an exercise room, and a barbecue pit. But we will make sure that our individual homes are arranged so that there is privacy if we want it. In other words, we won't be forced to be with everybody all the time and have our own space when we need it.

Actually, Mike's planned family compound with the central communal area has similar elements to another type of proximity-with-privacy housing known as cohousing.

Cohousing

Cohousing refers to a cooperative living arrangement planned and used by both extended families and nonrelated people who want to live in a communal development together. It features a cluster of single-family houses around a common building utilized for shared meals, child care, and guest facilities. The residents own their own units and divide duties for maintenance, gardening, and other chores. Most are intergenerational communities in urban centers or next to mixed-use developments. According to the Cohousing Association of the United States, over five thousand people dwell in about eighty completed cohousing communities in more than thirty states, with at least one hundred more communities in various stages of development. "The sizes range from half a dozen units on a fraction of an acre in Oakland, Calif., to 22 units on 260 rural acres in Hartland, Vt."[4]

There are a number of cases where members of an extended family have chosen to join nonrelatives in cohousing developments. Once again, it's important to do your homework to determine if this type of housing is right for you and your family. The Cohousing Association of the United States (www.cohousing.org) is a good place to start. Their website says that "Cohousing communities combine the advantages of private homes with the benefits of more sustainable living, including shared common facilities and ongoing connections with neighbors. These intentional neighborhoods, created and managed by residents, offer an innovative solution to today's environmental and social challenges." Indeed, these cooperative living arrangements can offer long-term savings through energy efficiency, as when neighbors share a car.

House Next Door

Living next door to family members can have similar benefits to many of the other types of housing already discussed in this chapter. Certainly, the extra space between the homes and separate ownership can make things easier too. A woman who lives in Northern California is delighted to live in the house next door to her in-laws. Linda is married, has four children, and is a homemaker and civic volunteer. Her husband grew up in the same house where his parents are now living on a small lake in the countryside. He liked the setting so much that he suggested to Linda that it would be a great place to raise their family. Twelve years ago, a house came up for sale, and his parents let them know about it. They bought it and have lived there ever since. Here is what she had to say about the "wonderful arrangement" of living so close to her in-laws:

Sharon: Please describe the physical layout of the two properties.

Linda: Years ago, my in-laws bought the lot next door to give them more space. So our house is actually on the other side of that empty lot. I think it was my mother-in-law's idea to put a walkway between our two homes, just knowing that there was going to be a lot of foot traffic back and forth. It's helpful because my husband is currently managing the family business. My father-in-law is still involved somewhat, but not in day-to-day operations. So I would say probably four evenings a week after work my husband will wander next door and they will have a chat about some business. Then usually family issues come up and there is an update on that.

Sharon: What do you like about your housing situation being so close?

Linda: Well, probably on a selfish note, it's so nice to have Nanna there if I need to park a kid somewhere and run out with another child. She is more than happy to do that for me. Just their influence on my children and the fact that my kids have such a close relationship with their grandparents is wonderful. Just as an example, Nanna is instructing my seven-year-old on how to play the flute. He and my twelve-year-old will be playing the ukulele that his grandmother taught him how to play and will be in the talent show. So it's time to rehearse, and they go over to Nanna's. It's just very cute. It's the older generation passing on skills and talent to the younger ones. It's really wonderful.

Sharon: Any other things that the other children do specifically with their grandparents?

Linda: Well, the family ranch is nearby. My mother-in-law is still part owner of that operation. There are horses out there and my oldest, Lana, and my youngest, Kelly, like to ride. I'm not a rider. So Nanna picks them up and off they go to the ranch, which is five minutes away. So that definitely is something that she has facilitated and passed on to them.

Sharon: What about Grandpa? Does he take them fishing?

Linda: My husband does that. Grandpa is the gardener. When he is out in the yard, that usually spurs the kids on to go out. "What are you doing? Can I help?" As I said, we do a communal garden between the two houses. Grandpa has always gardened that patch of yard, but in the last two to three years, his interest has dwindled. So then we have come in and picked up on it.

Sharon: What do you grow? How does that work?

Linda: We grow corn, tomatoes, and squash. We started growing our own pumpkins and decorate our home for Halloween. That's a big deal here. It comes alive on Halloween. We needed the corn stalks for that, so we've kept up the corn crop.

Houses across the Street and Behind

Another couple, Lily and Tom, not only have her widowed mother living in a house across the street, but they also have his parents in a house right behind them. The latter home is on a separate lot with its own address on a different street. They've added a connecting gate on the common fence between their homes. This arrangement works well for everyone right now. Eventually, their adult son and his family will probably live in one of the homes.

Sharon: In what ways do you help your in-laws? Do they travel very much?

Lily: Yes. They do travel. It is interesting how their lifestyle suits the arrangement we have with them. They have a beach house in Carmel and then a cabin in Boulder Creek. Both homes are thirty to thirty-five minutes away. So it's not unusual for them during the winter months to throw their stuff in the car and go to the beach for two nights. In the summer, they will go up to Boulder Creek for weeks at a time and park themselves up there. Then they are in Hawaii for two weeks out of the year. They like other venues, and they like their time together without the grandkids. That's important to them too.

Sharon: When they are gone, do you help them with the mail?

Lily: Sure. Mail and watering the plants. And they do the same for us. That's a real plus. We go to Hawaii for one week out of the year together as a family. Then there is one week in the summer when we piggyback with them to the cabin. But other than that, our vacations typically don't overlap. So there is that neighborhood watch, close-up and personal, that goes on.

Sharon: Would you recommend your living arrangement to others?

Lily: Certainly. As long as the personalities are such that you can live side by side.

Houses Next Door on a Cul-de-Sac

A cul-de-sac with no through traffic can be a great place for raising children. Think of that environment with grandparents nearby to help with babysitting. A young couple, Sam and Margaret, bought a house in a new development on a cul-de-sac for themselves and their three small children. They each told their respective parents what they were doing and invited them to consider buying the houses next door, one on each side of them. They did and have lived happily together now for the last five years.

Conclusions

There are certainly a number of helpful ways that extended families can live together. Having proximity with privacy is the primary key to success. Both Laura and Kathy talked about the importance of separate kitchens. Susan discussed the value of her detached accessory apartment when it comes to noise, as did Jack and Mary with their mobile home. Dan feels good about allowing school teachers free use of his accessory unit for vacations. Elena mentioned the benefit of separate entrances in her duplex housing arrangement. Lan is pleased about the mutual support and emotional well-being that the close proximity of town houses next door has to offer them. Karen is especially delighted that her family compound allows cousins to grow up with each other nearby. Mike is pleased with the design features of his family compound that allow for proximity with privacy. Linda extolled the mutual benefits of living in the house next door to her in-laws. Sam and Margaret enjoy the close proximity of both sets of parents living in houses next door to them on a cul-de-sac. Finally, Lily and Tom are so pleased to have their parents nearby to help them out when needed.

Our next chapter talks about extended family living in other countries, as well as different ethnic groups in the United States. Examples are given from American history. A view of related data from the U.S. Census Bureau is provided.

CHAPTER 8

Other Times, Other Places

The family is the oldest, most firmly grounded human institution. However great the changes may be in the proportion of the population that is married, in the age of marriage, or in the number of years people live within the family, whatever the size of the family may be, however much or little time members of a family spend together, and whatever else they may do individually, apart from all the others, still the family survives.

—MARGARET MEAD AND KEN HEYMAN[1]

S MARGARET MEAD and Ken Heyman put it so eloquently above, yes, "the family survives." But its form varies from place to place and from time to time. As conditions change, family structures adapt. And throughout history family residences have been built to accommodate these changes.

The obvious purpose of this chapter is to acquaint the reader with the variety of household structures (both physical and interpersonal) that have existed in different times in the United States and in different locales around the world. Of course, our discourse is not exhaustive—we don't have the space here. But the options we have listed below do serve our deeper purpose for this chapter. That is, we wish to open up your thinking toward creating your own best family and housing arrangements. The white-picket-fence thinking of the recent American past simply will not serve the immediate American future.

The Changing American Family

The Council on Contemporary Families (CCF) provides a concise summary of how families changed during the 1990s.[2] The number of people in the United States jumped from 249 million in 1990 to 282 million in 2000, and as you are reading this book, the number is now greater than 310 million. The changes in family structures have been substantial, including the percentage of traditional nuclear families actually decreasing during the 1990s. We expect the changes in the decades to come to be even more dramatic than those highlighted in exhibit 8.1.

As mentioned in earlier chapters, we see several forces converging to make multigenerational housing a preferred solution to the financial, demographic, and societal pressures of the baby boomers' retirement years. We can already see the changes happening. Indeed, a most interesting set of predictions were made about the changing American family in 1991 in William Strauss and Neil Howe's fascinating book *Generations*. Their prescience is remarkable. In the text quoted below, the authors label four current generations: (1) G.I.-born, 1901–1924; (2) Silent-born, 1925–1942; (3) Boom-born, 1943–1960; and (4) 13er-born, 1961–1981.

> The aging Silent will usher in a renaissance of the American extended family. More than at any other time in American history, 65-year-olds will have parents still living. Nor can the Silent count on their own children to leave home once and for all. Run the 13er "boomerang" child syndrome on fast-forward, and picture a continuing stream of young adults abandoning small urban apartments and returning to the large home of the Silent parents. Sooner or later, many a 13er live-in child will drop the hint, the parent will relent, and the master bedroom *coup d'état* will occur. The typical G.I. parent, who scrimped long years to afford household comfort, would never give in so easily. But the Silent are a softer touch. Having been empty-nesters rather early, they will attach less value to the privilege of living alone in a big home. Besides, the Silent will be culturally compatible with their children in ways the G.I.s were not. Around the turn of the century, these 65-year-old rock-and-rollers will get along just fine with their 35-year-old post-punk children. Grandparents will welcome the chance to help nurture a new generation of children—a task they realize they performed too young the first time around. Silent authors will do to the "art" of grandparenthood what they once did to the "art" of sex: They will scrutinize it endlessly, making it the subject of countless books, films, plays, songs, and paintings. And they will professionalize it with consultants, seminars, and global conferences.[3]

Exhibit 8.1. America's Changing Families

- In general, the percent of all households that contain just one person has risen over the last half of the twentieth century and into the twenty-first century. The percentage of such households rose from 13 percent in 1960 to 28 percent in 2011. While the percentage may not differ significantly from one year to the next, the overall trend has been an upward one. The percentage did decline, however, from 2008 to 2010.
- Between 2005 and 2011, the proportion of young adults living in their parents' home increased, according to the U.S. Census Bureau. The percentage of men age twenty-five to thirty-four living in the home of their parents rose from 14 percent in 2005 to 19 percent in 2011 and from 8 percent to 10 percent over the period for women.
- Of the 74.6 million children younger than eighteen in 2011, most (69 percent) lived with two parents, while another 27 percent lived with one parent and 4 percent with no parents. Of those children who lived with two parents, 92 percent lived with two biological or two adoptive parents.
- Among the children who lived with one parent, 87 percent lived with their mother.
- Of the children living with no parents present, 57 percent lived with at least one grandparent.
- In 2011, 10 percent of children under eighteen lived with at least one grandparent. Seventy-eight percent of these children also lived with at least one parent.
- Of the 67.8 million opposite sex couples who lived together, 89 percent were married couples, while the remaining 11 percent were unmarried.
- In 2011, there were about 7.6 million unmarried couples living together.
- In 2011, married couples with children made up 20 percent of all households, half what they were in 1970 (40 percent).
- In 2011, 23 percent of married-couple family groups with children younger than fifteen had a stay-at-home mother. This proportion decreased in the last few years during the recession. In 2007—before the recession began—the corresponding figure was 24 percent.

Source: 2012 U.S. Census.

In order to better understand the changes we see happening in American families today, it is worthwhile to view them in the greater contexts of history and other global patterns. We start with the first family structures, then move to historical ones in the United States, and finally on to how families manage themselves in other countries.

The First Family Structures

As best we can tell, the first prehistoric family households were formed by bands of hunter-gatherers. Reference to the Kalahari Bushmen in South Africa gives us a glimpse of how these original families might have worked, lived, housed themselves, and handled their elderly. Hopefully, you followed our recommendation in chapter 3 and viewed *The Gods Must Be Crazy*. James Michener provides a bit more detail in his description of Gumsto's clan in his historical novel *The Covenant*:

> The clan for which he was responsible numbered twenty-five; more would prove too difficult to feed; fewer, too vulnerable to attacks from animals. His consisted of himself as leader, his tough old wife Kharu, their sixteen-year-old son Gao, plus assorted males and females of all ages and all possible relationships. The safety of his clan was his obsession. . . .
>
> His immediate responsibility was to feed his clan, and this day he would mount an attack on the rhinoceros, kill it or be killed by it, then gorge his people with one gigantic meal and move them off to some better site. As he reached these basic decisions, his small brown face was wreathed in a contented smile, for he was an optimist: There will be a better location.
>
> Leaving the dying lake, he went to the living area of his clan, which consisted of absolutely nothing except a halting place beneath low trees. The terrain of each family was outlined in sticks and a few piled rocks, but there were no huts, no walls, no lean-tos, no paths, no shelter except grass rudely thrown across a framework of interlocked saplings. And each family's area contained only enough space for members to lie in hollows scooped out for their hips. The few possessions had been meticulously selected during centuries of wandering and were essential and tenderly prized: loincloths and skin cloaks for all, bows and arrows for the men, body powders and small adornments for the women. . . .
>
> There were weaknesses in the system. Since the husband had to be much older than the wife, there was in any group a surplus of old

widows whose men had died at the hunt or been killed by falls when searching tall trees for honey. These elderly women were welcome to stay with the band as long as they could function; when they could no longer chew or keep up with the march, they would be placed in the shade of some bush, given a bone with meat clinging to it, and one ostrich egg, and there they died in dignity as the clan moved on.[4]

Such a family form and function rendered some family problems easily solved. Housing might be changed to accommodate new kids, and so on, simply by moving about a few rocks and sticks. And health-care decisions about elderly members boiled down to which ostrich egg to leave behind with them. There was no yelling at kids about TV, video games, or cell phones. But the constant worry about starvation surely made life on the Kalahari Desert less fun than here and now.

Research on other hunter-gatherer tribes in Africa also unveils a reason for the greater longevity of women. We quote here from *Time* on why nature may have selected longer life for grandmothers:

Hence the "grandma hypothesis": maybe the evolutionary "purpose" of postmenopausal woman was to keep her grandchildren provided with berries and tubers and nuts, especially while Mom was preoccupied with the new baby. If Grandma were still bearing and nursing her own babies, she'd be too busy to baby-sit, so natural selection may have selected for a prolonged healthy and mature, but infertile, stage of the female life cycle.

To test this possibility, anthropologist Kristen Hawkes made quite a nuisance of herself among the hunting-gathering Hadza people of Tanzania, charting the hour-by-hour activities of 90 individuals, male and female, and weighing the children at regular intervals. The results . . . established that children did better if Grandma was on the case—and, if not her, then a great-aunt or similar grandma figure.[5]

Families in Historical America

Steven Ruggles, professor of history at the University of Minnesota, reported in an NPR interview that in 1850 some 75 percent of folks over age sixty-five lived with their adult children. That number dropped steadily to a low point of 15 percent by the 1990 census and has turned up in the most recent census.

Michener provides some color to Professor Ruggles's facts.

Maryland

James Michener's research and storytelling also allow us to take a look back at housing and families on the Chesapeake in centuries past.

> So for the first time she sailed across the river to Peace Cliff and walked up the oyster-shell path to the unpretentious, restful house that stood on the headland, and as soon as she saw it she understood what the brothers meant when they said *telescope*. The humble house built by Edward Paxmore in 1664 was still sturdy, but after his death the growing families of his four children merited additional space, so a larger block of four rooms had been added, with a higher roof line. And when the boatyard had prospered, a real house had been added, with an even higher roof line.
>
> The result was a house tall and solid to the left as one approached it, joined by a lesser middle section, which was joined by a noticeably smaller third. The three buildings resembled a collapsible telescope. "A giant could shove them together," Rosalind said approvingly as she studied the design. "It's neat, efficient, pleasing to the eye, and perfect for this cliff."[6]

Michener also described what family meant for slaves in America.

> The pitiful fact about slavery as it existed on the Steed plantation was its banality. On white and black alike the heavy encumbrances of custom pulled everyone down to a mournful level in which the most extraordinary situations were accepted as inevitable. An unbroken chain of black men and women was purchased for the plantation or bred there, and they existed through the centuries without family names, or recorded histories, or education, or variation, or hope. The male field hands formed an interminable succession of Toms, Jims, Joes; at the big house classical names were preferred, for these gave a kind of distinction to social life: Pompey, Caesar, Hannibal, Napoleon, Brutus. Women in remote fields often bore names that were rarely spoken by their white overseers: Pansy, Petty, Prissy, Pammy, Puss. Generation after generation were judged to be alike: treated alike . . . dressed alike . . . ignored alike . . . and buried alike.[7]

Michener also reports that the slave owners took a census and counted their wealth at the same time (see exhibit 8.2).

So back in the 1800s, landowning white folks lived in flexible housing—they had the room and often the means to expand in the agrarian society of

Exhibit 8.2. The Steed Slaves

| Classification | Males | | Females | | Total Value ($) |
	Number	Value ($) Each	Number	Value ($) Each	
Infants, 0–5	44	0	47	0	0
Children, 6–13	135	300	138	250	75,000
Prime, 14–52	215	2,000	161	1,800	719,800
Older, 53–66	72	1,200	65	300	105,900
Ancients, 67–	16	0	21	0	0
Total	482		432		900,700

Source: Chesapeake, James A. Michener (New York: Fawcett Books, 1978), 720.

that time and place. Meanwhile, for hundreds of years, black folks suffered. Their family relationships depended on the whims of their owners, and the "ancients" were literally valued at zero.

Texas

Now we head further south and west to the border area between Texas and Mexico, and to the mystical love story of Tita and Pedro. There, family structure brought objections, then questions, and eventually tragedy, as told in Laura Esquivel's *Like Water for Chocolate*. (The movie based on the book is also wonderful.)

> One afternoon, before Mama Elena told them they could leave the table, Tita, who was then fifteen, announced in a trembling voice that Pedro Muzquiz would like to come and speak with her. . . .
>
> After an endless silence during which Tita's soul shrank, Mama Elena asked: "And why should this gentleman want to come to talk to me?"
>
> Tita's answer could hardly be heard: "I don't know."
>
> Mama Elena threw her a look that seemed to Tita to contain all the years of repression that had flowed over the family, and said: "If he intends to ask for your hand, tell him not to bother. He'll be wasting his time and mine too. You know perfectly well that being the youngest daughter means you have to take care of me until the day I die." With that Mama Elena got slowly to her feet, put her glasses in her apron, and said in a tone of final command: "That's it for today."
>
> Tita knew that discussion was not one of the forms of communication permitted in Mama Elena's household, but even so, for the first time in her life, she intended to protest her mother's ruling. "But in my opinion . . ."

"You don't have an opinion, and that's all I want to hear about it. For generations, not a single person in my family has ever questioned this tradition, and no daughter of mine is going to be the one to start."

. . . Still Tita did not submit. Doubts and anxieties sprang to her mind. For one thing, she wanted to know who started this family tradition. It would be nice if she could let that genius know about one little flaw in this perfect plan for taking care of women in their old age. If Tita couldn't marry and have children, who would take care of her when she got old? Was there a solution in a case like that? Or are daughters who stay home and take care of their mothers not expected to survive too long after the parent's death? And what about women who marry and can't have children, who will take care of them? And besides, she'd like to know what kind of studies had established that the youngest daughter and not the eldest is best suited to care for their mother. Had the opinion of the daughter affected by the plan ever been taken into account? If she couldn't marry, was she at least allowed to experience love? Or not even that?

Tita knew perfectly well that all these questions would have to be buried forever in the archive of the questions that have no answers. In the De La Garza family, one obeyed—immediately. Ignoring Tita completely, a very angry Mama Elena left the kitchen, and for the next week she didn't speak a single word to her.[8]

So along the Rio Grande at the beginning of the last century, birth order determined elderly care roles. That is, Mexican American culture solved the problem by designating the last-born girl as the responsible one. This is in contrast to Chinese culture, for example, which demands that the eldest son take on the responsibility of his parents' care in his home. The Chinese solution also involves the difficult wife/mother-in-law interaction. But at least the constraint of celibacy as in the De La Garza family is not added to the burden.

California

Esquivel's poetic descriptions of family life along the old Rio Grande seem to be confirmed by the facts of our own California ancestors. We are sixth-generation Californians on our mother's side of the family. It seems our great-great-great-grandfather died in his youngest daughter's house and care sometime past his one hundredth birthday. His obituary read,

Jose Maria Amador, who was born in 1781 on the site of the City of San Francisco, died in Gilroy on Tuesday, at the home of his daughter.

He was the original owner of the San Ramonde rancho, covering the site upon which Dublin, Alameda County, stands; but for many years he lived at the Mission San Jose and at Watsonville. He has been married three times, his last wife surviving him. He also leaves seven sons and two daughters. (*San Francisco Bulletin*, June 18, 1883)

Shortly before Amador died, he delivered an oral history at the behest of Thomas Savage at the Bancroft Library at the University of California, Berkeley. The old pioneer's accounts of life on the rancho in the San Francisco area, including the slaughter of Native Americans, the early days of the gold rush, and the day-to-day activities of Mission San Jose, can all be found on a shelf in the Bancroft Library today. Savage provided the following preface to the book:

Don Jose Maria Amador of Watsonville, CA

One of the main objects I had in view in visiting Santa Cruz in June 1877, was to see this ancient Californian, said to have been born in 1781, that is twelve years after the foundation of the first mission in California, and only about five years after that of San Francisco.

I had been assured that Amador had a clear head, an amiable disposition, and a large stock of information which he would not withhold.

My disappointment was great on discovering that he had moved away from Santa Cruz years before, but was living in Watsonville. I went to see him, and found him on a small farm about four and a half miles from town, in great poverty under the care of his *youngest daughter* [our emphasis] who is married and burdened with many children. Amador is also quite crippled from the effects of paralysis which attacked him two or three years ago—the house was such as is found inhabited by the poorest class of Californian rancheros.

Such was the condition of the man after whom Amador County (California) was named, of the son of one of the original founders, Pedro Amador.

He had heard of Mr. H. H. Bancroft's labors in collecting material for a History of California, and did not hesitate one instant in furnishing what he remembered about the past of his country during the Spanish and Mexican domination.

I rode to his dwelling place every morning, and returned to town in the evening, during the seven or eight days, which were industriously employed by me in recording what he dictated—all of which appears in the following pages under the title *Memorias sobre Historia de California*.

Amador's memory was quite fresh and had it been possible for me to make a longer stay in that vicinity, I doubt not that from time to time he would have supplied me incidents, anecdotes, as they came to his mind, to fill up many more pages. As it is, his contribution may be called a substantial one. (Thomas Savage, for the Bancroft Library, 1877)

We are obviously proud of our deep California roots and often recognize the cultural influences of our Mexican/Spanish forebearers. Indeed, we note that Mary Ellen, the younger sister in our family, was headed in the general direction of caring for/living with our own elderly mother. But Mom died suddenly, living by herself in her own big home against our protestations.

New York

Now back to the East Coast for another "first family" story and to where American history offers another classic example of both how to and how not to practice multigenerational living. For example, a few years after Franklin Delano Roosevelt and Anna Eleanor Roosevelt were married, his mother offered to build them a house. According to Blanche Cook in her biography of Eleanor Roosevelt, mother-in-law Sara not only directed the planning of the Siamese-twin house, but also ran both homes after they were constructed.

On each floor, sliding doors gave Sara full reign of both houses. On the parlor floor, the dining rooms and drawing rooms could be opened onto each other to create a spacious party environment. On the bedroom floor, the children's floor, and the servants' floor, there were connecting passageways. The house was designed so that Sara could at any time intrude herself on every level into her children's lives. One never knew, Eleanor wrote, "When she would appear, day or night."

Shortly after they moved into the new six-story town house, Eleanor sat in front of her dressing table, looked into the mirror, and wept. She cried and cried, until Franklin appeared to find out what was delaying her for dinner. "I said I did not like to live in a house which was not in any way mine, one that I had done nothing about and which did not represent the way I wanted to live." Franklin made no effort to console his wife or comprehend her pain. He announced that he thought her "quite mad," and assured her she would "feel differently" as soon as she became calmer.[9]

Apparently, Eleanor survived her mother-in-law once she became "calmer." Or maybe it was after the move to the governor's mansion or the White House.

Some of the folks we interviewed also provided some interesting comments on families in America's past:

Tony: My house in Hartford was built in the 1920s in a neighborhood where the typical design included entry into a front hall, which had an open stairway going up. In the front hall there was a French door leading to the parlor. At the top of the stairway there was a landing and another French door. The reason for that design was so that if, for example, the breadwinner lost his job, then instantly the family home could become a two-family house. They could rent out one part, so that they did not have to lose everything they had.

Greg: Do you know much about the Amish? They have what they call *grossdaddi* ("grandfather" in German) houses. They will build a little house for the grandparents and systematically trade. As the younger generation's family expands, the older generation moves into the *grossdaddi haus*. Do you know the guy who makes granny flats, Ed Guyen, of Coastal Colony Corporation? He's never sold them on the West Coast. They are manufactured houses that you put on treated posts in the ground and put cement around them. He happened to live in Lancaster County, where the Amish live. He actually had Amish folks building these things for him. He sort of introduced me to this *grossdaddi* thing. As a matter of course, they trade in terms of family size. It's compelling from a marketing point of view.

Michener's description of the Chesapeake telescoping house was representative. In other words, the American household is constantly changing. Sean Mitchell of the *Los Angeles Times* not only tracks some of the most recent changes, but he also provides a bountiful meal of new ideas that will stimulate new options for the design of housing to fit your own multigenerational family (also see chapter 10 of this book). Please enjoy these excerpts from his article:

The Interior Landscape—Space

How big a house do you want? How big a house do you need? Americans have been trying to reconcile the answers to these two questions for as long as banks have been extending mortgages. Complicating the responses are family size and level of affluence, personal taste, fashion, and the ever-changing ways in which we live.

Through the years, while garages and bathrooms have multiplied and kitchens have grown in size and stature, living and dining rooms have all but disappeared. Outdoor space has been colonized, media centers have infiltrated, and the home office has nearly supplanted the practically quaint idea of an extra room for guests.

In the master-planned communities designed by Irvine architect Art Danielian, homeowners are rediscovering the modes of a century ago when the family, including grandparents, lived above the store. His 2,500-square-foot Spanish-style homes in the new Pasadera development in Palm Springs include a 240-square-foot detached casita, or little house, designed as a space for work or hobbies, "or a place for the mother-in-law," says the architect.

This design shift is directly influenced by the changing demographic of home buyers. Twenty-five years ago, traditional families represented 67 percent of the residential market, says Danielian, compared with today's new households in which 75 percent "are childless families—either empty-nesters, divorcees, late bloomers or singles."

Yet as the median family has shrunk from 3.11 people in 1974 to 2.59 in 2004, the median size of the single-family home in the U.S., as measured by new construction, has bulked up from 1,560 square feet to 2,340 during the same period, according to the National Association of Home Builders. "That's enough space for a family of four if you do it right," says Kurt Beckmeyer, an architect in South Pasadena. "But I have a lot of clients who really want big. I'm working on an 11,000-square-foot house right now."

"We're coming back slowly I hope from the excesses of the last 20 years in overscaled homes," says Duo Dickinson, a Connecticut architect and a leader of a downsizing movement to persuade Americans to think smaller in the face of such realities as available sites, swelling building codes and rising construction costs. "People have valued cubic footage over community, and extreme mediocrity has been rewarded with gigantic price tags."

Even one hundred years ago, the need for privacy was a consideration, and many early twentieth-century homes were designed with thick pocket doors that could seal off one large space from another.

"The notion of public versus private space has long been with us," says Robert Timme, dean of the school of architecture at USC. "And it has changed as a result of things happening in social customs. "Once, the kitchen was seen only by the cook or the woman of the house. But when people no longer had domestic help, breakfast rooms were added. And when cooking became part of the conversation, the great room was wrought. The den and the living room got married and became one room," he says.

In the tract homes that spread across the nation after World War II to provide housing for returning GIs and their baby-boom offspring, the den was also opened to outdoor light and the formal dining room was sometimes sacrificed to the new open floor plans, borrowed from Frank Lloyd Wright and other modernists.

In this country, the notion of living more efficiently in a smaller space goes back more than 150 years to the American writer Catharine Beecher, a pioneer in the field of home economics who favored utility over decor and put forth the significant idea that a small house, because it was easier to take care of, could be a more comfortable house—understandable from a woman's point of view since women were expected to clean and maintain it.

"Design is powerful and people deserve to take control of their spaces, but I don't see that happening on a big scale," Lockley says. Instead, he has noticed that clients are preoccupied with resale value, which often inhibits them from tailoring a house to their personal needs and style." A lot of clients are almost frightened by the next buyer," he says. "People tend to look at their houses as financial instruments rather than as homes."[10]

Families in Other Countries

Family forms and functions vary substantially around the world, even within individual countries. Consider the Belgian executive who lives with his mother, wife, and kids in a home in Brussels that his family has owned for the last five hundred years. Then there's the common practice of the high-income folks in Cairo buying an apartment house and filling it up with the extended family—grandparents, married siblings, cousins, and kids. Or how about the Japanese mother caring for her two children, pretty much by herself, often sleeping with them at night? Meanwhile, her husband catches up on sleep during his four hours a day commuting via train. And there's the American family in California, where both parents work like dogs to support their cars, closets, and kids in college, all the while worrying about aging grandparents halfway across the country in Texas.

Even the ratio of male to female children is affected by culture. For example, the percentage of boys aged one to six is 52 percent in India, and aged one to four is 55 percent in China. Obviously these ratios have long-term implications for families and societies. Moreover, the favoritism of boys is deep seated in such cultures as demonstrated by the Chinese *Book of Songs*, circa 800 BC:

> When a son is born
> Let him sleep on the bed,
> Clothe him with fine clothes.
> And give him jade to play with . . .

> When a daughter is born,
> Let her sleep on the ground,
> Wrap her in common wrappings,
> And give her broken tiles for playthings.

All these differences lead directly to differences in how children think and behave. For example, individualism is being taught the first night the American infant is tucked into her own separate bassinet. Values for egalitarianism are learned the first time Dad washes the dishes in front of the kids or Mom heads off to work or the toddler learns that both Grandpa and little brother are properly called *you*. In the last case, most cultures have at least two words for *you* that must be learned to speak properly. So a child in Spain learns almost immediately that social hierarchy is important—*usted* for some people and *tu* for others.

The Elder Years around the World

Yes, the form and function of the family varies around the world. But the fast aging of the American population is by no means unique. Exhibit 8.3 illustrates well how some countries are actually ahead of the United States in this regard.

Exhibit 8.3. A Graying Planet: Retirees (65+) per One Hundred Workers

Country	2010	2030
United States	18.2	27.0
Germany	25.0	34.5
China	11.2	20.4
Japan	26.3	33.4
Russia	16.3	25.6
Brazil	10.5	17.2

Source: U.S. Census, International Data Base, 2010.

We should certainly be watching Germany and Japan as they manage their aging population ahead of us. Now let's take a quick look at how folks around the world organize their families.

Ireland

What happens when there's a shortage of grandparents? In Ireland today 11.2 percent of the population is sixty-five or older, while in the greater European Union the percentage is 16.8. Big families were the norm in the 1950s in Catholic Ireland, and now several siblings are available to take care of the relatively small elderly population of today. Imagine yourself with eight brothers and sisters to share the responsibilities of caring for aging parents! So in Ireland today there is actually a shortage of grandparents. The following is a story about how one family adjusted to the problem:

The attending physician asked, "Who's his next of kin?" Anne Gallagher blurted out, "I guess I am." And ultimately the words made it so.

Seventy-year-old Dick Madden lay in bed in a Dublin hospital ward for indigents dying of pneumonia. The doctors kept him alive, but Anne saved his life. Anne is trained as a nurse, but now is perhaps Ireland's greatest connector. As founder of a peace-building organization that she named Seeds of Hope, she seems to know everybody on the island, North and South, Protestant and Catholic, ex-prisoners and policemen, rich and powerful, and folks in the direst of straits, like Dick. She finds common interests and makes introductions and thus strengthens the peace that's held in Northern Ireland during the last decades.

She also rescues people like Dick, a stranger she met on a cold and rainy street and helped to the hospital. She visited him during his recovery. When he was well, she and her husband, Jerry, moved him into a small flat near their home in a Dublin suburb and invited him to gain strength in their own home. The Sunday suppers sustained both his body and soul. They gave him a key to their front door and he helped out with their fourteen-year-old son, Jared. Both Anne and Jerry work full-time, with Anne spending days at a time helping to repair community in the still-divided Belfast in the North.

Indeed, the best part of the story is the "grand relationship" that developed between Jared and Dick. Jared's a youth champion at both hurling and Gaelic football, and his biggest supporter has been Dick. He never missed a game and was the community's most ardent fan. Thus developed five years of a growing three-generation relationship. During the last year, when Dick's health failed him again, he moved into Anne's house to die. She wouldn't let him go back to the hospital. Anne, Jerry, and Jared all helped keep Dick comfortable as he faded away finally.

So Dick died at home, surrounded by his adopted family. Jared was holding his hand when he passed, and he kissed his forehead at the services attended by scores in his adopted community. Dick is particularly missed by his breakfast bunch and his fellow sports fans and parents. Jared misses his best friend.

In such a way, in a land where a shortage of grandparents exists, Anne created a grandparent relationship for her son Jared. Anne's own dad had died a number of years earlier, and her eight siblings take good care of her mom up in Belfast these days. It wasn't a conscious act, but this very personal connection she made in her own family served all very well.

Norway

At least according to *Parade Magazine*, they apparently don't have a shortage of grandparents in Norway:

> A Norwegian woman is trying to auction off her father on the Web. "Giving away my dad to a nice woman in Trondheim," wrote 25-year-old Nina Melhum Gronland, who was looking to free herself of her father, Odd Kristiansen, 52. Odd had moved in with his daughter and her family after ending a long-term relationship. "Dad is tall, dark and slim and in his best age," she wrote. "I am tired of him living with me. Furniture comes with him. Serious!"[11]

France

Adam Gopnik reports in his entertaining book about his residence in Paris,

> The national craze for early retirement may be an employee's twist on an employer's gimmick, but its roots are cultural. Retirement isn't scary here. In America one unmentioned aspect of the Social Security debate is the feeling people have that to stop working is, in a sense, to stop living. It is the vestibule of death. In France there is no equivalent anxiety—and there are no great Florida-style gulags for the elderly. One of the striking things about Paris is that it is filled with old people who actually look old: bent, fitted out with canes, but dining and lunching and taking the air and walking their small, indifferent dogs along with everybody else. The humiliations visited upon old people in America— dressed up like six-year-olds, in shorts and T-shirts and sneakers, imploding with rage—aren't common here. The romance of retirement is strong. The right-wing *Figaro*, for instance, though editorially

opposed to the move for very early retirement, ran a series of pieces about the "young retired"—people still in their forties and fifties who have managed to stop working. The series described people who at last have time to "reflect"; it was written in exactly the same admiring spirit that an American daily might use for a series about old people who are as busy as all get-out.[12]

Belgium

European economists decry the lack of mobility of their labor force. Folks just won't move to follow the jobs. Indeed, the family of a friend at a Belgian university has lived within five hundred meters of the same spot for five hundred years—that's immobility at its worst, or perhaps best? The story is related by Jean-Paul, a forty-five-year-old father of two.

John: You talked about three-generation households being more common in Belgium. Can you talk about the rest of Europe and about the economic sense of the lack of mobility and desire to stay in one place? In the States, we are all commuting.

Jean-Paul: I have the feeling this is more of a Catholic thing that at least one child stays at home. I'm telling you this because I had some Dutch girlfriends and the moment I started talking about relations, future and marriage, the opinion of their parents was that there are two moments when children should leave the house. One moment is when they start to study, they go to another city and they don't come back anymore. The other moment is when they get married, then they should move out. I saw this happening much more in the Netherlands, particularly in the north. There more people are Protestant. So I think it's a little more . . . maybe an old-fashioned Catholic thing where you stick together, where the family has to be closely connected. Maybe it's more of a Protestant thing that you say families are important, but not that important.

John: What do you think the advantages are of having three generations in one household?

Jean-Paul: Since we were living in a very large family house with a lot of space, there was also a lot of emotional space. I think in our modern culture this is an important condition. If you don't have that condition, it doesn't work. It's completely impossible. A lot of times this practical stuff creates a big limitation.

In our house, we don't use the same bathroom or the same kitchen. We have a totally independent living level on the first floor and a totally independent living level on the second floor. If we would have a little bit of an intense situation, my wife would live completely downstairs without going upstairs and my mother could live upstairs without going downstairs. That gives a big psychological advantage.

John: You talked about the relationship between your mother and the kids already. But can you see anything that affects the kids' behavior and values and things like that? Maybe in Protestant Europe the kids don't have the grandparents in the house or even in the province. They seldom see them and there is no passing on of the values, for example.

Jean-Paul: That is where that wonderful, old, wise person comes in. It's not a threat; it's not a policeman dictating to you what to do. It's an old, wise person who says, "I have no power anymore. Allow me to show something of my experience." Then they go out of the room and they suddenly see their parents differently. I remember that from my grandmother until my father died. My grandmother was ninety-nine. She did not live in our home, but it was always wonderful to talk with her.

John: She lived right in the neighborhood? So did you go there in the afternoons?

Jean-Paul: She lived very close by. I'd visit her once a week, Sunday or . . . I remember that sometimes I would talk with her other times as well.

John: Is there anything you want to add on this topic?

Jean-Paul: As I said, I think it's wonderful, but it's difficult because there is no standard recipe to do it. For people who have their parents in the home or one of their parents, it's a wonderful tool to teach yourself how to handle people in general. Then, when you look into a company, an organization, you see all kinds of variations of people there. It makes you sometimes a little bit more wise.

Jean-Paul lives in the house of his ancestors with his mother, wife, and two children. The arrangement has its ups and downs, but it all seems quite natural for all. The benefits are there for all three generations. And such an arrangement is common in many areas of Europe, particularly so in the Catholic areas. Indeed, when we lived in Spain (Sharon in the 1970s and

John in the 1990s), we saw the Spanish kids living at home well into their twenties—usually not moving out until marrying, if then.

China

Peter Hessler in his wonderful book *River Town* compares how things work in rural China and America:

> The families I knew in Fuling were arguably closer than the average in America, because individual members were less self-centered. They were remarkably generous with each other, and often this selflessness extended to good friends, who were also drawn into tight social circles. Collective thought was particularly good for the elderly, who were much better cared for than in America. In Fuling I never saw older people abandoned in retirement homes; they almost always lived with their children, caring for grandchildren and doing what they could to help out around the family farm, business, or home. There was no question that their lives had more of a sense of purpose and routine than I had seen among the elderly at home.[13]

Our own recent observations in one of Beijing's *hutong* districts also demonstrate the emphasis the Chinese put on family and how housing has been adapted accordingly. The term for this old district in Beijing comes from the Mongolian word *hottog* (that is, "water well" in English). Originally, villagers built their homes around convenient sources of water. The word *hutong* literally means a narrow lane or alley. In fact it is the passage between homes called *siheyuan* (a compound with houses built around an inner courtyard). Before 1949 these courtyard housing compounds were used by extended families, including some servants. However, after the communist takeover, these high-income houses were converted to multifamily apartments with huts filling in the courtyards to save on precious space.

We visited a family living in the district in August 2003, shortly after the SARS ban was lifted allowing tourism to begin again in Beijing. The quarters were tight, Mr. and Mrs. Xin living in a large twenty-by-twenty room that included their bed in one corner and dining and entertainment area in the other. There was a separate small kitchen area for cooking and food storage. They shared bathroom facilities with the ten other families living in their compound. Both were retired and in their seventies and had lived in the house since 1949. They had raised a son there and now their teenage grandson was visiting. He often stayed there as well. They had a large color television and a microwave oven both beside the kitchen table. The teenager, like so many Americans his age, had a cell phone in his pocket. That day the Xins were also caring for a neighbor's (same compound) six-year-old son. The boy obviously had the run of the house and kept Mr. Xin laughing.

Before the Beijing Olympics in 2008, there were all kinds of pressures to demolish the *hutong* districts, which many believed to be important cultural treasures. Some were saved by Beijing's new millionaires, who bought the compounds from the multifamily residents, cleared out the courtyards, and reestablished the traditional extended family compound idea. But the land is precious, and only 260 *hutongs* with 2,000 *siheyuans* survived the redevelopment projects; this despite sit-down protests by middle-aged and elderly residents like the Xins.

Perhaps the most interesting challenge facing the Chinese these days is not housing redevelopment—that's proceeding at a breakneck pace. The real conundrum for the society will be the consequences of the one-child policy on elder care during the coming decades. They are fast headed toward a demographic scenario where one child is supporting two elderly parents and four ancient grandparents. The good news is that the prospective grandparents are investing big time in their "little princes," and the latter are enjoying the blessings of four grand relationships.

Finally, we think it is quite worthwhile to include a few wise words from anthropologist Edward T. Hall's still pertinent book *The Hidden Dimension.*

> Fixed-feature space is one of the basic ways of organizing the activities of individuals and groups. It includes material manifestations as well as the hidden, internalized designs that govern behavior as man moves about on this earth. Buildings are one expression of fixed-feature patterns, but buildings are also grouped together in characteristic ways as well as being divided internally according to culturally determined designs. The layout of villages, towns, cities, and the intervening countryside is not haphazard but follows a plan which changes with time and culture.
>
> Even the inside of the Western house is organized spatially. Not only are there special rooms for special functions—food preparation, eating, entertaining and socializing, rest, recuperation, and procreation—but for sanitation as well. . . .
>
> Actually the present internal layout of the house, which Americans and Europeans take for granted, is quite recent. As Philippe Ariès points out in *Centuries of Childhood*, rooms had no fixed functions in European houses until the eighteenth century. Members of the family had no privacy as we know it today. There were some spaces that were sacred or specialized. Strangers came and went at will, while beds and

---

Room for Thought 8.1.   Is It a Tsunami or an Earthquake?

Wang Fuchuan lies in bed wearing a quilted black jacket, with two comforters pulled up to his chin to keep out the chilly November air. The heating at the Beijing Songtang Caring Hospice is broken, and the 90-year-old's nostrils are stuffed with toilet paper to stop perpetual dripping. Cockroaches scurry across the floor of his room, which has no toilet or running water. His possessions, a few articles of clothing, are in a plastic bag under his bed next to a pink plastic wash bowl with a sliver of soap. His only entertainment is a transistor radio.

Wang counts himself lucky. While he has no family or savings, he fought against the Japanese and the Kuomintang in the 1940s, so the government pays the clinic's monthly fee of 2,000 yuan ($315). His 200-yuan pension buys food. "A lot of people my age can't afford to be here," Wang says. "The food isn't too good, but I have nothing else to complain about."

The latest government census shows 178 million Chinese were over 60 in 2009. That figure could reach 437 million—one-third of the population—by 2050, the United Nations forecasts. In the past the elderly would have been cared for by their children, but urbanization and the one-child policy have eroded this tradition. "It's a demographic tsunami," says Joseph J. Christian, a fellow at Harvard University's Kennedy School of Government who specializes in housing issues for seniors in China. "The whole multi-generational housing model has disappeared."

Source: Frederik Balfor with Natasha Khan, "China's 'Demographic Tsunami,'" *Bloomberg BusinessWeek*, January 9, 2012.

Unlike an earthquake, a demographic disaster does not strike without warning. Japan's population of 127m is predicted to fall to 90m by 2050. As recently as 1990, working-age Japanese outnumbered children and the elderly by seven to three. By 2050 the ratio will be one to one.

Source: Schumpter, "Land of Wasted Talent," *Economist*, November 5, 2011.

---

tables were set up and taken down according to the moods and appetites of the occupants. Children dressed and were treated as small adults. It is no wonder that the concept of childhood and its associated concept, the nuclear family, had to await the specialization of rooms according to function and the separation of rooms from each other. In the eighteenth century, the house altered its form. In French, *chamber* was distinguished from *sale*. In English, the function of a room was indicated by its name—bedroom, living room, dining room. Rooms were arranged to open into a corridor or hall, like houses into a street. No longer did the occupants pass through one room into another.

Relieved of the Grand Central Stations atmosphere and protected by new spaces, the family pattern began to stabilize and was expressed further in the form of the house.[14]

Conclusions

Except for the United States during the last fifty years, three-generation households have been the norm around the world and throughout history. Different cultures have solved the problem of caring for the elderly in different ways: For Bushmen it's ostrich eggs and shady spots. In Hispanic cultures it's been the youngest daughter, in Chinese the oldest son. Here in the United States of the twenty-first century, we are blessed with the freedom to set up households pretty much any way we want if we allow ourselves to think creatively. We particularly appreciate the sentiments expressed by Professor Constance Hilliard in response to the census data we presented at the beginning of this chapter:

> How weary I've become of living in the shadow of nuclear war—not global thermonuclear annihilation, but the explosive detonators imbedded in the American nuclear family.
>
> As the number of school shootings perpetrated by young people from middle-class, intact nuclear families grew, I waited for the real debate to begin. I do not mean the humdrum political haggling over gun control, youth violence and gangsta rap, but a thoughtful, penetrating examination of the nuclear family itself. But it didn't happen.
>
> As an American of African descent, I have long harbored a cultural prejudice against mainstream America's *Leave It to Beaver* nuclear-family ideal. The difference between the extended-family structure more characteristic of my own subculture and the nuclear form is far deeper than a mere calculation of the number of adults and children per household. Parents in nuclear families may offer children economic privileges, but this familial structure sometimes devolves into tightly shuttered, emotionally isolating cells. Vulnerable, lonely family members can be so damaged by material indulgence and emotional neglect that they lose touch with reality; meanwhile, no one is around to defuse or even notice their explosive angers and resentments.
>
> In contrast, subcultures that value the extended-family structure commonly believe that children need far more unconditional love than any two parents, however devoted, can give. Grandparents and other relatives often share child care with parents, providing an ineffable ingredient often missing from parental love: something sometimes

called "being-love," which is not possessive or contingent on what a child "does" in life. This unconditional love is a powerful self-esteem builder for a young person entering into the complexities of modern adult life.

Of course, extended families have their own special problems. As children within extended families grow into young adulthood, for instance, they sometimes feel an excessive responsibility to become immediate breadwinners rather than delay entrance into the workforce in order to gain more education.

The federal government spends vast sums on family-related research. Rather than "pathologize" extended families or simply ignore them, it's time to examine them more closely—and to cast a more critical eye on the increasingly volatile nuclear norm.[15]

Designing and Remodeling Your Home for Privacy

Virtually everything man is and does is associated with the experience of space.

—EDWARD T. HALL

UR COUSIN FRANK is a retired writer who has planned ahead for himself. He currently lives alone on Kangaroo Island in Australia, while his daughter lives with her family one thousand miles away in Sydney. When Frank goes to visit her, he likes to stay for a few weeks. With his daughter's permission, he had an apartment with a separate kitchen and its own entrance built onto her house for himself. Frank paid for it and gifted it to her. He is pleased to have his privacy, along with peace and quiet during his long stays with his daughter, her husband, and their three active children. Eventually, Frank will move there permanently when he can no longer take care of himself. Until that time, he plans to visit his daughter and her family and stay with them in his own attached apartment.

Whether you are thinking of remodeling your home to add an accessory apartment for your elderly parents or adult children, or even planning ahead for your own future needs as Frank did, you can accomplish this in a variety of ways. In many cases, a separate dwelling unit can be carved out of your home or added to it. You can extend existing bedrooms, close off walls, or convert surplus garage, attic, and basement space. If your single-family homesite has the land or space, you also can build a cottage in the backyard. Furthermore, if you live on property with an existing barn, you can convert it into housing for family members. Given the American preference for privacy and independence, the accessory apartment is a type of architecture that allows families or individuals to live together and apart at the same time.

Home Conversions

Research indicates that one-third of American houses have the space to add an accessory unit. Patrick Hare, a national expert on accessory apartments, took data from the 1987 American Housing Survey and determined that 32 percent of all single-family homes with five rooms or more were occupied by two persons or fewer. The term *rooms* does not include basements, garages, or attics, all of which offer additional space for accessory units. On the basis of those figures, he concluded that 32 percent, or almost one-third, of American homes have the potential of creating new accessory apartments.[1] As both the size of new homes and the elderly population have increased during the last three decades (+17 percent and +29 percent,[2] respectively), the numbers of homes that might accommodate an accessory apartment have ballooned as well.

The relatively minimal cost of creating a dwelling unit out of existing interior living space makes it more affordable than other types of remodeling projects that involve extending walls or raising the roof to add a second story. For instance, for as little as five to ten thousand dollars in material costs, an outside door can be added to a single-story home, a laundry room can be converted to a small kitchen, an existing bedroom can be used as a living area, and another existing bedroom and bathroom can be used as such. The apartment can be made private with the installation of a wall with a lockable door at the beginning of the hallway leading to it, effectively closing it off from the rest of the house. Because these types of units use existing space, they typically can be installed for one-third the cost of constructing a standard rental unit.[3]

An illustration of an inexpensive and simple single-family home conversion is depicted in exhibit 9.1. With minor modifications, an addition is added to an existing bedroom on a first floor and a second living unit is created.[4] A more elaborate ranch house conversion is shown in exhibit 9.2. Here a first-floor wing of a large house is turned into an accessory apartment.[5]

Indeed, there are a variety of ways to add a second living unit to an existing single-family home. For a surfeit of ideas, you might tune into HGTV's *Income Property* or order a copy of Michael Litchfield's excellent

Exhibit 9.1. Typical Single-Family Home Conversion.

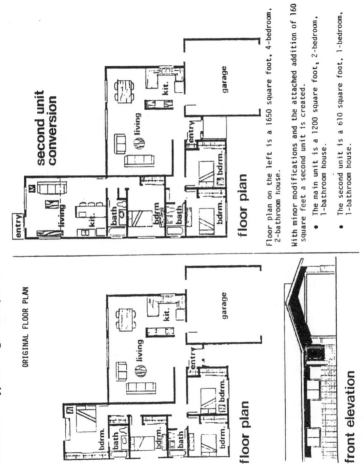

ORIGINAL FLOOR PLAN

second unit conversion

entry

living

kit.

bath

bdrm.

garage

floor plan

front elevation

floor plan

Floor plan on the left is a 1650 square foot, 4-bedroom, 2-bathroom house.

With minor modifications and the attached addition of 160 square feet a second unit is created.

- The main unit is a 1200 square foot, 2-bedroom, 1-bathroom house.

- The second unit is a 610 square foot, 1-bedroom, 1-bathroom house.

Source: Bert Verrips, *Second Units: An Emerging Housing Resource,* POS Housing/Greenbelt Alliance, Technical Report 2-E (San Francisco: People for Open Space, 1983).

book *In-Laws, Outlaws, and Granny Flats* (2011, Taunton Press). In addition to the architectural floor plan shown on pp. 150–51, Patrick Hare also includes in his book *Creating an Accessory Apartment* drawings of a split-level house lower-level conversion; a two-story house second-floor conversion; and a town house basement conversion. His book is an excellent resource for more details about converting homes to include accessory apartments.

When working with an architect or designer to remodel your home to add an accessory unit, there are a number of ways you can prepare for the initial meeting. You will want to think ahead about your space needs, lifestyle issues, and home layout. Also, figure out which family member will be the project manager. Noreen, a Northern California architect, had this to say about working with one of her clients.

Noreen: When I worked with Paul, he wanted to modify his existing single-family home so he could live there with his daughter, her husband, and their child. The young family was to live in the main house, and Paul would have his own private apartment with a separate kitchen and entrance there too. They did want to have the two units connected with a door, as well, to be convenient and provide easy access to his grandchild and the public area of the main house. It allows five-year-old Gail to come over to see him when she wants to, without having to go outside.

When I first started working with them, we talked about their space needs. How did both families want to use their public and private areas? We determined where people would sleep and work. Paul wanted a room with a big table where he could spread out drawings related to his work. It also has a foldout hide-a-bed for guests. His son-in-law Tom also needed a separate office to work in. As I said, they both wanted their own kitchens. Paul did not want a dishwasher. His bathroom has a shower. His daughter wanted a tub for young Gail's bathroom. We installed plumbing for a shower in the tub for her to use when she got older as well.

When working with clients, we also look at lifestyle issues. Those who live in California are inclined to want "California casual"—a combined living, dining, and kitchen room. In the east, lifestyles tend to be more formal and separate.

In addition, we see how the house is laid out. Do they want the laundry room in the house or in the garage? Where do they want the sleeping, work, and play areas?

Also, we research building code requirements. For example, in some municipalities, if a second unit is added, fire sprinklers are required throughout the house. Off-street parking also comes up, along with square footage requirements. Furthermore, in some cases, the owner has to live on the property if a second unit is put on it. That has to be part of the title.

Sharon: What about noise issues in remodeling homes when a second unit is added?

Noreen: We put in sound insulation between the floor joists. Any connecting walls or floors call for sound insulation. Also floor coverings are important. Carpeting is obviously quieter than wood or tile floors. Also, the installation of quieter plumbing pipes with insulation is important. Room furnishings, such as draperies and upholstered couches, can also affect sound.

Sharon: Do you have suggestions for people considering remodeling their home to add an accessory apartment?

Noreen: Don't be afraid to go to a professional beforehand for guidance. You're talking about quality-of-life issues. I've talked with clients who have a baby on the way or a mother-in-law about to move in with them. Plan ahead; don't be frozen into inactivity.

Lina, a divorced seventy-year-old secretary with an insurance company, paid for an apartment addition to her daughter's home in Connecticut in 1999. Lina's daughter, husband, and their two children live in the main house. She was originally planning to go to Florida to live after she retired, but her four adult children did not like the idea of her living so far away by herself. After a medical incident left Lina hospitalized for two months, they finally talked her out of it. Here's what she had to say about her involvement with remodeling her daughter's home to accommodate her joining the family:

Lina: My problem was the housing in the area was so expensive, particularly for a single person with a limited income. A friend suggested I sell my house and use the proceeds to build an apartment attached to my daughter's home. My daughter thought it was a great idea. The folks at city hall didn't object as long as I lived in it—it couldn't be built as just a rental unit. The place is about a thousand square feet with a kitchen, a living room, and a half-bath downstairs. Then I have a bathroom and bedroom upstairs. I put my washer and dryer upstairs as well. Also, I have my own separate entrance.

Sharon: You paid for the remodel. Did you have choices on what color to paint the walls?

Lina: Yes, I designed it. I have a friend who is an architectural designer and she helped. I was very careful to include my daughter and son-in-law in the process. I would ask, "Would you mind if I did this or if I added that?"

Exhibit 9.2. Ranch House Conversion

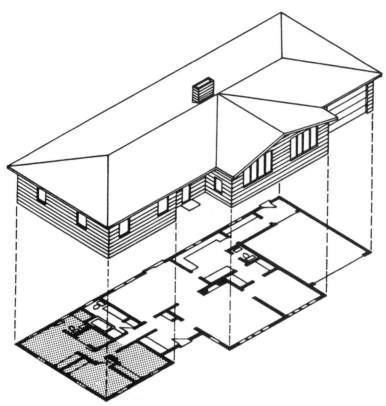

Ranch House - First Floor Conversions.

The sprawling wings of many one story houses can often be turned into accessory apartments. A plan for the conversion of the bedroom zone of this one level house is shown on the opposite page. This would require creating a new bedroom for the Main House which could be done by subdividing the Family Room. Conversion of the garage area would also be feasible.

Separate entries are easy to accomplish because both units are located at grade.

Source: Patrick H. Hare and Jolene N. Ostler, *Creating an Accessory Apartment* (New York: McGraw-Hill, 1987).

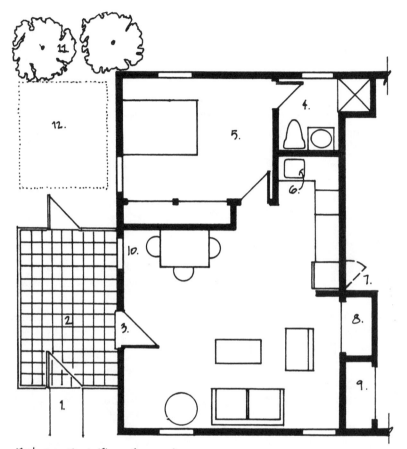

Features: First Floor Conversions

1. New Path to Street.
2. New Gate and Patio.
3. New Front Door Replaces Existing Window.
4. Existing Bathroom.
5. Bedroom Located Adjacent to Bath.
6. Kitchen Sink on Existing Plumbing Wall.
7. Soundproof Door to Main House (behind refrigerator).
8. New Closet for Acoustical Privacy Between Units.
9. Existing Coat Closet in Foyer of Main House.
10. Optional New Window at Dining Area.
11. Landscaping to Screen Apartment from Backyard.
12. Optional Gardening Area for Apartment.

I think it's a whole-house look. It's part of their house. I want them to know and to feel that this is their house, even though this section is mine. I just try not to be a pain.

Sharon: Anything you would change about your addition?

Lina: Yes. I don't have a basement or a garage. So even though I have a lot of storage spaces, there are some things I don't have places for. I miss the space. On the other hand, maybe that's good because then I don't clutter too much.

Sharon: But storage space is still something to think about in terms of making an addition to a home. If possible, be sure to create more storage space.

Eric, a young college student living in Wisconsin, told the story of his parents adding an upstairs apartment with two bedrooms, a kitchen, and a bathroom to their home for his grandfather to live in. It has an outside entrance and worked fine until the grandfather could no longer physically navigate the stairs. He then decided to move in with another family member nearby. Eric helped his grandfather move out before he moved into the accessory apartment himself and started to remodel it.

Eric: I like the fact that it's something I can fix up. You know, if you rent a place you're not going to fix it up. So I try to upgrade it, since I know it will help my parents.

Sharon: So you are actually helping out by doing a little bit of remodeling stuff?

Eric: Yeah, we put in a new kitchen sink and new flooring, stuff like that. I like doing it. I am learning a lot by fixing up the place.

Sharon: Well, it's kind of a win-win situation, because you're helping out, but you also get to live there.

Margaret, an interior designer living in Illinois, remodeled her current home to include an accessory unit for her mother with a small wet-bar kitchenette, a living area, two bedrooms, and a bathroom. It includes a stairway, but also the space to add an elevator should her mother need to use one in the future. Here's what she had to say about it:

Margaret: We originally considered getting a condo for my mother that is just a short distance from here, within the neighborhood. Then we got to thinking about how difficult it would be to have to run back and forth all the time. Also, the condo would not be a single story for her. She would have to go up and down the stairs so many times because the bedrooms are all on the upper level and the living space is down on the ground level. Since we have a very large house here to start with [3,600 square feet] we thought, "Why not add on to this?" It certainly made sense in terms of investing the money here rather than buying another place. It would increase the equity in our own place. She would be close at hand, and if anything came up, we would be right here.

So we built an addition of about 1,500 square feet so my mother could come and live with us. We did that in 1999. It took about eight months to get everything in order. We moved her here from Los Angeles. She loves her little place with us. It gives her privacy; it gives us privacy. She can come down when she needs to. She used to eat every meal with us. But now she has to watch her sodium intake, and in order to control that, she fixes her own meals and eats all of them upstairs.

Sharon: Anything you would have done differently?

Margaret: Well, there is one thing I probably would have stuck more to my guns on. When we first wanted to build this addition on our house, we encountered problems with the property line on one side of the house, where we were planning to push out and do a one-story addition. There was a question about the property line, and who owned from the ridge of the hill down to the water, which is not usable to anyone, really. But there is a setback. If you couldn't use that as a setback, then you had to come back another ten to fifteen feet from that edge of the hill. That wouldn't have allowed us enough room to put the addition out in that direction. I would have waited a little longer and pushed a little harder to have that happen as a single story for her. Then she could have had an exterior entrance and would feel a little more independent, as well as not have to go up and down the stairs.

Sharon: You have covered the bases though with your idea of providing space for an elevator that could be installed if needed.

In a further example, a middle-aged couple who live in Illinois remodeled their home and put in an accessory apartment for the wife's parents downstairs. The parents were invited to come and live with them and did so.

Room for Thought 9.1.   There Are Limits

Three years ago, landlord John Callaghan was granted city permits to enlarge a South Los Angeles single family home, creating three apartments. But he didn't stop there. He crammed as many as 44 rental rooms into a warren of narrow hallways, tiny, shared bathrooms and communal kitchens. Now, as the holidays approach, dozens of renters who paid as much as $500 per unit are being ordered to vacate the burnt orange three-story complex, in a neighborhood about a mile from the Coliseum.

Tenants and city officials agree that the place is potentially unsafe, but some city officials are asking what took inspectors so long to figure it out. "Clearly, someone was not doing their job," said Councilwoman Jan Perry, who represents the area where the building is located and has demanded a formal inquiry.

Construction began on the 49th Street building in 2008, records show. The city issued a temporary certificate of occupancy in 2009 for three units. It's not clear when the owner transformed the interior, a third-floor attic and a carport into a hive of rented bedrooms and shared kitchens and bathrooms. Pflaster, the attorney for the tenants, said she has spoken to one tenant who moved in as early as the fall of 2009. By the summer of 2010, according to tenants at the building, the third floor, which the city has found is illegal, was occupied.

Attorneys for the tenants said they believe the building has 44 units. City officials said they cannot confirm that because they do not recognize them as housing units since they are illegal.

Source: Jessica Garrison and David Zahniser, "Tenants Ordered Out of Home Crammed with Units," *Los Angeles Times*, December 17, 2011.

Subsequently, the mother developed a medical problem that required her daughter's help on a daily basis. Because of the living arrangement they had set up ahead of time, and because the daughter worked out of her home as an editor, she was easily able to help her mother. Also, her parents did not need to suffer the additional anxiety and stress of moving to a senior facility.

Cottage Additions

When possible, for privacy, it is preferable to have completely separate living quarters on the same property.[6] Many people are building a detached cottage or guesthouse on their property to allow aging parents or adult children to join them now or in the future. Todd and Lynne own and operate two nursery schools in Colorado. They are building a large house for themselves and their two young daughters, and also plan to include a cottage for Todd's parents. Originally, his parents were going to buy their current house from them and live nearby. However, his parents have since reconsidered. They want to simplify their lives, to downsize to a new and smaller place that doesn't require the expense of remodeling or as much upkeep. Todd explained how they are including their parents in the process of designing the guesthouse on their new property.

Todd: Actually, my stepdad is a professional home designer and is not only designing our house for us, but is also planning the guesthouse. So it will be entirely what they want for themselves. We still need to check with the city about the possibilities. There might be a limit to what we can do.

A young Northern California couple planned ahead for their parents' future care by building a cottage in their backyard. In the meantime, it has become a revolving-door guesthouse, with different family members and friends living there for several months at a time. Diane is a young homemaker and community volunteer. Here's what she had to say:

Sharon: How did you get involved in building it.

Diane: It started out with the idea of having an extra bathroom and shower for the children near the swimming pool. But, knowing my dad was ill and that my mom would be coming more often for long periods of time, we also wanted a space for her to stay. So the guesthouse idea came up and we drew up plans. They were approved by the town. We decided to put in a Murphy bed instead of making it a full-time residence or guesthouse. It became an extra space, kind of a hangout place for the kids. But then it could be used for someone to stay for a short period of time. Along with the living area and a foldaway bed, it has a little kitchen and a bathroom with a big closet.

Sharon: Anything that you would change if you could about the guesthouse?

Diane: Add a washer and dryer. But I think if we do that people would stay too long.

Another young couple living in Oregon put in a guest cottage for his mother, who babysits their daughter while they are traveling for their work. Jim and Christine, along with his mother, Madeline, talked about how they worked together to design and build the cottage.

Madeline: We met with the builders and looked at apartments and different floor plans to try to figure out what was too small, what was too big, and try and get some ideas. Jim and Christine then came up with the final floor plans. They did a great job. I was able to bring with me my important furniture pieces and be surrounded with my things. They even designed a wall at an angle to accommodate my favorite antique carved wooden chest from China.

Christine: When Madeline moved into her new cottage, almost all of her original stuff went with her. So she now is surrounded by 95 percent of it.

Sharon: What about wall colors for the new place? Who made those selections?

Jim: We encouraged her to pick out all the colors as well as the carpets and the flooring. The only thing that we selected was the cabinets.

Sharon: So that gave you more of a sense of it being your home?

Madeline: Yes, it is eight hundred square feet. It has one bedroom, a living room, a kitchen, a bath, a laundry room, and a very large walk-in closet off the bedroom, which is almost big enough to fit a bed. It also has small covered patio. The cottage is absolutely lovely.

Garage Conversions

It is possible to convert a garage into an accessory apartment. However, before doing so, it is advisable to hire an architect or building designer to conduct a feasibility study. You will want to determine if there is enough space available on your lot for a "habitable living area" addition and whether the conversion will conform to all building codes required by your local planning and zoning office. Also, you may want to request a zoning classification for the site, along with papers describing zoning regulations and the application-and-approval process.[7]

Be aware that one of the issues that comes up with garage conversions is where you will park your cars in the future. Do you have enough room for "tandem parking," that is, one car parked behind another? You would need twenty feet in front of the garage for an extra parking spot or "20 feet from the leading edge of this parking stall to the front property line."[8] Will cars evicted from the old garage have no place but the street to park? What impact would this have on your neighborhood? You might want to talk to your neighbors beforehand to see what they think of your plans.[9] Also, you may be required to have covered parking for one or more cars located at least twenty feet in from the front property line. If there is enough space available, you could consider building a carport in front of the former garage or somewhere else on your property. Be sure to find out what your city requires in the way of parking, including setbacks, number of spaces, and building dimensions. Typically, the minimum width for a single-car garage is twelve feet.[10]

If you are considering converting a portion of a two- or three-car garage into a studio apartment, there are special conditions that must be met when constructing a wall between the new room and the remaining garage. The new wall must meet fire-resistant building codes that are even more strict than an interior wall in a house. Moreover, in some cases, a garage cannot open directly onto living quarters, so you won't be allowed to put a door between the new room and the garage. Again, look into what your own city planning department requires.[11]

In short, although there are not a lot of code requirements for a garage because it's just a storage area, there are many code requirements for a space that will be inhabited. It has to be both safe and comfortable to live in. Besides the basic structural, electrical, and plumbing requirements, there are also "habitability" codes that regulate ventilation, natural light, insulation, floor covering, and minimum room sizes.[12] To be livable, your apartment must be weather-tight, well ventilated with windows, heated in winter, and furnished with comfortable lighting and flooring. Depending on the space available, two types of garage conversions are depicted in exhibit 9.3.[13]

In many instances, people are converting garages into apartments for rental income. In one case, Helen, a single Northern California Realtor, remodeled her garage into an apartment with an outside entrance, bedroom, living area, kitchenette, and bathroom. It has the potential for many uses. She uses it now as a rental, but in the future someone could live there and take care of her. Likewise, a single friend of ours has remodeled her garage into a smaller, four-hundred-square-foot "sonny flat." Our friend's three-bedroom home was becoming too cramped for her bookkeeping business and two teenage children, so she created the new studio apartment for one of her sons. When he moves away, she plans to use the unit for rental income.

Susan, a divorced college professor in Southern California, initially had her garage made into an apartment and rented it out for income. When her daughter and husband needed a place to live while completing their graduate degrees, she offered the space to them. Subsequently, they had a baby. Here's what she said happened next:

Susan: It soon became evident that the three of them over in this little tiny apartment, and me in this great big house, was kind of silly. So there was a

Exhibit 9.3.　Garage Conversions

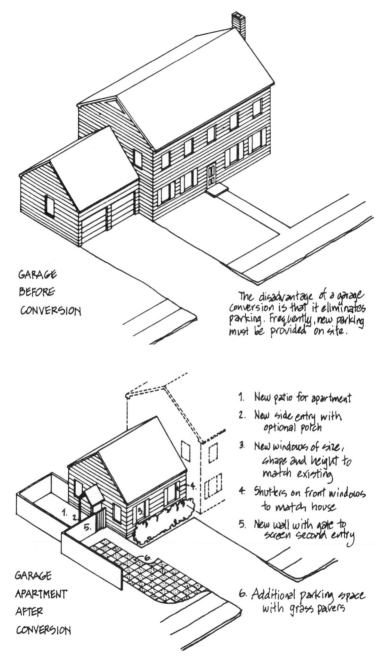

GARAGE
BEFORE
CONVERSION

The disadvantage of a garage conversion is that it eliminates parking. Frequently, new parking must be provided on site.

1. New patio for apartment
2. New side entry with optional porch
3. New windows of size, shape and height to match existing
4. Shutters on front windows to match house
5. New wall with gate to screen second entry

GARAGE
APARTMENT
AFTER
CONVERSION

6. Additional parking space with grass pavers

Source: Patrick H. Hare and Jolene N. Ostler, *Creating an Accessory Apartment* (New York: McGraw-Hill, 1987).

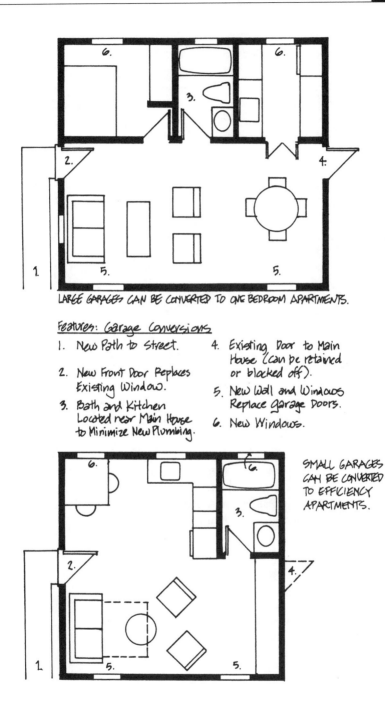

LARGE GARAGES CAN BE CONVERTED TO ONE BEDROOM APARTMENTS.

Features: Garage Conversions

1. New Path to Street.

2. New Front Door Replaces Existing Window.

3. Bath and Kitchen Located near Main House to Minimize New Plumbing.

4. Existing Door to Main House (can be retained or blocked off).

5. New Wall and Windows Replace garage Doors.

6. New Windows.

SMALL GARAGES CAN BE CONVERTED TO EFFICIENCY APARTMENTS.

point when they moved into the house, and I moved out to the apartment. But that transition was relatively difficult. By the time I moved out to this apartment, then it was much better. And I'm very separated in the sense that I don't even hear the kids crying during the night. Furthermore, I had sort of lost interest in keeping the big house up. I didn't want to remodel or make any serious changes. Whereas, with my new apartment, I've had a great time remodeling and having everything new and bright and shiny and lovely.

Sharon: You did remodel your apartment yourself; you put in a sunroom.

Susan: Right. Then I put in one of the storage walls, which is beautiful and made out of maple. Then I did a completely new kitchen, and finally finished the floors to match the ceramic tile floor in the sunroom. That's been kind of fun and makes it really nice.

Sharon: How would you describe the physical layout of your apartment?

Susan: The main apartment was sort of the bedroom and kitchen. That's where I've done most of the remodeling. Also, there's a bathroom beyond that. It's more like a Pullman kitchen. It's not a big kitchen, but it's very well laid out. You walk through my sunroom into what you might call my sitting/living room/kitchen. I had a whole wall installed for storage. That's what you end up being short of when you go from a big house into a cottage. By the way, my sunroom is the place where I entertain.

It's also possible to build an accessory unit above a garage. A young couple living in Utah have benefited from her parents' making this type of addition to their home. Brenda, an elementary school teacher, and her husband, Joe, a Realtor, are living there rent free in order to save money to buy their own place. They described their living situation.

Brenda: Well, it's an apartment right next to my parent's house. We have one bathroom. We moved in just after we got married. We've been here for about six months.

Joe: It's above the garage. It's attached to the house, but it has a separate entrance. It's attached by a walkway. We have our own kitchen, living room, central area, bedroom, and bathroom. It has lots of light and high ceilings, like a quaint little chateau.

Sharon: Was someone living here before you?

Brenda: No. Relatives would stay here when they came to visit. Five years ago we had a couple living here who babysat.

Sharon: What about the washer and dryer? Do you use their washer and dryer?

Joe: We have our own downstairs in the garage. Her family set that up.

Sharon: Do you have any friends who are also living with their parents to save money?

Brenda: I have a lot of friends who have lived with their parents when they got married, mostly in separate basement apartments with their own kitchens.

Joe: A lot of the basement apartments are big. It's just a very common thing. In our town, it's very difficult to find accessory apartments because of restrictive zoning. But I'll get a lot of calls from people on an ad just because it has a mother-in-law unit. That would be the thing that drew them. If you are listing a house, that's always a major draw. A place with a mother-in-law unit is bound to be nice and big and people like that. It seems like more parents are getting them for their adult children or the other way around.

Paula, an administrative assistant living in Northern California, and her husband recently converted their garage into an apartment for her mother and niece. Her mother had just sold her home and plans to move out-of-state once she retires. She needed a transitional place for a couple of years. She also wanted to have a place to stay when she comes back for visits with her daughter. The unit has a living area, one bedroom, a bathroom, and a small kitchen. Paula talked about why and how she remodeled her garage.

Paula: My mother was about to retire and said to us, "Well, you have a garage and it's detached. It has a bathroom in it. Why don't I fix it up and stay in it?" My husband and I were already thinking about doing that anyway, just so that we'd have an extra room separate from our three kids. They are only eleven, eight, and six. We wanted a little hideaway place for us. So we decided to move forward with it.

My mom and my husband worked on the project together. They came up with a plan and hired a contractor to do the work. It's a two-car garage and it had a half-bath, which was just a toilet and a sink. We had to install a shower and the kitchen. Fortunately, the plumbing was already there, since we had our washer and dryer out there. She has her own little yard. We have our own backyard, so it's really convenient in a way.

Basement Conversions

In a town near Boston, Massachusetts, a sixty-three-year-old grandmother was able to convert a walkout basement space in her home into a place for her grandson and his wife to live in while they both attended a local community college. For an investment of about seven thousand dollars, including building permits, she hired a contractor to make the conversion, complete with a kitchenette and separate entrance. To make ends meet, she did need to charge them a small rent each month to help pay the cost of utility bills. Fortunately, her area is zoned for multifamily houses and rental apartments are legal.

Lou Manfredini, in an article he wrote about basement conversions for *USA Weekend*, said,

> It's important that the apartment conform to building and fire codes. A basement should have windows to escape through in a fire, as well as an exit other than a staircase. Walk-out basements are ideally suited for this, because they're mostly raised above the ground anyway.
>
> Start by providing plenty of light. If a basement does not have full-sized windows, they sometimes can be added. Window wells can help bring in natural light so the basement doesn't feel like . . . well . . . a basement. A creative architect or contractor can help.
>
> Floors should be built above the concrete slab using an underlayment that creates air spaces, which will go a long way toward making a place feel warm and dry. Walls should be constructed in front of the foundation walls to create air space. The result can be a streamlined set of rooms that look like any other part of the house.[14]

Other Conversions

Not only can garages and basements be converted to accessory apartments, but also you can create housing in barns, stables—even chicken coops. Across the country, unused farm structures are deteriorating, collapsing, being torn down, or finding new life in being transformed into housing. Although we did not personally interview people who had made such conversions, we found numerous examples on the Internet. *This Old House*, a television home-remodeling show, has featured several accessory apartment remodels the past couple of years, further indicating the increasing national trend for this type of housing. Two articles titled "Barn Storming" and "A Cottage in Concord" describe how the *This Old House* crew turned a two-story barn in Massachusetts into an "in-law" apartment for a couple's parents.[15]

In short, barn conversions can be very rewarding, but also more expensive than building a new house. To keep in line with modern-day regulations, they almost always need major structural alterations. Furthermore, in most cases a lot of work is needed to meet roofing and insulation standards. Nonetheless, a completed barn conversion can be a lovely sight and give the owner a great sense of accomplishment and pride at completion.

Green Building

There are affordable ways to remodel and build these days to conserve energy, reduce waste, and improve air quality. "Over the last few years, prices for such things as installing photovoltaic solar panels on the roof for pollution-free energy or using recycled materials and sustainably grown wood are getting close in cost to the conventional alternatives."[16] Depending on where you live, incentives are available to help reduce costs. In some areas, state and federal incentives can bring down installation costs by as much as 50 percent. For example, in 2006 the federal government began to give 30 percent tax credits for residential solar installations (for details, visit www.california solarcenter.org).[17] In addition, during the same time period, the federal government offered tax credits "for energy-efficient air conditioners, heat pumps, furnaces, water heaters, windows, and insulation."[18]

Using recycled or salvaged materials is often less expensive than using new materials. Not only can green systems and materials save money to begin with, but they can be cost effective in the long run. Examples include the following:

- Radiant heating systems can save space and costly framing labor by not needing big chases and additional furnaces that might be needed for forced-air systems.
- While cellulose insulation (made from 90 percent recycled newspapers) is initially more expensive than fiberglass, installation costs less because there's no need to provide air spaces around the insulation.
- Cotton insulation costs more than fiberglass, as do most environmental materials; however, environmental materials save on energy bills in the long run.
- The easiest and cheapest way to save on energy bills is to add insulation in attics and walls to avoid artificial heating.[19]

In fact, homes constructed with sustainable building products can save up to 90 percent of monthly utility costs. These zero-energy homes "generate their own electricity with photovoltaic systems, and reduce energy consumption through on-demand hot water heaters, radiant roof barriers, high efficiency furnaces and appliances, tightly sealed ducts, extra insulation and low-E windows."[20] Installing fluorescent light fixtures is another option. "They use one-fourth the energy of regular lighting and last 10 times longer."[21] Also, you can put light switches in rooms "that can be programmed to automatically turn off the lights when sensors show no one is in the room."[22] Furthermore, installing ceiling fans in key living areas can cut down the need for air-conditioning. Likewise, programmable thermostats will save on utility bills. Certainly, converting unoccupied rooms of a large house into an apartment for extended-family living can help reduce energy and resource consumption in general.

Policy Issues

There are a number of factors to investigate before moving ahead with plans to add an accessory unit. Included are local codes or regulations, zoning, permit processes, tax, and insurance issues that can complicate your project. The first step is to check with your local building department to see if the conversion or addition is feasible for your property. Are accessory units allowed? How are they classified? What are the tax ramifications? Most cities define an accessory unit as a space that has its own entrance and kitchen similar to that of an apartment. Different municipalities have different regulations regarding their installation and use. Depending on where you live, some cities encourage the building of such units, while others put up barriers against constructing them. Requiring extra parking for automobiles can be one of the biggest barriers. Other obstacles include minimum lot size, setback requirements, and requirements about what percentage of a lot can be covered with living space. For example, the city of Los Angeles requires a minimum lot size of 7,500 square feet, while neighboring Pasadena requires double that. Also check to see if there are limits on the number of occupants and rules about lease terms.[23]

Depending on your needs, you can select a licensed architect, a designer, or a design/build contractor to work with on your project. It helps to get referrals from friends who have had positive experiences. You can also contact the AIA (American Institute of Architects), the ASID (American Society of Interior Designers), and the NARI (National Association of the Remodeling Industry) for referrals. Be sure to look for someone who has remodeling experience. If that person happens to be from outside your area,

---

Room for Thought 9.2. Local Restrictions Are Easing

Many of the laws are modeled after one advocated by the AARP and passed by Santa Cruz, Calif., in 2003 that prompted other cities in California and the Pacific Northwest to follow. Seattle began allowing detached backyard cottages in December 2009, and it received permit applications for 55 of them last year, plus 96 for attached units. But it's not just a phenomenon on the West Coast. ADU laws have recently passed in many places in the East, including Virginia's Arlington and Fairfax counties, and elsewhere. In June, Denver revised its housing code to allow second units, and in July, Hudson, Wis., gave the nod to garage apartments.

"It's very widespread," says Michael Litchfield, author of a book, *In-Laws, Outlaws and Granny Flats*, who lives in an in-law suite with 12-foot ceilings and quarry-tile floors in Point Reyes, Calif.

He says many of these units are converted garages, attics, unused rooms or basements, while others are additions or detached cottages. He surmises that most are illegal, citing the time and money involved to get permits. "There are a lot of these, but we don't have (Census) data," says Arthur Nelson, director of the University of Utah's Metropolitan Research Center. "People are doubling up, even tripling up," he says, because of tight budgets or economic worries.

Source: Wendy Koch, "In-Law Units Help Homeowners Pay Bills, Care for Relatives," *USA Today*, August 17, 2011.

---

make certain that individual consults your local building department for requirements before drawing up your plans.[24]

When working with a home architect/designer, it is wise to determine your budget for the project in advance. The cost of adding a unit can be far more expensive than just adding a single room. Be sure to allow for the extra costs of putting in a kitchen with the required electrical and plumbing work, along with the possible installation of separate utility services. Also, your unit may require additional insulation between ceilings or adjoining walls, depending on municipal codes. According to Leo Cram with the Missouri Gerontology Institute, the costs of a home conversion vary significantly based upon

- the amount of remodeling work required,
- the ratio of do-it-yourself to contracted-out work for materials and labor,
- the amount of prior furnished space available, and
- luxury of the living accommodations provided.[25]

Once you have your detailed architectural plans in hand, if you are not already working with a design/build contractor, you will need to select a licensed and bonded home remodeler to do the work for you. One source for finding these people is your own homeowner's insurance company. You can request a list of local contractors that they recommend. Once again, the National Association of the Remodeling Industry provides information and referrals to people who want to remodel their home. Also, you can ask your architect/designer or friends for recommendations. It's a good idea to get price quotes from more than one builder and compare them, making sure they are bidding on the same items. Take the time to go and look at projects your prospective builders have done.[26] Another thing to consider is hiring a contractor you would like to work with, someone who is a good listener and has a professional business. It is very important to establish solid lines of communication early on. It helps to provide as much information as possible to the contractor with drawn-up, detailed plans at the beginning of a project. You will want to write down the details of any communication with your contractor, so if disputes do arise, there is a reference to what was agreed upon.[27]

After you've selected your remodeler, it can be a good idea to hire an attorney to draw up and/or review the contract. Make sure the contract specifies the start and completion dates.[28] It's important to allow adequate time for construction. Many homeowners underestimate how long it will take to build a unit before they can begin to use it. If you want to save time and know the budget in advance, you may want to consider working with a design/builder/remodeler instead of an outside architect.

Before attempting any home improvements, whether they be plumbing, electrical, or structural, you (or your contractor) will need to obtain the necessary permits from your local building department. Finally, after the work is completed, be sure to follow up with the required inspections by your local building department. Good luck with your project!

Conclusions

Certainly, there are a number of ways you can add a self-contained living unit to your property. You can reconfigure space inside an existing single-family dwelling or add on to it. Spaces that have the greatest potential for conversion include attics, basements, and garages. You can also build a new cottage in the backyard or remodel an old barn. Examples have been given of all of these conversions. Finally, policy issues related to building accessory apartments have been outlined. It's important to find out what your local municipality requires before starting your project.

On the other hand, if you should decide it is not feasible for you to become involved in remodeling your home, what other options do you have to house family members? Our next chapter discusses how to find and buy housing with accessory units. You will learn about the innovations that are already happening in housing and developments around the country.

How to Find, Buy, or Build Housing

We have bigger houses and smaller families, more conveniences, but less time.

—GEORGE CARLIN

OR MANY the remodeling option described in the last chapter won't work. This is particularly so if you're living in an area like Southern California, where land values aren't calculated in terms of money anymore, only limbs. In many places around the country, like Southern California, spare land will cost you an arm and a leg, maybe even a neck.

So this chapter is about finding and buying or building properties with contiguous residences. We've divided the chapter into four main topics. First, we discuss finding existing homes with attached, adjacent, or neighboring units, giving special attention to the stories of motivated citizens who are succeeding in changing restrictive twentieth-century statutes and regulations. Next, we consider how residential real estate developers are anticipating the needs of the baby boom generation. Third, we take a look at the lucky folks who can afford to custom build three-generation housing. We close the chapter with a quick summary of the restrictions local governments and other authorities place on three-generation housing.

The Existing Stock of Multigenerational Housing

We'll start with the stories. The people we've talked to have been quite creative in their searches for roofs for their extended families. Their stories fall roughly into three categories: (1) some folks looked for and found two adjacent units, (2) others just moved in with family with big places and stayed, and (3) several just bought the house next door.

Adjacent Units

Nancy: We lived in a large home for thirty-five years, and it came to the point where we would have to redo a lot of the house. It was getting tired. We were tired of taking care of the garden. We decided we were going to sell the house. Our son-in-law was very much a part of this whole decision because I would not have done this with just my daughter and me working something like this out. An in-law thing can be a very difficult thing. We were going to buy a small house in our neighborhood and our son-in-law said, "Let me look for a home with a guesthouse and see if maybe we can find something that will fit us all."

We found this. We saw several others that were not appropriate at all. I remember walking in the door here and saying, "I could live here very comfortably." Everything turned out right. The original owners didn't want to move right away. We weren't in any great hurry. It was October. Prices were coming down a little even though this was before the big rush. By the time we purchased it, it was a wonderful buy for us and the timing was great. We had a huge estate sale. We sold most of our furniture, just walked in, and have enjoyed it so much ever since.

Families with Big Places

Here are stories from members of three families lucky enough to have big places:

Kathleen: When I graduated from college in 1988, I came back to Los Angeles. My parents had initially bought an apartment building in Santa Monica that had a little house in the front and an apartment building in the back. They did it mainly for my older brother to have a place to live. He was also finishing school, and he was back east. He had met a girl and ended up deciding to stay back there for a while. So when I graduated, I took one of the units, and then I got married. My younger brother ended up moving into another unit while he was at UCLA, because he couldn't get housing. Then he got married and lived there. Next my older brother came back from New York and moved into another unit. He was not married at the time. So we were all three siblings living together again.

Then my husband and I ended up buying our little house two years later and moved out. My brothers were still living there. In fact, my younger brother moved into the little house in front that we had used. Then he proceeded to have children. When he and his wife were looking for a house, they started looking in our area. It just so happened that the house right next door to us came up for sale, and they bought it a year ago.

Marian: I lived with my parents in a house in Indianapolis. When I was five and my sister was three, my grandparents (my mother's parents) asked if they could build a house next door to us on the property. They did. So we ended up with a family compound, combination yards and that sort of thing. As time went on, we all appreciated the advantages of the setup.

Dorrie: Our house was designed with an in-law quarters downstairs. The family who lived there before and built the home had the mother-in-law living in it. They had teenage children who had their separate bedrooms upstairs. So that is how they designed the house, with the upstairs and downstairs as two separate houses. Tim and I loved the location and many things about the place. We just decided to take the size along with everything else. Little did we know, fifteen years later, we would have our daughter and her three children move in with us. We now all live in every inch of the house.

The House Next Door

Sylvia: We finally got a place near the lake. My in-laws mentioned, "Keep us abreast of any homes that go up for sale. We would love to move out to the lake too." My mother-in-law grew up on a family ranch where there were three families on a compound. So that situation was one that she's very familiar and comfortable with. So anyway, back in 1988, the neighboring home came up for sale. It was a private matter. It was never put on the market. It was just by word of mouth that we heard that our neighbor wanted to sell her home. They negotiated a deal, bought the house, but didn't move in right away. They had renters in the home for a year or two before they actually moved in.

Dana: When we were looking for a place for my grandmother to live, we basically went to our neighbors and said, "What is it going to cost us to get you to move?" They had two children and it was a small house. We had heard that they were getting ready to put on a second story. We decided we better jump on this. It worked out so well for them because they were given the opportunity to buy a much bigger, better house. We paid them significantly more dollars to move. So they benefited and we benefited even more, because we really needed that house. I wanted my grandmother to be close by.

So we've described three basic types of existing housing: contiguous houses/duplexes, compounds, and houses with cottages. Most folks we interviewed didn't work through a Realtor, but some did. And, of course, calling a Realtor in your neighborhood of choice will provide you the best information about how to find your particular preference. And such options vary substantially by neighborhood depending on land prices and age of the housing. If you're interested in buying either of your next-door neighbors' places or perhaps the one across the street, one of the three will typically come up for sale about once every four to five years.[1] So those opportunities are precious. You'll generally find houses with casitas in older neighborhoods where they've been added over the years, or in new, upper-end housing tracts built since the late 1990s. In the latter case, builders have been recently giving buyers the option of a third garage or a casita with a separate entrance in homes of more than three thousand square feet. Such options are the subject of the next section of this chapter.

Room for Thought 10.1.   Multigenerational Housing Is Hot

Family reunions are taking on a new meaning in the real estate market. According to a recent survey by Coldwell Banker Real Estate LLC among its network of real estate professionals, in the last 12 months, 37 percent of sales professionals surveyed noted an increase in homebuyers looking to purchase homes to accommodate more than one generation of their family. In addition, almost 70 percent of Coldwell Banker sales agents believe that economic conditions may cause greater demand for multi-generational homes in their market during the next year.

Furthermore, the Coldwell Banker January 2010 survey respondents cited financial drivers as the no. 1 reason why home buyers or sellers are moving into a house with other generations of their family (39 percent). Twenty-nine percent said that health care issues are the primary reason, and six percent cited a strong family bond as the main factor.

"While saving money is certainly an incentive for buying a home that accommodates multiple generations, the benefits go beyond just financial reasons," said Diann Patton, Coldwell Banker Real Estate Consumer Specialist. "With two or three generations living under one roof, families often experience more flexible schedules, quality time with one another and can better juggle childcare and eldercare."

Communicating with family members and consulting with their real estate professional is key, as well. "Talk to everyone involved and determine how comfortable the family members are about sharing bathrooms, office space or common areas, and let that guide your search," Patton advises. "All of these topics are incredibly important in finding the right kind of home to fit the family—like one that has four bathrooms or one that has three."

Helpful Hints

- Sellers with "mother in-law suites" or additional spaces that could accommodate a family interested in a multi-generational living arrangement should highlight this aspect of the home. Whether it's a garage apartment or refurbished basement, this separate space can help one home stand apart from the others on its block.
- Buyers must be clear about their exact needs. Some families may just want an extra bedroom or two for family members, while others require areas with a separate kitchen, entrance, handicap accessibility or even a larger garage for additional cars. Desired location may also be influenced by proximity to local hospitals, senior centers or other important activities to family members.
- Extended families purchasing a home together should consider signing a written contract outlining everything from finances to chores and childcare. Each family should assess their situation individually and find a plan that works best for them.

Source: Coldwell Banker, "Coldwell Banker Survey Identifies Multi-Generational Homes as a Trend in Real Estate," news release, March 30, 2012, www.coldwellbanker.com/real_estate/learn?learnPage=DETAIL&contentId=14550986.

How Residential Developers See Multigenerational Housing

The housing boom peaked in 2005 at 1.3 million new units sold. During 2009–2010 home builders sold less than 400,000 each year. Home builders can see the baby boomers retiring, but they are still figuring out what they'll want in the way of housing. Those who don't recognize the generations-uniting trend we are talking about in this book mostly build and advertise for recreational needs like hiking and biking (in addition to the more traditional, but sedentary, golf), along with broadband communication facilities allowing continued home-based employment. Most builders are still making the mistake of planned isolation of the generations. Even in the housing innovation center of the planet, Orange County, California, most of the new communities are segregated by unit size and so on. In other words, the creative mixing of small units with large ones, attached with detached, and owned with rental units remains taboo. They're putting the 1,200-square-foot single-story units in separate villages from the 2,800-square-foot family homes, even if both kinds are in the same development. In the upper-end developments—three thousand square feet and larger and over one million dollars—granny flats are listed as options, but even then they don't often include kitchen facilities or separate entrances. And, worst of all, in high-density California billions of dollars are being wastefully invested in *upstairs* "artists studios" that accommodate the boomerang kids well, but make absolutely no sense for the future flood of grandparents, who will have trouble with all those stairs.

Luxury homebuilders such as Toll Brothers offer in-law suites ranging from twelve to thirty-six thousand dollars in their new homes. Competitor Pulte Homes offers detached casitas in its new developments in Nevada and Arizona at around thirty thousand. Toll Brothers has recently started to mix housing types, including larger single-family homes and smaller single-story homes aimed at older folks. An executive there reports, "We have master plans across the country where there is both product for the growing boomer family (and for) parents who might be retired at this point. That wasn't the case five years ago. Now we do a lot of that because of market demand." Andrew Kochera, senior policy adviser at AARP's Public Policy Institute, suggests that Toll Brothers' high-end innovations will spread: "A lot of the features that start appearing in the upper-end homes tend to drift down toward other homes in the market. Large kitchens and bathrooms started in upper-end homes, large window casings, all those sorts of things gradually filter down as builders increasingly try to offer those to other people."[2]

An Interview with Executives at Standard Pacific

John had the good fortune to talk with two executives at Standard Pacific, one of the leading residential builders in the country, renowned for their innovations, high-quality homes, and excellent consumer satisfaction. Below are the comments of Scott Stowell and Ralph Spargo:

Room for Thought 10.2.   The New Home Builders Are Finally Getting the Message

A new kind of home is being marketed to multigenerational households, a category that increased by 30 percent from 2000 to 2010, according to the U.S. Census Bureau. KB Home, Lennar, and Pulte Group are among builders that offer models with second master bedrooms, kitchenettes, and separate entrances. Those features may help lure buyers at a time when new residences are selling at a record slow pace. The number of new single-family homes sold sank to 323,000 last year, the fewest since the Commerce Dept. began tracking data in 1963 and down from a peak of 1.28 million in 2005. "This is a niche area that appears to be solid and growing," says Stephen Melman, director of economic services at the Washington-based National Association of Home Builders. "It's a demographic thing."

A steady stream of visitors toured two of Lennar's Next Gen models at a grand opening in the Rosena Ranch community in San Bernardino, Calif., on Nov. 5. Prices start at $318,890 for a three-bedroom house with a built-in suite equipped with a kitchen and living room, as well as its own entrance. Mary and Marty Nachman, retirees from Apple Valley, Calif., say the two-unit Lennar home may be preferable to the house they bought in 2007 in one of Pulte's senior communities. Where they live now, the Nachmans are restricted from hosting guests under 55 for more than two months—a rule that might prevent them from taking in one of their five grown children if they hit a rough patch. "The way things are right now, there are a lot of young adult children who need to move back home for a while," says Mary Nachman.

While duplexes, granny flats, and guest houses have a long history, the two-homes-in-one models are new for mass-market builders, says Jeff Roos, president of Lennar's Western region. Lennar unveiled its first Next Gen homes in September in the Phoenix area and expects to offer them in as many as 40 communities by year-end. Besides Phoenix, the company is targeting California's Inland Empire and Central Valley; Las Vegas is next. These are all areas that have suffered some of the biggest price declines since the U.S. housing bubble burst, so there's a need for new designs to boost sales. Says Roos: "We think it will compete very well vs. a foreclosure or distressed sale."

Source: John Gittlesohn, "Making Life with the In-Laws Bearable," *Bloomberg BusinessWeek*, November 28, 2011.

John: What I'm seeing in the current stock of new housing are the granny flats or at least there is a downstairs bedroom. The one place I'm thinking of is in Turtle Ridge, where you walk up a set of steps and there is an office area that could be a separate bedroom.

Scott: We have an option for that.

John: So you must have done market research to come up with that. People are asking for that kind of option?

Ralph: Yes. But primarily for us it is because we think that potential customers are doing it because their married children might come to stay with them for five years.

John: So you are recognizing that kids are coming back.

Scott: That's the bigger trend that we see versus the one you are talking about—the parents moving in with their kids—which we think will happen later. We're not seeing a whole lot of that yet.

Ralph: Let me just comment on that real quickly. The challenge that we are also going to have is that twenty years ago when lots were much bigger, it was easier to do that. Today, especially in California, as land gets really expensive, lots are getting smaller and smaller. We are not nearly as flexible as we were when we were putting in pool houses. That's going to be a challenge. The land use is going to be the limiting factor. Things are going to become more vertical.

Scott: I think what you are seeing more of now is the adult children who have just started their families, who have trouble finding a house to live in around here. So some of it is necessity driven. The baby boomers don't want their kids to move to Temecula where they can buy a house. They would like them to stay here. If they don't, they're not going to see the grandkids as much as they would like to. So I think a lot of that is happening, even before the grandkids arrive.

Ralph: Right. They're investing in their kids now. We are seeing a tremendous transfer of wealth from baby-boomer parents to their children. They are going to transfer the wealth anyway at some point in time. They're gifting it now so the kids can buy a home and be close, versus moving inland to Riverside County or out of state to Phoenix, where the housing is cheaper.

Scott: Del Webb puts out a report every year. Historically, the seniors they focus on have retreated to the large retirement communities to get away from everybody. Now Del Webb is reporting some important changes. In a recent survey, 30 percent of boomers would prefer retiring to an urban community. Another 29 percent would prefer a mixed community that included a multigenerational neighborhood. Also, more than half would be "happy to help" if either their parents or children needed to move in with them.

Ralph: The report talks about being an empty nester for a long period of time. Male baby boomers are more likely than female baby boomers to indicate they will be happier once their children leave. But it's only less than a quarter; only about 20 percent of the people want to see them leave. The other 75 percent don't.

John: There are a lot of nasty terms floating around in the popular press, like "boomerang kids." So how long ago did you notice this trend?

Ralph: We probably have been seeing it for fifteen years.

Scott: I would say that at least for us at Standard Pacific, division presidents along with the marketing staff really have a lot of influence on the design principals used in our housing. We look to trends plus our own experience with our sales people. But I would say that, probably ten years ago, we were designing houses that had both an office and a guest room downstairs. This gives enough flexibility that you could have a parent move in with you and be down on the first floor, if they were handicapped or couldn't negotiate the stairs. And you didn't have to give up your home office or den to do that. Then the third-car garage option allows people to combine that space with the guest room and make it into a suite. You could have the room plus a converted third-car garage and create a whole guest suite that would include a kitchenette.

Ralph: So we've been designing houses for flexibility to accommodate families that needed to come together.

John: How about universal design?

Scott: We are looking at universal design where it makes sense. There are certain elements of universal design that are really bordering on handicap design, being able to lower cabinets and things like that. Things like how you situate tubs, how much turning space you give in bathrooms, how wide your hallways are, these kinds of things are fairly easy to integrate into a house. In fact, in many cities, we're actually required to prepare a list of what universal design things there are in our homes. And other new laws are coming into effect on these issues.

Ralph: For example, there's a new California state law. . . . I'm not quite sure how it's going to affect things, but all municipalities are going to have to have some acknowledgment of what elements of universal design builders have included. It's not going to tell what they have to include, but they have to tell people about what they have done. Things like backing for grab bars. We do a lot of that anyway: raising plugs to sixteen inches rather than twelve inches, lowering switches from fifty inches to forty-six inches. I mean, some of these things are very subtle, and it just takes a little bit of attention to detail. But it isn't a major change in the design process.

Scott: We hired Ralph to help us build our active adult business. So we are focused intently on designing housing for this baby-boomer generation that we know is going to buy different housing. We have not been as focused on designing houses for their kids to accommodate the parents moving back home. However, if what you are saying is really right, we probably need to be thinking more about designing houses for families that can accommodate parents coming home. We do that already, but maybe not to the extent that you are suggesting.

Ralph: I agree with the whole thesis that the baby boomers are going to change the way the market works all over. The numbers are bearing this out. What we are trying to do is figure out what that means because we know it isn't just one answer. It's not just, "Why don't you go build them a seniors' community out in the desert." I think the numbers already show only 10 percent of that population want to do that. Most of those are government workers that have got their retirement pensions. They don't want another job. Most of the baby boomers don't see themselves in classic retirement. They're going to rejuvenate, reinvent, redo, recreate themselves in other ways. How we accommodate that is where the opportunities are.

Scott: Let's say you are seventy years old and go back and live with your kids. You can invest in your grandkids or your great-grandkids perhaps or help out at home. That's going to put tremendous pressure on families' abilities to get along.

As their comments suggest, the folks at Standard Pacific are looking toward the future housing needs of baby boomers and their extended families. In particular, they are noting and responding to the changes in the preferences and needs of American families, including (1) the fading attractiveness of senior communities and (2) the appeal to many of multigenerational arrangements. Others are noticing as well. On the first point, Strauss and Howe in their amazingly foresighted book *Generations,* predict that "'Seniors Only' living communities will become more uncommon and controversial, perhaps even objects of legislative or judicial attack."[3] On the second point a recent AARP study reports that 80 percent of adults over the age of forty-five think it's important to live near their children and grandchildren.[4] When asked in a poll sponsored by Century21.com about whom folks would prefer as next-door neighbors, more than half said "a family member."[5] And at a recent conference of architects and builders sponsored by *Residential Architect* magazine, topping the list of fifteen emerging trends in home design was "Housing should accommodate more activities, types of people, and living arrangements, and it should be multigenerational."[6] Finally, researchers at Vision Group reported that nearly half of the Americans they interviewed thought they would have parents or other relatives living with them over the next ten years.[7]

Further, as we will see toward the end of the chapter, home builders generally complain that outdated zoning and building codes restrict their creativity in responding to the changing demographics and preferences of their customers. Despite the obstacles, many new developments around the country demonstrate the wonderful ways that residential builders and architects are able to accommodate the coming revolution in American housing arrangements. Below we excerpt three descriptions of new communities.

Courier Place (Claremont, CA)

Courier Place Apartment Homes in Claremont, California, is an affordably priced, transit-oriented development (TOD) and will also be a LEED (Leadership in Energy and Environmental Design) certified community. Laura Archuleta, Jamboree Housing Corporation President, says Courier Place represents a development milestone for the company. "This is a very special community for Jamboree and I believe Courier Place will help pioneer a new generation of housing that will be sustainable, affordable and intergenerational," she said. "Without the partnership with the City of Claremont and the participation of the funding sources that share our vision of Courier Place, we would not be breaking ground for this innovative community."

Courier Place is being developed on a 3.4-acre infill site that is the former location of the *Claremont Courier* newspaper. The three-story, garden-style community will offer apartments for both working families and seniors. The workforce housing apartments will be offered on a priority basis to people who work in Claremont but live elsewhere, thus shortening the length of their commutes and helping the environment by reducing vehicular emissions. Mixing workforce with senior housing is also a big plus for the city because it promotes Claremont's emphasis on providing quality, affordable housing for people of all ages and income levels. "Our goal is to provide a diversity of housing for everyone who wants to work and live in our city and Courier Place's intergenerational concept certainly helps us meet that goal," Elderkin said.

As an intergenerational community, Courier Place will be home to both seniors and working families who earn between 30 percent to 60 percent of the Area Median Income (AMI). The seniors building will feature 38 one-bedroom apartments, an elevator, and recreation space. The family apartments will be encompassed in two buildings and consist of 36 two- and three-bedroom apartments, each with two bathrooms.

"Intergenerational living is based on the idea that the blending of families and seniors builds a community and offers a lifestyle that enhances health and happiness," says Michael Massie, Jamboree's Housing Development Manager. "Although intergenerational housing is not a new idea, it is only recently that we have started to see these projects become more popular in California and only a few have been affordable. We are pleased to be the developer that introduces this concept to the City of Claremont and its residents."[8]

Highlands' Village Gardens (Denver, CO)

Ryan Chittum writes about "'Smart' Redevelopment Plans" in the *Wall Street Journal*:

The ideal of what has come to be dubbed "smart growth" is a project that combines environmentally friendly construction, affordable housing, parks and walkways, a variety of housing styles, preservation of historic sites, and quick, easy access to mass transit—all in an urban setting.

More cities are helping spur such projects in an effort to keep high-income earners in town, increase property-tax revenues, and use existing infrastructure like sewers and roads instead of building new, expensive public works. In the case of Highlands' Garden Village, the city of Denver will recycle property taxes back into the project to the tune of about $5 million over 20 years to help finance the $85 million development. Most of the money from the city will go toward the renovation of a historic theater and carousel housing on the site, which was an amusement park for more than 100 years, and to help pay for the parks that wind through its 27 acres.

Highlands' Garden Village residents are encouraged to give up their cars, or at least limit their use, by the proximity of mass transit and the availability of two Zipcars, fueled by compressed natural gas, on-site that can be rented for $4 an hour and 40 cents a mile.

Younger people who are rejecting the suburbs in favor of a more urban lifestyle are a driving force in the demand for this type of development, Ms. Poticha says, along with aging baby boomers who "don't necessarily want the responsibility of a big house on a big lot on the fringe of a big development."

Developments built on the principles of New Urbanism do have their share of problems. One obstacle to broader appeal is concerns about the quality of public schools in many cities. "Public schools are an essential issue where people want to raise a family," Mr. Rose says. "The suburban lifestyle may work better for a family with two parents and kids," he says, "but those families are less than 25 percent of the households in America."

But the demand for projects like Highlands' Garden Village is apparent in how quickly its units have sold and the prices they have commanded. The units sold before they were built, and sale prices increased 25 percent annually from 1999 to 2002, while the surrounding neighborhood's sale prices increased 10 percent a year. The multifamily units are 99 percent occupied, while Denver's overall rate is 88 percent.[9]

Green Orange Renaissance

Finally, the most comprehensive thinking we have seen in new housing development is represented by a new company, Green Orange Renaissance:

California's recently enacted climate change laws AB 32 and SB 375 have targeted ambitious greenhouse-gas reductions by 2020 and carbon neutrality by 2050. Rising to the challenge, Green Orange Renaissance (GOR) designs and implements socially responsible investments of mixed-use infill development that create and spread healthful, vibrant "eco-hamlets" featuring triple-bottom-line value. Key innovations include (1) exploiting social media and Google Maps for crowdsourced community-based envisioning and planning, public communications and education, and marketing; (2) high-quality design and LEED-certified multifamily housing manufactured in plants to reduce the length of conventional onsite construction and disruption to mere days of preprogrammed site installation; and (3) an IT-enabled global web of value creation activities aimed at a minimum 75 percent "Made Locally in USA" product, achieving zero waste and zero inventory. GOR's competitive advantage lies in integrating product and process innovations to shorten the real estate development cycle, requiring only four to six months instead of the conventional three years or more. GOR's market potential extends to other cities in California and other states, as well as emergent international markets where there are the double benefits of market access and arbitrage in the global value chain.

To various customer segments (renter, owner, investor), GOR offers smart investment choices amid growing market demand for work-live, multigenerational, aging-in-place, and long-term care housing types. GOR's site analytics, synched with Google Maps–based locator websites to generate candidate infill regions or multiple opportunity sites, can efficiently assess real estate development potential and project feasibility. In its emergent phase, GOR would target sites in the diversely and densely populated cities of car-dependent central Orange County, California, where plentiful opportunities exist to improve the land use and value of vacant and underutilized properties. Site design via public-private collaboration would incorporate suitable iconic urban design features such as recreational public commons ("mini-parks") that doubly function as nodes in a network of interconnected transportation options (e.g., transit adjacency, walking, biking, on-demand full-service taxis, IT-enabled shared car fleet).

GOR's "open source" approach to planning is intended to engage a wide swath of stakeholders, virally engage public awareness and public input, and expand community support of promising infill projects. In recognition that public scholarship is essential to knowledge diffusion, GOR engages select academic institutional partners in creative research to guide and promote best practices and benchmarks for sustainable development. GOR's tagline—*"Proliferating Profitable (& Cool) Planetmarkings"*—conveys the urgency of climate-healing action and the immediacy of GOR's redesigned business structures and processes to adapt and retool America's manufacturing capacity for the new green economy. See www.GreenOrangeRenaissance.com for more details.

Designing and Building Your Own Multigenerational Housing

Depending on where you live and the extent of your family's resources, building your own three-generation housing may make the most sense. A few of the folks Sharon interviewed for our book have done that and also suggested design features. First we hear from Sarah and then Paul's family:

Sarah: When his dad and Carl built this house on a cul-de-sac, the plan was that Carl would live in the lower-level apartment with the kitchen. His parents would live above in the main house until we got married. Then we would switch with them and his parents would go downstairs.

Paul: Structurally, I wish this house had more [sound] insulation. I really believe people ought to be able to live within reason the way they would like to live. Unfortunately, if they want to play their music louder, our home is not well enough insulated from floor to floor for them to do that.

Charlotte: Yes. Walking on the floor sometimes wakes them up downstairs.

Stacie: Every time.

Paul: Not in bare feet. But if we walk with shoes on, they hear it.

Stacie: Just adding to the insulation thing, it goes both ways, from upstairs to downstairs and downstairs to upstairs. We can hear conversations almost to the word that my parents have together downstairs, particularly at this end of the house. Despite the fact that there is a locked door, there is not much privacy.

Indeed, it's no wonder the long-crowded Japanese culture avoids shoes worn in the house. It's a matter of cleanliness, but also noise! But such cultural matters are the subject of chapter 12.

Back here in the States, there are a wide and growing variety of approaches to new home design. For the tighter budgets, innovations in manufactured housing are making that option more attractive and flexible, allowing new modular combinations. New notions are also traveling here from abroad. For example, there's a new mini-kitchen available that combines a portable sink, stove, and refrigerator in a fifty-by-forty-one-by-twenty-six-inch cabinet for about three thousand dollars—great for a guesthouse—and so on. (See www.edeskco.com for more good ideas from Europe.)

We will discuss the latest thinking on ECHO (Elder Cottage Housing Opportunity) housing in chapter 11. Another interesting approach is prefabricated housing. These differ from manufactured housing because while the pieces are built in a factory, the house is assembled on the lot. Note this description of one "put together" by Michelle Kaufman, a San Francisco architect:

The house that emerged was a long, low-slung, understated dwelling—
a marriage of Californian warmth and Japanese precision—with a
slanted roof and a long wall with a series of 8-foot-wide sliding-glass

doors that can open onto a view or close off the interior from the elements. Louvered panels slide into place over the glass to create protection from the sun while still letting the breeze in. With only 1,344 square feet, the home includes a long great room that includes a kitchen, an eating area and a living room, as well as two bedrooms and two baths—one with his-and-her stainless steel basins and a giant slate shower.[10]

And if you have the financial resources, you can really have some fun, as did one family in northern California described in the *San Francisco Chronicle*. It's a great story, so read on:

A Full Table

It's 5:55 on a Sunday afternoon at the house in Fairfield. Five-year-old Grace Curry walks around ringing a small bell to summon everyone to dinner.

By 6 p.m., they're all seated around the dinner table: Grace's parents, Bernadette, 37, and George Curry, 42; her brother, Jack, 3; her aunt and uncle, Teresa, 41, and Steve Lavell, 42; their children, Jennifer, 15, Michael, 13, and Danny, 11; and her grandparents, Gretchen, 70, and Joe Shilts, 72. The family dog, Roxie, also shows up. They all live in a 6,800-square-foot house on 4.8 acres along the Putah South Canal. The Shiltses live downstairs, and each of the other two families has an upstairs wing.

The idea for the family compound started after Joe was diagnosed with Parkinson's disease in 1999. The five Shilts daughters had all moved out and married, so the Fairfield house where they had grown up was too big and too much work. In the meantime, the Currys and Lavells were outgrowing their Fairfield homes.

Teresa Lavell came up with the idea of everyone living together. She and Steve had moved all over the world while he was an Air Force pilot. After he had completed his service, "She said, 'We're moving back to Fairfield, and then we're going to live together,'" Gretchen Shilts said.

Three of the Shilts daughters and their families had moved away, but the three Fairfield families were already spending time together, "so there was a natural integration of our lifestyles," Bernadette Curry said.

The search for a site began in 2000 and ended with the purchase in November 2000. Next the family settled on an architect, Jacobson, Silverstein & Winslow in Berkeley. "We spent hours not only talking with them but also poring over books" to get ideas, Gretchen Shilts said.

Finding financing for construction was difficult. The family invited loan officers to lunch to explain the dream, but possible default was a worry. Finally a loan officer from First Northern Bank agreed to lend the money. "He caught the vision," she said.

The project cost $1.4 million—the equivalent of $466,666 per family—for the land, design and construction except for the pool, landscaping and solar panels.

The Shiltses used some of Joe's retirement money to buy the land, and all three family groups pitched in for the down payment after selling their houses. They own the house as joint tenants, and each family contributes to a joint account that pays for the 15-year mortgage and other shared costs. Although the new house is unique, Joe Shilts estimates that buying three new Fairfield houses suited to each family's needs would have cost "at least twice what we paid." New single-family detached houses in Fairfield can cost anywhere from about $600,000 to more than $1 million.

If the families had built three separate houses, they would have had to buy three lots because city zoning allows only one house on the lot they have. Shilts estimated that three lots would cost a total of $100,000 more than they paid for their land. Construction costs would have totaled nearly $500,000 more.

The entryway is flanked by a hall spanning the center section. The hall is lined with book shelves beneath large windows on the outer wall and openings into the great room with its two-story-high ceiling. On the left end of the great room is a conversation area with a fireplace, TV, piano, a window seat and another wall of windows overlooking the backyard, which has decks, pool, lawn and a dry, grassy hillside sloping down to the canal.

The center of the great room is dominated by a long dining table that can seat up to 20. It was the first joint purchase because of "the communal value of sharing a meal," said Bernadette Curry.

This table also has allowed the family to have Thursday night soup suppers during the winter. They started with friends and neighbors who sometimes brought others along, making for lively discussions. "It was a way to have a wider community," George Curry said.

Each family chose the colors for its living area. Colors and other details for the communal areas were collaboratively chosen. "It was work," Gretchen Shilts said. Everyone would meet around the Shiltses' dining room table to make decisions during construction.

Collaboration is a huge key to the success of this living arrangement. Families take turns cooking dinner for a week at a time. Everyone is on his own for breakfast, lunch and Friday dinner, which often winds up to be leftovers or pizza. The family that cooks also plans the menus and does the grocery shopping.

Housekeeping tasks for the communal areas are divided eight ways and rotate weekly, excusing Joe and the Curry kids. Each family takes care of its own area.

Eating dinner together at 6 p.m. is "quite an experience for the young people," Gretchen Shilts said. It gives everyone a chance to talk about the day.

It's also a chance to head off conflicts, she said, noting that the family spent a lot of time talking about that issue before moving in. The family also tries to have regular meetings for everyone, but the kids are excused when finances are involved. "The chemistry is here to make it work. We have the commitment to one another," said Gretchen, a nurse who works on call as a lay Catholic chaplain with North Bay Hospice.

In planning the house, "we saw it as a marriage of families" and a way "to be there for Mom and Dad," Steve Lavell said. "This isn't an experiment. We're going to make it work."

George Curry agreed. "No matter what happens, we can work it out. It's a more impressive family than it is an impressive house."[11]

We have a few more suggestions. Chapters 7 through 11 of this book are intended to stimulate your creative juices when it comes to designs for living. Also, you might want to visit HGTV's website (http://frontdoorhome plans.com). There they have some twenty-one thousand house plans you can explore, including twenty-six for accessory units and 615 duplex units. If you find one you really like, you can buy the detailed plan for around $575. But it's just fun to cruise around their "virtual neighborhood" for ideas. Both Chittum's article and the HGTV website will add useful options to your plans. Finally, having written all this about designs, three design features are crucial: (1) avoid stairs, (2) allow for separate kitchen facilities, and (3) provide separate entrances.

Fighting the Codes

Any innovation is disruptive. Even though the successful ones improve life overall, some folks will always see them in a negative way. It is certainly no different with innovations in housing. Everybody in the business complains about the codes—zoning and building—that inhibit flexibility and creative solutions to the changing demographics and lifestyles of Americans. Here's a representative taste of the comments from folks we interviewed:

The Families' Views

Joe (a Realtor): Here in our town, it's very difficult to get accessory apartments because of restrictive zoning. But I'll get calls from people all the time. They'll inquire about an ad just because it had a mother-in-law unit. That was the thing that drew them. If you are listing a house, that's always a major draw. People are interested in these units for their adult children or their elderly parents.

Lina: A friend of mine said, "Why don't you try and have your daughter buy a house that already has the unit in it." That is what they originally tried to do. But they couldn't find anything with a unit that was within their price range. So that's when they bought this house that had the space to add one. Then they had to go through the normal procedures with the town hall. The town didn't mind it being an in-law suite, but didn't want it to be used for rent.

Nancy: Our town fought us adding on an in-law unit. In fact, when we were moving in here, they were very restrictive. The town said you could only live in them thirty days out of the year. They did not want people living in places like that.

The Builders' Perspective

Even the largest homebuilders have their complaints about the restrictiveness of the codes. Here Scott Stowell and Ralph Spargo at Standard Pacific opine:

Scott: My biggest problem is the zoning codes, the building codes, don't allow this. They restrict this. Zoning codes were set up to separate people, not let them combine.

Ralph: And getting the state and the local jurisdictions to change their building codes is not an easy process, particularly in the environment of crowding here in California. We are currently in kind of a no-growth orientation in most communities today.

Scott: The other part is you have zoning codes and building codes. They don't necessarily go together. You can get a lot of zoning say for mixed use, but the building codes say nothing about mixed use. They don't know how to interpret it. It goes the same way all the way through housing. You cannot have two families in a house unless you are zoned for that. You are recognizing a social change that doesn't have zoning or building codes that would allow it to happen, when it should. It will be a slow, cumbersome process. California is the worst in the country. If we solve it here, it will work anywhere.

Community Action

In order to adjust the housing stock of the country to reflect the baby boomers' retirement and the associated growth in extended-family living arrangements, changes will be required in long-existing and mostly local housing and building codes and associate ordinances. The main battle line in this political fight is over accessory apartments. Public debate and political battles are being fought, won, and lost around the country over making changes in codes that not only allow for but actually promote the construction of accessory apartments in existing neighborhoods and in new developments. Below we report on recent events primarily in crowded California, the "neighborhood" we know best. Hopefully, restrictions in your area are less onerous, but we do know that similar issues are being discussed around the country. We just hope with more civility!

The Fundamentals of the Disagreement

According to housing expert Martin Gellen, accessory apartments produce two kinds of problems. The first concerns physical impacts, such as increased parking and traffic and architectural changes that are seen as disruptive to a neighborhood. The second relates to social and cultural issues. The accessory apartment deviates from the traditional way of looking at housing, family, and the neighborhood. It stands for a change in the way the single-family house is used, a departure from the conventional meanings connected to residential zoning categories.

Residential zoning gives a community control over its social and economic composition and gives continuity to the character of a community. American zoning caters to the separation of single-family housing from apartments. It does so in order to retain a system of land use that favors a perceived "natural progression": that is, climbing a ladder from renting an apartment to the ultimate goal of owning a home. However, today that traditional mind-set is being challenged by both changes in family structure (particularly the growth in multigenerational family living arrangements) and the economics of housing. Still, people's beliefs about what housing and family should be have stayed somewhat fixed; accessory apartments challenge these beliefs.

Moreover, there is a historical problem that needs to be overcome. Even though today accessory units are seen by many as an attractive housing alternative, they were once viewed as an indicator of neighborhood blight. Years ago, they were found only in run-down areas. But even if its connection with urban blight could be eliminated, the accessory apartment would still be shunned. Since it allows multifamily use of a single-family home, it violates the sanctity that many people attribute to the single-family house and neighborhood. This cultural perception has been difficult to alter and has acted as a deterrent to accessory apartment zoning.

When the rational basis for exclusive single-family zoning is examined, an important question emerges: What public purpose is served by preventing individual homeowners from adding accessory units in answer to changing lifestyles and economic needs? In fact, zoning regulations "must have a substantial relation to the health, safety, morals, comforts, convenience, and general welfare of the community." If so, then "zoning is to a large degree an instrument of social policy and must therefore serve legitimate social ends." Zoning needs to serve the needs of the people and keep up with the times.[12]

Barriers to the Construction of Accessory Apartments

The San Francisco Bay Area's Double Unit Opportunity (DUO) Program has developed the most comprehensive listing of specific deterrents to creative housing options.[13] One-half of all DUO clients dropped out of the program without filing for a second-unit permit. Many who did not proceed were discouraged by the required additional parking; limits on the accessory apartment's size, type, and occupancy; deed restrictions; and the cost of fees and permits. Building costs were another important deterrent; many were shocked at the cost of construction in general. Elements of all the obstacles described below are mirrored in the comments of the stories reported above.

1. **Additional parking** is the single factor most likely to block planning approval of a second-unit project. Zoning and building regulations specify the number of additional spaces required, along with their size and location on the lot. Feasibility is also determined by the local topography and lot size. Unfortunately, with few exceptions, most Bay Area ordinances require two or more additional parking spaces for a second dwelling. DUO found this requirement to be unnecessary, as

its clients owned an average of 1.67 cars per household, with 1.3 cars owned by tenants living in completed DUO units.

2. **Unit size and type** can be restrictive deterrents to building second units. All ordinances define minimum and maximum unit size—generally from three hundred to seven hundred square feet—and mandate that the addition be subordinate to the primary dwelling. Some municipalities use a 10 percent cap on the floor area for the second unit, discouraging such buildings in homes of less than 3,500 square feet. Others prohibit detached units, which doesn't make sense on a large suburban lot where a well-designed unit could easily be placed.

3. Cities often place **occupancy restrictions** on accessory apartments. The most common is to require that the homeowner live in either the main or second dwelling. This requirement means that the owner must record a deed restriction limiting future use of the property, causing some to drop the project or proceed illegally. In other cases, the homeowner, seniors, family members, or servants must occupy the unit. Some communities also limit occupancy to low-income tenants and set rent levels. Such controls have the effect of limiting the use of the new housing and reducing the future salability of the property.

4. **Use permits** can act as major obstacles to building accessory apartments. Even though a second unit tends to be a small remodeling project, it typically receives greater scrutiny because it is considered to be a new dwelling. In most cases, those adding an accessory apartment must apply for a so-called use permit before applying for a building permit. The use permit application requires secondary materials, including a map of the neighborhood, site plan, floor plans, and elevations. In some instances, there are additional requirements for "engineering surveys, soil and seismic safety reports and detailed descriptions of vegetation and other environmental features."

Taking Action at the Community Level

Former California governor Arnold Schwarzenegger "terminated" legislation (Assembly Bill 2702) that promoted accessory apartment construction in California. Despite such major setbacks, a growing number of local communities around the country have changed codes to allow for and even promote accessory apartment construction: Boulder, Colorado; Westport, Connecticut; Montgomery County, Maryland; and Santa Cruz, California, are often mentioned. Building *cross-community coalitions* has been crucial in getting codes changed in these and other areas. You will need to recruit partners such as affordable housing groups, local chapters of Parents Without Partners, the AARP, and other associations with self-interests such as real estate agents, remodelers, architects, home builders, disabled advocates, home health-care agencies, hospitals, bankers, and environmentalists.

The DUO well describes what to ask for in changes to codes:

- Exempt second-unit applications from use permit and public hearing requirements if they meet the development standards of the ordinance.
- Require a *maximum* of one additional parking space per bedroom in the new unit.
- Permit tandem parking.
- Allow parking in the setback areas.
- Reduce the size of the parking space to compact-car standards.
- Eliminate occupancy restrictions and deed restrictions on properties with second units.
- Permit all types of second units (conversions, attachments, and detached) as long as they are in scale with the existing house and lot.
- Eliminate arbitrary limits on unit size.
- Assess second units in accordance with their size and scale, not as new single-family dwellings.
- Consider waiving or reducing fees as an incentive to second-unit development.

Two local examples provide an optimistic glimpse at success: First, the Bridle Creek development in Pleasanton, California, offers a detached second unit on the same property as the single-family home. The sales manager for the complex said that the City of Pleasanton required the developer to provide twenty of the 111 units with accessory apartments in order for the project to be approved.[14] In cities like Pleasanton where there is space for new housing developments, the inclusion of accessory apartments as part of these developments is a strategy that can build affordable housing for these communities. Certainly, such a requirement would help the town meet its affordable housing quota required by California state law.

Second, what about communities that are built out or don't encourage large new housing developments? The town of Woodside, California, fits that category with its 5,600 people and 1,000 horses. It recently took a look at accessory apartments, some even in barns, as an answer to its affordable housing needs. In June of 2000, residents were surveyed about their interest in creating new rental units. Some 3,000 mailers drew 560 responses, a response rate of almost 20 percent. These responses provide a profile of residents' thoughts about extra living quarters. Key points included:[15]

- A total of 209 properties contain 244 accessory living structures; 62 are being rented now, with most of the others being occupied by guests, family members, or caretakers.
- Fifty-seven of the additional living quarters are attached to the main residence, 176 are detached, and 11 are in barns.
- Eighty-three respondents are interested in building new accessory living quarters, 59 of which might be for rent. Another 110 said they might be interested.
- Respondents suggested incentives for building new living units: 185 want clearer information on the town's rules, 201 would welcome fee waivers, 175 support floor-area allowances, 66 want units in barns, and 66 would welcome low-interest loans.
- Some respondents worried the additional units might hurt the rural quality of Woodside and impact traffic, parking, and the environment.

The planning commission considered this survey information in its proposed amendments to ordinances controlling accessory living quarters and rental units. The proposed new rules balance more flexibility with more restrictions on the overall level of accessory buildings allowed on a lot. Proposals that would allow more flexibility include:

- Allowing living units in barns, at least for people taking care of livestock.
- Allowing rental units of up to 1,200 square feet instead of the present maximum of 720 square feet.
- Allowing rental units in the R-1 zone (smaller lots of mostly half an acre or less) to occupy 30 percent of the main building instead of the current maximum of 10 percent. Detached units still would not be allowed.

Proposed additional restrictions include:

- Only one accessory living unit on lots smaller than three acres.
- Reductions in both size and number of accessory buildings on lots smaller than three acres.
- Requirement that the owner live on any property with a rental unit—either in the main house or the accessory unit.

Proposed amendments that clarify many definitions and provisions of the current ordinance include:

- Requirement that accessory living quarters contain a full bathroom with interior access from the main room and a sink and counter space in a separate room with outlets for kitchen appliances.
- Requirement that the unit must be at least four hundred square feet in area.

Ultimately, amendments that are approved will be used to update Woodside's housing element when complete. The town staff believes some of the proposed modifications to rules for accessory apartments could help the town obtain state certification for its housing plan. Woodside's state-mandated quota is to provide forty-one units of housing affordable to people with low or moderate incomes between 1999 and 2006. As of August 31, 2006, the town had exceeded its quota and issued permits for fifty-six accessory units.[16]

It can be done!

C H A P T E R

11

Making Your Home Accessible to Seniors

Planning is bringing the future into the present so that you can do something about it now.

—ALAN LAKEIN

O MANY OF US are living now in Peter Pan housing—built as if no one ever ages. The typical single-family house is designed for people who will never grow old. It is not a good place for someone who can't drive, use stairs, or do simple household maintenance. Most of us will lose some, if not all, of these abilities before we die. In fact, these days we all have a long *disabled* life expectancy.[1]

Consequently, in making your home accessible to seniors, it is important to include design features that can meet future disability needs. For example, an accessory apartment installed above a garage that would require the occupant to climb stairs would not be functional for a mobility-disabled person. In any case, stairs present a major obstacle to those with walking difficulties. Also, for a wheelchair-bound person, it would be important to install thirty-six-inch doorways to allow for passage. Adding grab bars in bathrooms near the shower and toilet would be another option. Moreover, kitchens can be set up for people in wheelchairs with lower counters, and bedroom closets with adjustable double-hung clothes racks and lower shelves.

An alternative to remodeling an existing house is to design and build a new one to meet the requirements of a disabled individual. Our Aunt Alice Graham did just that by having the wisdom and foresight to plan ahead for her impending need to use a wheelchair. She helped design and had built a small, two-bedroom, single-story home that includes a level front entry without stairs, wide doorways, grab bars in the bathroom, and low counters in the kitchen. She lived in this house with her son for several years before her death at eighty-six and certainly benefited from those innovative features, which enabled her to perform the routine activities of daily living.

Universal Design

Faced with a growing population of people advancing in years and disabilities, designers and builders are finding a growing market—and growing legal pressure to incorporate what are called *universal design* features in new or remodeled homes. Universal design "is used to describe products or environments that accommodate people of all ages, sizes, and abilities, and allow them to live and function independently. This is accomplished by eliminating or modifying those features that may be obstacles or dangers for the user, while also adding considerations for their safety, comfort, and ease-of-use."[2] It is intended to benefit all people throughout their life span at little or no extra cost. In fact, universal design features are generally no more expensive than traditional features, if incorporated by the designer at the conceptual stage.[3]

Along with thirty-six-inch doorways and wider hallways, homebuilders are beginning to brace walls for the later installation of grab bars. Curbless showers are being constructed with sloped floors and a five-foot radius that allow for walkers or wheelchairs. Lever-style handles are being installed as doorknobs or faucets. Unlocking doors is being made easier with keyless systems that use a keypad or magnetic card. Homes are being constructed on one level without steps inside or out. If stairways are constructed, they are being made wide enough to allow for an electric-chair track system. In some cases, space is being designed for a future elevator. For example, an executive at home builder Pulte Group, Inc., reports, "Lately we work to deliver the elevator shaft as a possibility for conversion down the road with removable floor plates . . . and stacked closets on the first and second floors."[4] Kitchens and bathrooms are being planned with adaptable counter levels, including removable drawers to allow space for future wheelchairs. Other features include storage space at lower levels and good lighting throughout the home. All of this is being done in ways that look attractive and not institutional.[5] Ultimately, universal design is intended "to reconcile the artistic integrity of a design with human needs in the environment."[6]

Eleanor is a professional ASID (American Society of Interior Designers) interior designer, who has incorporated universal design in a number of in-law units. Eleanor also built an attached apartment for her in-laws when she lived in Southern California with her husband and son. They were with them from 1986 to 1993. She told us why they decided to live together and how they did it. Her stories and suggestions are very useful if you are considering making your home accessible to seniors.

Eleanor: My in-laws had moved to Arizona, and my mother-in-law was not in good health. She was almost ready to be in a wheelchair full-time. We felt it was time to bring them closer to us, so we moved them into our home. We created a seven-hundred-square-feet addition onto our home that had a separate exterior entrance and was all on one floor. It was self-contained and had a bathroom, kitchen, dining area, and living room. They also had two small bedrooms because they wanted their own privacy from each other. They liked to watch different TV programs and also had different sleeping times. One liked to read, and the other was more of a television person. We decided to build it as a handicapped ADA-compliant type of a unit, also utilizing universal design principles.

Sharon: In your professional life as an interior designer, have you had many requests from clients to build new homes with accessory units?

Eleanor: Yes, I have consulted with many families who have considered doing this. I think there are a lot of questions that people don't think to ask themselves. If you are going to move your in-laws or your parents in, what is the situation? Are they ill? If mom or dad is already in a nursing home, you may have to equip your house in a certain way to accommodate them. If they have certain types of problems, you have to think ahead about special design needs before you do the construction. Also, if there are health considerations, it's much less expensive to prepare the house for that when you build than it is to go back and retrofit. Retrofitting is very difficult sometimes.

Sharon: So, if possible, plan ahead.

Eleanor: You really do need to plan ahead. Make sure the design includes features and fixtures that allow for your parents' changing needs. Your parents may be fine now, but in another five or ten years, they may have special needs. At the time you build a new home, incorporate such elements as blocked walls to handle grab bars, heavy-duty carpet that stands up to wheelchair or walker use, and wide doorways and halls. Pocket doors take up less space. Also, you can install the light switches and thermostat lower on the wall so they can be reached by someone in a wheelchair. Lever handles on doors are easier too. All those things need to be considered, otherwise you could be facing an expensive remodeling project down the road.

Sharon: Anything else you'd like to add?

Eleanor: One interesting thing that I haven't mentioned is the story about a friend of ours who came to see the apartment that I did for my in-laws and brought her father-in-law with her. He made some comments about it that I thought were very revealing about how well the place works for older people. He said, "I love this place. I love being able to stand in the kitchen and reach things on both sides without having to move. I like knowing that there is a grab bar all the way down the hallway in case I need it. I like being able to stay all on the same level."

Joan lives with her husband and their child in South Carolina, and in the early 1990s they built an addition for her mother onto their home (see exhibit 11.1). Here's what she had to say about why they decided to live together and how they created a separate unit to accommodate her mother's needs:

Joan: Back in 1990, my mother was living in a home near Charleston. My father had passed away in 1980. So for almost ten years, she maintained the

Exhibit 11.1.   Joan's House with the Attached Addition for Her Mother to the Left of the Garage

Source: Photo by Sharon Niederhaus.

house by herself. That worked out fine, until my husband and I began seeing that it became more difficult for her to find people to mow the lawn, clean the gutters, and so forth. We did what we could, but we weren't always able to provide much help. We started wondering what her long-term housing situation would be. We knew from a financial perspective that she would not be able to afford a long-term care facility. My father was ten years older than her. He retired in the late 1960s. He was a blue-collar tradesman in Manhattan. So she basically was on Social Security. He did not have a pension transferred over to her because that was not available in those days. It's very much the plight of people from that generation. So we were looking at it from the perspective that she could not afford assisted living.

When we bought this house, it had a garage with an entrance that went out to the side of the property. It was a piece of land that we never knew how to landscape because it was not really that wide. We thought about putting in a pool. But we also thought that it was kind of a natural area to put on an addition, where there would be an entrance from the garage into what we called the guesthouse. There was access to it from the house, but not from the main part of our home.

Sharon: Have people called on you for advice since you've done it?

Joan: Some people have, yes. They've come and they've looked. I've talked to them about how to care for an aging parent and how you plan for it. In terms of planning, since my mother had her own house, we tried to plan it so that some of her furniture would fit into her new surroundings. Since she wasn't completely selling everything and starting new, she was able to pull from her past. That worked quite well. We probably have a little bit less than one thousand square feet. We were able to put in a fully equipped kitchen, a living room, a dining room area, a utility room where she has her own washer and dryer, along with a bathroom and a nice-sized bedroom. In the bathroom, we planned ahead. We put in a tub and later we also put in a grab bar. From the design perspective, I think it's important that the materials you use hold up well and are easy to care for. Think about what type of countertops to use for a vanity. Try to use products that you don't have to replace, that are dependable.

Remodeling

According to the National Association of Home Builder's (NAHB) Remodeling Council, as the baby-boom generation is reaching retirement age and beginning to look at issues of home safety and comfort, remodeling needs are changing dramatically. In response to this rising demand, the organization has begun a training program for remodelers to do the kinds of home modifications homeowners require as they grow older in their homes. The first fifty certified aging-in-place specialists (CAPS) were awarded credentials following training sessions in Orlando, Florida, in May 2004. These specialists are now equipped with the marketing, technical, and customer-service skills required to make a home accessible to seniors. Examples of jobs for these specialists range from placing grab bars and adjusting counter heights to creating first-floor master suites and installing elevators.[7] Also, the NAHB offers a "Directory of Accessible Building Products" through their website at www.nahbrc.org/about/bookstore or by request at (800) 638-8556.

Entryways

For proximity with privacy, we encourage you to build an independent entryway for any addition to your home. In order to make it user friendly for seniors, where possible build a covered, well-lit, and level-entry approach.

Fumbling with keys, packages, the mail—all can distract and unbalance someone entering or exiting a home. In addition to providing lighting at entryways, be sure to have a table, bench, or other surface nearby for putting things down.[8] Where space is tight, you can also install a shelf for packages on a wall near the front door.

Eleanor created a separate entrance and flat pathway to the street for her in-laws' apartment. This allowed guests of her in-laws, as well as the Meals on Wheels driver who delivered her lunch, to access their place separately. They didn't have to traipse through Eleanor's house. Joan had a similar story to tell about her mother's separate entrance:

Joan: Our housing situation works. What makes it work is that we designed it so that my mother has her own front entrance. Right now, when the caregivers come, they are not coming through our house. I think it's intrusive enough to have someone you know around you. So they are not actually coming into our house. My mother has her own independent living and we have ours.

Ramps

We've already mentioned the importance of thirty-six-inch doorways to accommodate wheelchairs. If you are in a situation where you need to provide a ramp for someone in a wheelchair, the Internet offers a website with information; "www.wheelchairramp.org posts a manual for design and construction of a modular wheelchair ramp, including information on long-tread, low-riser steps to improve safe home accessibility. This site includes the manual, success stories, videos, articles, and links."[9]

Stairs

Stairs can be especially dangerous for older people living on more than one level. Use sturdy handrails on both sides of all stairways if possible. Since carpeting can increase the risk of slipping, removing it can be helpful. Also, make sure a staircase is well lit with light switches at the top and bottom.

Well-defined steps that show where the edge of the tread is can help prevent falls.[10] Moreover, "stair treads deep enough for the entire foot can ensure more stable footing and support when climbing steps. . . . The tread of the step shouldn't extend out beyond the riser to avoid the risk of tripping. A stair rise of 7 inches or less can make it easier to climb steps."[11] When it becomes more difficult to climb stairs, consider installing long-tread, low-rise steps outside your house. Doing so will decrease the amount of energy that is needed and allow for space to walk with a walker.[12]

Stairlifts

If stairs are a barrier in making your home accessible to seniors, you might want to consider installing a stairlift. The February 2004 *AARP Bulletin* carries an ad regarding Bruno stairlifts. It states that "Bruno is the leading manufacturer of indoor curved and straight rail stairlifts . . . and now we have the only 400 lb. capacity outdoor model! Stay in the home you love!" Features listed include "battery operated, onboard diagnostics, no stairway modifications, fast installation available, easily fastens to stair treads." For further information, call (800) 462-0664 or go to their website at www.bruno.com.

However, stairlifts are not for everyone. Some individuals need help getting in and out of them. Also, carrying along such things as a walker can be problematic. In many cases, it's better to move yourself or your aging parent to the ground floor of your home and make sure that the kitchen, bathroom, and bedroom are easily accessible.

Elevators

One couple planned ahead for later housing needs by installing an elevator sooner rather than later. Bob and Sarah bought their home fifteen years ago in the San Francisco Bay Area, when they were in their sixties. At the time they purchased it, they remodeled and added both an accessory apartment downstairs and an elevator. When asked why they had done so, Bob responded that it would be a place for people to live who could take care of them later in life. Also, since they had a lot of stairs, an elevator would help them now and later too. They currently use it for hauling groceries and luggage. Had they waited until they were older or disabled, they probably would not have the energy to deal with the stress of remodeling.

The good news is that as baby boomers are facing disabilities the demand for elevators in single-family homes is going up and prices are going down, no puns intended.[13]

Grab Bars

Grab bars were not always as stylish as they are today. Awhile back, you could only find them in hospitals and nursing homes. They all looked alike and were pretty unattractive. However, today you'll find a variety of grab bars in fancy private homes and hotels. "Some are straight, while others are curvy. Some attach to the wall at both ends. You can move others out of the way when you're done with them. And grab bars now come in enough colors to satisfy every decorator."[14] Universal design plans for the future. Even though you may not need a grab bar in the bathroom now, you can install plywood blocking in the walls to make it easier to attach a bar later. The plywood should be nailed into the studs. It should be three-quarters of an inch thick and six to twelve inches wide. You can also attach a grab bar directly to your wall studs.[15]

Grab bar installation should be done according to the user's needs. If personal assistance is given, this also needs to be considered so that placement will benefit everyone in the household.

Grab bars must be installed according to the manufacturer's instructions. Professional assistance is necessary if one lacks the knowledge and skill for proper installation. Designer styles and colors are available.

Features to check when selecting and installing grab bars:

- "Fit" for a user's hand. A round or oval shape, one and a half inches in diameter, fits most people's hands best. Bars are also available in one- to one-and-a-quarter-inch diameter, which may be more comfortable for young children or adults with smaller hands. It's necessary to evaluate the user's hand.
- Safety clearance from the mounting surface. Clearance between the grab bar and its mounting surface should be large enough to allow comfortable reaching and gripping but small enough to prevent an

arm from sliding down between the bar and the wall. A clearance of one and a half inches is a good guideline to follow.

- Placement. The user's physical capabilities, mobility equipment, and the constraints of the room layout will affect the shape and placement of grab bars. Helpful considerations include:
  - What range of reach is comfortable?
  - Does the user need to lean, push, or pull for support with the transfer?
  - Does the individual have a preference or necessity to have the grab bar on a particular side of a fixture?
  - Will more than one grab bar be beneficial?
  - Will horizontal, vertical, and/or angled mountings be best?
- Material and grip. Bathroom grab bars should be made of stainless steel to resist mold, mildew, bacterial growth, and corrosion. High-impact plastic bars and metal bars coated with plastic also meet this requirement. When installing metal bars, be sure the screws and other fasteners are of a compatible metal type to avoid corrosion where the two are in contact. Where hands will be wet and/or soapy, use a textured grip surface.
- Ability to support the user. Grab bars must have proper reinforcement to prevent them from bending along their length or from pulling out of the wall. Grab bars should be mounted into wall studs or support blocking, not just into drywall or tile. Some bar lengths (eighteen, twenty-four, and thirty inches) don't match the standard sixteen-inch spacing commonly used for centering wall studs in most homes. Stainless steel grab bars are typically designed to support 250 pounds anywhere along their length.

An adequate grab bar system must provide support throughout the tub and toilet areas and must be located at a height that provides good body mechanics. The grab bar should not be angled, as a falling person can slide down the bar rather than be stabilized. It's recommended to install parallel, horizontal bars along the long tub wall, one for standing and the other one for sitting in the tub.[16]

Hallways

Be sure to install extrawide forty-two-inch hallways where possible to allow for wheelchairs or the installation of grab bars. Eleanor told us about the hallway she built for her in-laws' unit:

Eleanor: We had the hallway built extra wide to accommodate a wheelchair. We had blocking put in the wall so that it could hold a grab bar all the way down the hallway. Initially, it gave her a place to hold on to all the way up and down this little hallway to do exercise, walking, and other movements that her doctor wanted her to be doing. We installed a full-length mirror from the ceiling on one small area so that she could see if she was standing straight.

Doors

She also described the doors she had placed in her in-laws' unit:

Eleanor: All the doors were thirty-six inches wide to accommodate a wheelchair. We put lever handles on all of them. We installed pocket doors in the bedroom walls because that eliminates the area you need for doors to swing open.

To make it easier to open a pocket door, place a tassel on the opening bracket that can be pulled. Also, use hollow-core pocket doors, as they are much lighter and easier to open. To assist with opening a regular door, you can install a power door operator.

Windows

Sometimes it can be difficult for seniors to open and close conventional windows. According to Lew Sichelman, a nationally syndicated housing and real estate writer, "Old-fashioned hand-cranked casement windows with extra-large handles have replaced the sash-type windows most builders use today." In an article he wrote about the LifeWise Home, he quoted Chad Garner of the National Association of Home Builders Research Center as saying, "It's easier for many seniors to crank than it is to push up."[17]

Also, you will want to consider the accessibility of window coverings such as blinds and drapes for people with limited mobility. It is possible to have blinds made with longer cords and handles to make them reachable for someone in a wheelchair. In addition, you can have motorized draperies installed for large windows.

Bathrooms

There are many innovations available now to people with special needs in the bathroom. If a wheelchair or walker will be used, it is important to have enough clear floor space to make a 360-degree turn (at least thirty by forty-eight inches; sixty by sixty inches is ideal).[18]

Toilets

For those who have trouble squatting or sitting, it is helpful to install toilets that are about two inches higher than a standard toilet—about seventeen or nineteen inches off the ground versus sixteen inches. Various manufacturers offer the taller version (called "comfort height") for approximately $450 to $620.[19] Grab bars near the toilet need to be put in at a height that is easy to reach and helps with transfers. Do not use towel bars in place of grab bars, as they are not strong enough.[20]

Also, as a temporary solution, you can put a portable, elevated toilet seat on top of a regular toilet seat. A friend has one available for her mother-in-law when she comes to visit. It is a locking raised toilet seat manufactured by Guardian (model #30270) with padded arms for additional support. The wraparound foam padded armrests allow a sure grip and comfort, along with support. The device raises the seat height five inches above the toilet. She says it is easy to use, and the locking system does not require tools. It is lightweight and made of polypropylene resin, which is easy to clean.

Vanities

For those who have trouble bending over, bathroom vanities can be raised from the standard thirty-inch model to thirty-four inches tall. Building supply stores or the Internet can tell you where to find such models.[21] Also, they can be sloped or angled to accommodate a wheelchair (see exhibit 11.2).

Sinks

If a wheelchair is being used in a bathroom, a sink with a vanity does not permit close access, although it can provide good counter space. An alternative is to install a wall-hung sink that can allow closer accessibility. "A sink mounted no higher than 34 inches with a minimum clear knee space of 29 inches and a minimum width of 31 inches (preferably 36 inches), with plumbing out of the way, is desired. When plumbing pipes are exposed, be sure to insulate them to prevent burns."[22] Also, a single-handed faucet control reduces the chances of scalding at the sink. This type of lever is easier to use on faucets than the traditional knobs.[23]

A medicine cabinet or mirror placed no more than forty inches above the floor allows access to someone seated in a wheelchair (see exhibit 11.3).[24]

Exhibit 11.2. Thirty-five-inch Bathroom Vanity

Source: Photo by Roger Hardy. Courtesy of Harrell Remodeling.

Exhibit 11.3. Mirror Placed Forty Inches above the Floor

Source: Photo by Roger Hardy. Courtesy of Harrell Remodeling.

Tubs

Taking a bath used to be extremely difficult for some elderly until a company called Premier Bathrooms came up with a solution: a walk-in tub! Their ad shows a picture of a man about to enter one of their tubs. He is quoted as saying, "It's so easy, I just open the door and step in. . . . I really used to enjoy having a bath but I realized as I got older that the fear of slipping, or the effort of pulling myself up after I had finished bathing was becoming a real problem. . . . Premier Bathrooms has the largest range of walk-in bath tubs in the country, and buying one helped me regain my independence."[25] For more information, call (888) 777-2209 or check their website at www.premier-bathrooms.com.

On the other hand, there is a variety of adaptive equipment that you can use to make an existing tub work for showers or baths, including a shower chair, tub-transfer bench, tub slide, and hydraulic bath lift.

- Wall grab bars in the front and side of the tub area are recommended at a height that makes transfers safe and can be easily reached. Use of a grab bar on the back wall of the tub area can also be helpful. Grab bars that clamp onto the side of the tub can substitute for installed wall grab bars or be used in addition.

- Use of nonslip decals or a bath mat on the tub floor is recommended to prevent slipping.
- It is also possible to convert a bathtub into a step-through handicap shower access with a cutout portion of the side of the bathtub. This will decrease a fourteen-inch step to a few inches. This method utilizes the original bathtub and keeps the walls, floors, and plumbing intact, which can also save dollars over conventional bathroom remodeling.[26]

Joan told us she had both a tub and a shower installed in her mother's addition.

Joan: When my mother first moved into the unit, she was able to use the tub and she enjoyed taking baths. Then she got to a point where she was not able to get out of the tub. She could get in, but her knees couldn't support her enough even though we had a rail in there to get out. So the stall shower is another great thing that we put in because she can walk into it and walk out of it. We now have a person who comes in the morning and helps her with her shower and getting her laundry done.

Showers

For those who don't like bathing in tubs, another option is to replace existing tubs with showers that someone can walk into without having to step over a big barrier.

- A sixty-by-sixty-inch square is the recommended size for roll-in showers (thirty-six by sixty inches is the minimum). Slope the floor at a maximum of a quarter inch per foot for water flow.
- Walk-in showers should be large enough to accommodate a shower chair, at least thirty-six by thirty-six inches. If a shower with a built-in seat is desired, check the location and the height of the seat for safe transfers. The seat height should be a minimum of seventeen inches from the shower floor and positioned for a safe reach of water controls while seated. A walk-in shower with no more than a half-inch threshold is ideal.
- If personal assistance is needed, be sure that the size of the shower will accommodate an additional person.

- Grab bars in the front and at the side of the shower are recommended at a height that can be easily reached and used with transfers. A grab bar at the back can also be useful.
- Controls should be no higher than thirty-six to forty-eight inches from the shower floor.[27]

Of course, sitting down while showering will lessen the risk of falling down. Fold-up seats attached to the wall can make a shower more flexible for multiple users. Using nonslip decals or a bath mat on the shower floor is also recommended to prevent slipping. A handheld showerhead can be installed so you can bathe while seated. An eighty-inch hose mounted on an adjustable-height vertical bar is preferable.[28] "A hand-held showerhead is often easier to use for someone with limited mobility than a fixed showerhead" (see exhibit 11.4).[29]

Eleanor told us about the shower she designed for her in-laws:

Eleanor: The shower was the most challenging because it was a space issue and we didn't have a lot of room. But we did install grab bars in the shower.

Exhibit 11.4.   Handheld Showerhead

Source: Photo by Roger Hardy. Courtesy of Harrell Remodeling.

We also gave her the ability to sit in the shower and have my father-in-law bathe her with a flexible showerhead he could hold in his hand.

However, if someone needs a lot more support than a shower seat, there are automatic pulley devices available that lift frail individuals into a bathtub or shower. They're made by companies like Waverly Glen and prices run about $4,500, including installation. Some states will even provide financial assistance to qualified needy families to pay for such things as lift systems.[30]

The AARP recommends that people put in antiscalding devices to keep water temperatures low. They can cost as little as fifteen dollars and are easily installed into a showerhead or bath faucet. Importantly, they can prevent someone from being burned by scalding water.[31] A single-handle, pressure-balanced faucet control is not only easier to use than two-knob faucets, but can also reduce the chances of scalding.[32] Another option is to turn down the hot water heater to 115 degrees Fahrenheit or less.[33] The newer faucets and shower valves are antiscalding.

Bedrooms

It has been said that people spend more money on their coffins than on their beds. Certainly, one of the biggest considerations in making your home comfortable for seniors, or anyone for that matter, is choosing the right kind of bed. One product advertised in the September 2006 *AARP Bulletin* looks worthwhile. It is a flexible bed that can be bent into a sitting position with a remote control. There are many other flexible bedding options out there as well. For more information about Flex-A-Beds, call (800) 787-1337 or go to their website at www.flexabed.com.

It's ideal to have at least a 3-foot clearance by the bed to allow enough room for transferring from a wheelchair. A bed height of 20–22 inches allows for more level transfers. If the bed is too low, evaluate use of "furniture extenders/risers" that attach to the legs of the bed frame and raise the height.

Having a roll-in or walk-in closet with lowered rods and shelves (2–4 feet from the floor) will also provide easier accessibility. Removal of closet doors or installation of pocket doors will allow easier entry when closets are too small.[34]

Closets with adjustable rods and shelves can allow for more flexibility. Also, it's a good idea to have a chair in a closet so you can be seated while putting shoes and socks on and taking them off.

Kitchens

Universal design has evolved over the past two decades in response to the growing population of the elderly and disabled. However, it does not require that every counter be lowered to wheelchair height. Instead, it can mean having one section of the counter lower and another higher, enabling an elderly mother and adult child to prepare meals together. Our Aunt Alice and her son Sterling had such an arrangement in the kitchen they had built for the two of them to use. The concept has worked so well that recently the National Kitchen and Bath Association revised its guidelines to incorporate universal design.[35]

Workspace and Counters

For a kitchen to be a safe and efficient workspace, it is important to avoid wasted motion. You want to create a kitchen where you'll spend less time walking, turning, bending, lifting, and cleaning. If a wheelchair will be used, you will need a five-foot turning radius in the kitchen. Also, there should be adequate lighting and counter space. Under-cabinet fluorescent task-lighting can make working in the kitchen a lot easier.[36]

An efficient kitchen is generally designed around a work triangle formed by the location of three basic work centers: the refrigerator, sink, and range. Ideally, these centers should be arranged to follow the natural sequence of work for food preparation and cleanup. Basic patterns that accommodate this sequence include: U- and L-shaped, galley, and island/peninsula work centers. Good counter space next to each of the work centers is very important. As a general guide,

- one-and-a-half-foot wide countertop next to the opening side of the refrigerator is desired as a minimum,
- three feet of counter to the right of a sink, and two feet to the left (assuming a right-handed user) is desired, and
- two feet of countertop on both sides of the stove is ideal.

Having a countertop section at least 30 inches wide that is lower will allow for working from a seated position (approximately 28–32 inches above the floor with open knee space). If this is not possible, use of a high chair or stool makes it easier to sit while working at standard height counters. Pullout cutting boards can also provide a work site. When there are no pullouts, a kitchen drawer can be converted to a work surface by fitting a cutting board on top of it. Stabilization of the cutting board with nonskid materials is helpful.[37]

Better hardware now exists to make the cutting board level and rigid. If possible, the cook top and sink should have roll-in areas available that are free of plumbing or other exposed fixtures that could injure knees and legs.[38] For an example of such a cabinet with retractable doors, see exhibit 11.5. Another option is an adjustable kitchen sink from Populas (www.populas furniture.com) that features push-button control to both raise and lower the sink for those standing or using a wheelchair. Also, for safety, place a fire extinguisher within easy reach of the stove.

Storage Areas

Storage areas need to be at the right height for wheelchair-bound users. Unfortunately, this is difficult to do in most kitchens. The so-called prime reaching zone for people is between the waist and the shoulders. Typically, this area is devoted to work space in a kitchen, not cabinets for storage. If you have the room, it is advisable to put in a pantry closet for storage. If not, you can add shallow shelves on top of a countertop or put in hooks under

Exhibit 11.5.   Kitchen Cabinet with Retractable Doors

Source: Photo by Sharon Niederhaus. Courtesy of Harrell Remodeling.

cabinets above the countertop to hang small pots and pans. Tambour doors or "appliance garages" can be used to enclose shelves on top of a counter. Also, you can install pullout shelves, Lazy Susans in corner cupboards, and adjustable-height cupboards to allow for easier access to utensils and supplies. It's advisable to use wide loop pulls with ample finger space instead of knobs or small handles on drawers and cabinets. They are much easier to grab for someone with limited strength or dexterity.[39]

Appliances

For limited reach, consider a side-by-side refrigerator, front-or side-located controls on the stove, and side-mounted water faucets. Side-swing oven doors make it easier to be positioned in front of the oven for easier loading and removal of food. A pullout shelf underneath the microwave or oven creates an immediate counter when removing foods.[40]

The microwave and dishwasher should be reachable (drawer-style dishwashers are excellent alternatives that really save a person's back).[41]

Installing a microwave at counter height is recommended. Also, you might want to consider putting in lever-style faucet handles at the kitchen sink, along with an under-cabinet jar opener and electric can opener.[42]

Eleanor told us what she did for her in-laws' kitchen.

Eleanor: I designed it so that they could have a cooktop and a microwave. If they needed to, they would use my oven, which wasn't all that often. At that point, my father-in-law was doing all the cooking for them because they had their own likes and dislikes. I designed their kitchen to be very user friendly. We put in drawers below the counter, instead of cabinets with doors. When you have a drawer, you can pull it out and easily look down into it; you don't have to bend over. We put in full-extension glides on the drawers, so that they could be completely pulled out without falling out of the cabinets. That worked really well. We put in a single-lever faucet with a pullout spray at the kitchen sink. That's much easier to use than two-knob faucets. They had a miniature refrigerator and a mini-dishwasher as well. It looked like a doll-size dishwasher, only fifteen inches wide. They also had overhead cabinets that were easy to reach, along with under-cabinet lighting.

It's also possible to put in a raised, regular-size dishwasher that can be loaded and unloaded with much less bending, if elevated off the floor twelve inches or so.

Laundry Rooms

The ideal spot for doing the laundry is on the main floor of a house, near the bathroom and bedroom(s). One solution for those who have trouble bending or squatting is to "lift appliances off the floor," according to Roy Wendt, president of Wendt Builders, an Atlanta-based construction company that specializes in homes designed for seniors. For example, instead of top-loading washing machines, Wendt uses front-load washers and dryers in his homes. He installs them on a platform "to make it even easier to get at clothing. We raise them by about sixteen inches," he says. "You put them on a raised platform covered in tile. It's a pretty subtle feature."[43] Also, use of these front-load appliances can make reaching inside them easier from a wheelchair. An accessible-height countertop nearby can be helpful for folding clothes as well. Good news! A lot of the new washers and dryers being sold today are not only front-loading but much higher off the floor than older models!

Living Rooms

The "lift chair" is one of the best pieces of furniture being sold these days for the mobility impaired. A friend's mother has one that looks like a beautifully upholstered lounge chair. It comes with a remote control device that will gently raise her into a standing position, as well as lower her to sit down. They are priced at $550 to $1,500 and can be found not only in medical supply stores but also in regular furniture shops. In some cases, Medicare or health insurance companies will cover some of the purchase cost. Pride Mobility Products is a major manufacturer of lift chairs. It even sells some of its models with heaters and massagers. For more information go to their website at www.pridemobility.com.

Following are other tips for the living room:

- Having three to five feet between pieces of furniture provides enough room to move when using mobility devices. Ensure there are clear passageways and ample maneuvering space with furniture placement.
- A height of nineteen to twenty-one inches with favorite chairs or couches makes transfers easier and more energy efficient. A firm, dense cushion can increase the sitting height. If the furniture is too low, "furniture extenders/risers" can be used.
- Use of remote control units can be helpful for controlling lights, as well as the TV, DVD, and entertainment center.[44]

Floors

Tripping and slipping are two major safety concerns in a home. According to AARP, in a single year, Americans sixty-five and older had some 1.8 million falls that led to emergency room visits. More than half—about 55 percent— of these falls occurred in their homes. Fewer than half—49 percent—of all dwellings with an older person who has a physical limitation of some sort have been modified at all to make the home safer. And only 10 percent of homes had made two safety improvements.

You can make floors slip-resistant by adding nonskid mats under area rugs or getting rid of them entirely. Also, it is important to eliminate potential tripping points like thresholds whenever possible, or to lower their height.[45] Floors should be level with a nonslip surface, not sunken or raised. For those who use walkers, low-pile carpeting is safest so the walker doesn't catch on deep pile and cause a fall. Ultimately, for both walker and wheelchair users, hard-surface flooring, such as hardwood floors, tile, or linoleum, is the best option.[46]

Eleanor described the type of flooring she used in her in-laws' unit.

Eleanor: I used linoleum in the kitchen and a frieze type of carpeting in the rest of the house. Frieze carpet is trackless or track resistant. The yarns are tightly twisted in order for a wheelchair or a walker to go over it and not leave a track. It's comfortable to walk on; you would use a jute pad for a firmer walking surface. The elderly are more prone to turn their ankles or trip, so this firmer surface works well for them.

Joan also gave a reason not to use wall-to-wall carpeting.

Joan: Initially, we had carpeting. We put wall-to-wall over the hardwood flooring in her bedroom and in the dining area. A few years ago we took that out. Why did we do that? Not because of tripping, but because of overall cleanliness of her unit. Elderly people run into incontinence problems, which is a major problem. Wall-to-wall carpeting is not the way to go, unless you want to have a professional cleaner out once a month. Being able to have hardwood flooring was just great.

Lighting

Often ignored, adequate lighting is another important feature in senior-friendly homes. It is advisable to place extra lights in places like the edge of the bed or the bathroom, where it's easy to fall. Added lighting near steps or the front door is a good idea too. Illuminated rocker or touch-sensitive wall light switches are easier to use than the standard toggle light switches. Consider placing them lower on the wall, so they are reachable from a wheelchair. In this day and age of electronic equipment, you can even put in remote-controlled lights and dimmers, enabling you to turn on lights from your bed or chair without having to cross a dark room to find the switch. Hardware stores carry them and installation does not require an electrician.[47]

Eleanor installed overhead recessed lights in her in-laws' unit. She said this type of lighting eliminates the need for lamps and dangling cords. Also, you might want to consider installing skylights or clerestory windows. They can add natural light to a home, creating a bright and cheery atmosphere. Eleanor said that windows are not only important for letting in natural light, but also for keeping people connected to what's happening outside. Windowsills that are about twenty-four to thirty inches above the floor allow people to see outdoors while seated or standing.[48]

In comments about the design of her mother's home, Joan confirmed what Eleanor had to say.

Joan: One thing we did in the entry was put in a half wall. That allows sunlight from the front entry window to come in further. If you have a light and airy atmosphere, that can help a person not be depressed. I think sunshine is very cheery. We did put in skylights as well.

Color Schemes

When Eleanor designed the cottage for her in-laws, she was careful to select colors that would be visually appealing even as their eyesight changed. Here's what she had to say about color schemes for the elderly.

Eleanor: I wanted to take into consideration the color of walls and paper, because as the eye ages, the lens yellows. Things you're looking at won't appear to be white whites. They'll be yellow. That issue of the "aging of the eye" is a very important issue when you are dealing with designing for the elderly, whether they be in a facility or in their own home. By the way, when they have cataract surgery, that opens their eyes to the point where they have white as white again, instead of creamy yellow. I learned this through my father-in-law having cataract surgery.

However, if you put someone in a room and their eyes view everything through a yellow filter, the room could look very unappealing and even make them unhappy. It changes the coloration of the foods they eat. Foods could become "distasteful" to their sight, and therefore they might not want to eat them. For example, if a carrot was made purple, you probably wouldn't find it very appealing. So the coloration that you put in a person's home is something they are living with and seeing on a daily basis. You want them to have it either be soothing or a color that they feel good about. So, as a designer, you don't go in and say, "Well, I think such and such color would be wonderful here." You have to consider if the client's eyes are aging, and how that color is going to look to them.

In some cases, it is advisable to use bold and contrasting colors to make things easier to see.[49] You can make walls a different color from baseboards, as well as use contrasting borders on floors, around cabinets, and along countertops for extra definition and depth perception.

Communication

One of the benefits of living in an electronic age is that technology can be put to work to help us in a number of different ways. Monitors are used by many people caring for their elderly parents. These can range from a simple, low-priced baby monitor to a customized setup. An easy-reach buzzer at the side of someone's bed is another alternative.[50] In the case of communicating between two separate houses, certainly the telephone is one way to do it. A cell phone could be used. Another option to consider is an intercom system. If you're building a house, it's cheaper to install the wiring during construction than it is to install it later. Radio Shack also has a wireless intercom system that costs very little.

It is important to have telephone jacks accessible and located in necessary rooms. Use of portable phones is recommended.[51] Also, there are specialized telephones and devices to help people who have difficulty hearing, seeing, moving, speaking, or remembering. These phones can turn up the volume, flash incoming calls, make dialing easier, allow hand-free calling, display conversation in text, and remember numbers.[52] For information about availability, it is suggested that you call your local phone company.

Safety

There are a number of features you can install in your home that deal with safety issues. In case of fire, the use of audible/visible smoke alarms is strongly advised. If you are concerned about doors being left unlocked, put in a security system. Also, for everyone's peace of mind, it is a good idea to have some sort of medical alert system in place. There are medical alert devices available that can be worn around the neck to summon help at the push of a button. Seniors feel more comfortable knowing they have a panic button to use to get twenty-four-hour help seven days a week without ever touching a phone. Call Life Alert for such a device at (800) 404-5474.

Transportation

Five years ago, a woman who lives in Connecticut with her husband and three small children bought the house next door for her grandmother. Dana, the granddaughter, is currently a full-time mom and community volunteer. She had been raised by her grandmother after her own mother died when she was three. She talked about transportation issues related to making her home accessible to her grandmother. Dana came up with a creative way to transport her grandmother to and from their house next door.

Dana: My grandmother is here at our place for breakfast, lunch, and dinner. Depending on the weather, I will either go over and get her and bring her back, which is literally sixty-five seconds, or my son will. He has an electric golf car, and he'll use it to go get her for me. Most of the time I make her walk on purpose to get the exercise.

Sharon: Would you say she's about a hundred yards away?

Dana: Yes. From here to the end of the driveway. She can walk and she should walk. So I try not to cater to her.

Robotic Elder-Care Products

The "Technology" section of the May 17, 2004, *San Francisco Chronicle* featured an article about *Wired* magazine's NextFest technology expo. However, the 110 new technologies on display at the expo were not for sale. The point of NextFest was to expose the general public to new technologies that usually only scientists, military leaders, or journalists get to see.

Honda Motors showed off its Asimo, short for "Advanced Step in Innovative Mobility." The 4-foot-tall robot is the latest in an 18-year-long research effort by Honda to create a robot that moves as smoothly as a human. A crowd of students attending NextFest cheered Asimo as it danced the disco and walked up and down stairs. But the robot is still far from becoming a household item like Rosie the Robot in "The Jetsons," said Jeffrey Smith, a senior corporate affairs and communications manager for American Honda Motor Company. Honda believes there is a future market for robots that can, for example, assist elderly or disabled people with daily tasks. "We really think that someday it's going to be, 'Asimo, get me my medicine,' or 'Asimo, get me water,' or 'Asimo, walk the dog,'" Smith said.[53]

Many of the innovations at NextFest still need a lot of work before they can become everyday consumer products, if they ever do.

On the other hand, according to an earlier March 5, 2004, article in the *San Francisco Chronicle*, robotic elder-care products are gaining popularity in Japan. High labor costs are helping the trend gain acceptance in a nation that has the world's most rapidly aging population. Reminiscent of the old steam machines for bodies, washing machines for humans are now available in Japan. Yes, machines that wash people! Here are stories of how they work:

> With an electronic whir, the machine released a dollop of "peach body shampoo," a kind of body wash. Then as the cleansing bubbling action kicked in, Toshiko Shibahara, 89, settled back to enjoy the wash and soak cycle of her nursing home's new human washing machine. "The temperature is just right—the bubbles are really comfortable," she said, happily sealed up to her neck inside Sanyo Electric Co.'s latest elder care product. Turning to an attendant hovering around the pink, clamshell-shaped "assisted-care bath," she asked, "May I have a bit more water, please?"
>
> "It automatically washes my body, so I am quite happy about it," said Kuni Kikichi, an 88-year-old in a wheelchair who is paralyzed on her left side after a stroke. "These bubbles are good for the massage effect."[54]

Yukiko Sato, the general manager of a large chain of nursing homes, tells why his company decided to purchase the machines:

> Residents say it is really good because they warm their whole body; they can take the bath on their own; they can protect their privacy. As for the staff, it means less burden on their backs. Also, they can save time, because the whole procedure can be done in a very short time.[55]

In fact, the washer works like an MRI. "The person sits in a chair that is rolled backward into place. The sides of the machine then close like a clamshell, forming an instant tub with the person's head sticking out the top. Shampooing and drying off are done by hand."[56]

Along with the human washing machine that retails for almost fifty thousand dollars, Japanese companies will soon be selling "a 'robot suit,' a motorized, battery-operated pair of pants designed to help the aged and infirm move around on their own." In addition, "there is the Wakamaru, a mobile, 3-foot speaking robot equipped with two camera eyes. It is used largely by working children to keep an eye on their elderly parents at home." It is projected that "these devices and others in the works will push Japanese sales of domestic robots to $14 billion in 2010 and $40 billion in 2025 from nearly $4 billion currently, according to the Japan Robot Association."[57] Let's see what the future brings!

ECHO Housing

For those who don't have the time, energy, or financial resources to remodel their existing home to accommodate a senior, another option to consider is ECHO (Elder Cottage Housing Opportunity). An ECHO house, often called a "granny flat," is a small, portable, self-contained house designed to enable older people to live on the property of relatives or close friends so they don't have to be placed in an institution. It is a low-cost alternative since the homes are factory-built and there is no land cost. Installation of an ECHO unit takes two to three days. The main benefit of an ECHO house is that it allows an older person to live independently and privately in their own home while living near family caregivers who can keep their own privacy—a win-win for all.[58]

To find out if there is an ECHO program in your area, you can contact your local HUD (U.S. Housing and Urban Development) office. Depending on where you live, ECHO units are owned and rented-out either by the government or nonprofit organizations. You could also buy your own prefabricated cottage or trailer to put in the rear or side yard of your single-family home. However, be aware that zoning often limits ECHO housing or trailers to large lots and rural areas.

In New England and the Hudson Valley, the Home Store is the largest builder of custom modular homes and offers ECHO in-law apartments with over forty universal design features. One of their clients tells the following story on their website:

> My parents have now been living in an ECHO in-law apartment with me for about 2 years. It has actually turned out better than I ever expected it could, and that's why I'm telling the story, so that others who might be thinking about this can know how we did it and how we make it work, both financially and emotionally. . . .
>
> The first step was to get estimates for the job. Originally, we were just going to have a conventionally built addition. Dad got a quote

from a builder he knew and trusted for a 526 sq. ft. completely self contained one bedroom apartment. The price was unbelievable! We were all shocked. My folks could never afford to go to Florida if the cost of the apartment was going to be so high, and I was, unfortunately, not in a position to help finance the apartment with my oldest son getting ready to start college. We agreed that we would always provide a home for my folks from this time forward, and help with their care whenever they needed us.

Fortunately, Mom and Dad came across an AARP publication titled "ECHO Housing." It described affordable free-standing modular homes and in-law apartments that were specifically designed to meet the needs of elders. Both are built with Universal Design features that make the homes accessible for people of all ages, sizes, and abilities. The publication described how the modular homes are built in a factory and trucked to their destination. The amazing thing is that they can easily be removed if the family is relocating or no longer needs the ECHO home. The idea seemed intriguing. Mom and Dad remembered seeing a modular home at a home show a few years back and inquired with that builder about his cost for the same size apartment. The Home Store, who built the home-show house, was able to beat the local builder's price by thousands of dollars. It helped a lot that The Home Store has a specialty in universal design and ECHO housing. We were also pleased they were able to do everything that needed to be done from start to finish.

We then had to go before the Zoning Board of Appeals to get the O.K. to add a supplemental apartment. In addition, we had to inquire about any restrictions on the size of the apartment. We did not have any difficulty getting approval for our addition. Our neighbors and the town were supportive of the idea, and are pleased with how seamlessly the ECHO blends with our home.

Now that our ECHO apartment is here and lived in, we have found that the quality and sturdiness of the modular home is exceptional. I learned that the reason the modular addition feels so solid is that it has to be built to withstand the trip from the factory and being lifted by a crane and placed on its foundation. That apartment does not have one single spot that squeaks or creaks. My home, on the other hand, squeaks and creaks everywhere we walk.[59]

For more information, you can call the Home Store at (413) 665-1266, extension 13, or see their website at www.the-homestore.com. If you live outside the geographical area mentioned above, you can contact the Center for Universal Design at North Carolina State University at (800) 647-6777 or online at www.design.ncsu.edu/cud/.

Conclusions

This chapter has provided you with multiple options for creating an elder-friendly home using universal design features. Examples include grab bars, thirty-six-inch doorways, lever handles on doors and faucets, hardwood floors, lower counters, and many more. All of these innovations can increase the accessibility of your home for people of all ages and abilities. Such design enhances the ability of people to limit obstacles and maximize independence for as long as possible. Planning ahead to include universal design features can make the changes more affordable, as well as make your home more functional and accessible now, and in the future. It pays to plan ahead!

P A R T

The Challenges

C H A P T E R

Overcoming Cultural Stigmas

Four Curses and a Blessing

In the progress of personality, first comes a declaration of independence, then a recognition of interdependence.

—HENRY VAN DYKE

E HAVE IDENTIFIED four kinds of barriers to getting together again with your extended family. We will discuss the (1) *financial and legal* ones in some detail in the next chapter. We summarized (2) the *constraining building and zoning codes* at the end of chapter 10. We've mentioned (3) the *psychological* obstacles in many places in these pages. That is, extended-family living will not work for everyone—some folks just cannot get along because of the mix of personalities. And now we turn to the fourth kind of barrier: (4) the *cultural* kind. The good news for Americans is that the cultural barriers are beginning to fade.

Earlier we described how almost all people on the planet have always and are still living in multigenerational households. Moreover, in this country we also used to live in predominantly multigenerational households. How is it then that twentieth-century America became unique among societies? The answers to this question reveal much about taken-for-granted aspects of American thinking. The answers to this question also reveal the path to a new freedom that will allow us to live together again and enjoy doing so. Let's start the story with the latest symptom of the fluidity of American culture, the so-called boomerang kids.

Boomers, Boomerangs, and Barriers

The *Zits* cartoon says it all (see exhibit 12.1). You can bet that Jeremy's *fear-appeal* will yield tons of the sweet stuff. In fact, we know that what fear-appeals do best is get your attention. They may make you fearful or just plain mad, but they do get your attention, they elicit an emotional response. Indeed, look at today's politics. Republicans tell us we should be afraid our international neighbors will kill us. Democrats tell us we should be afraid our international neighbors will steal our jobs. But what's really going on in all these cases is that journalists themselves also realize that fear headlines and disputes sell newspapers. And Americans often disagree about the so called "boomerang kids." In the Room for Thought boxes in this chapter, you will see a sampling of the differing opinions elicited by a *New York Times* article titled "The Whole Family under One Roof?" from December 26, 2011. Thus, we see a profusion of confusion about twenty- and thirtysomethings still living at home, or the so-called "boomerang kids." Take a look at a sampling of recent headlines and book and movie titles:

> *Adult Children Moving Back Home: Don't Let Them Derail Your Goals*
> *Returning College Kids Shake Things Up at Home*
> *Look Who's Back*
> *The Coddling Crisis: Why Americans Think Childhood Begins at Age 26*
> *The PermaParent Trap* (perhaps the scariest)
> *The American Dream Runout: The Cluttered Nest*
> *Home Sweet Home—Again*
> *Hi Folks, I'm Home! As College Grads Move In, Some Parents Are Put Out*
> *Mom, Can I Move Back In with You? A Survival Guide for Parents of Twentysomethings*
> *When Our Grown Kids Disappoint Us*
> *Failure to Launch*

The worst consequence of the popular media's negative interpretation of the boomerang kids phenomenon is the pain it delivers to our kids. Our interview with Southern California family therapist Dr. Terri Maloney delineates the problem:

Exhibit 12.1.

Dr. Maloney: We see a trend in two groups of new "home again after college individuals." Maybe a little more than one-third of my practice this year involves kids in this age group—from the ages of twenty-two to thirty-two and mostly twentysomethings. One of the types I see is overgrown adolescents. They seem to be waiting for the world to knock on their door and provide opportunities that they can pick and choose from. These individuals have been indulged with too much money too soon in their lives without the rites of passage, without the capacity to really earn or understand the fact that they're not automatically entitled to such luxuries. They tend to come from very dysfunctional families and often display alcohol and/or drug addictions and sometimes bipolar depression. So sometimes a difficult combination of symptoms makes such cases quite complex.

The second part of that age group, the other individuals that I see, are more of the "I grew up in this family and I deserve what my parents have" types. Their families developed the capacity to earn enough money to live in Newport Beach in the last ten years of their children's lives. Then the kids went off to nice private colleges to get their degrees. And now they've graduated and feel like, "If I've done this, I'll have it made." They are the ones that display a kind of chronic, low-level, vague sense of directionlessness and feelings of loss and, by the way, abandonment: "I've been duped. They've lied to me. So here's my college degree and where's all my success? Where's my job and where's my great apartment?"

They identify with the characters on the sitcom *Friends.* I had one individual refer to that television show. She imagined her twentysomething life as, "I'll have my own place. I'll have this great job that I'll go off to when I feel like it. Otherwise, I'll just sit around and shoot the breeze with my friends." Then we talked a little bit, and she began to see the distinction between the television show and her very real life.

So we have the media and society and everybody kind of promising those things, and the kids really feel let down. They feel abandonment and loss and disappointment. I actually enjoy working with them because they are of the mind now, they have the brain capacity and judgment to take in some of the data points that we've discussed about what's happening to kids in their age group. I ask them about their friends. I had one patient who was twenty-five who said that out of ten friends seven of them are living at home. And the numbers appear to be growing.

Scary, indeed! The negative headlines get everyone's attention. The headlines deliver angst to us all, particularly the kids. But, these headlines misrepresent reality. The reality? Perhaps it's not all that bad? Perhaps it's

---

Room for Thought 12.1.   Parents' Complaints about Boomerang Kids

---

Lorenzo
New York
Sounds like hope triumphs over experience. America has been taken in with this culture of positive thinking and happy thoughts. Believe me if your allowing your 34-year-old to stay home and hang around until they have a meaningful position your really enabling them to be loafers and losers. So tell them to go take the Starbucks barrister position and when they find something better quit . . . but not before.

Banty
Upstate New York
Being an engineer, I work with a lot of men. And the view I've gotten from them about the period of parenthood where we are preparing our kids to launch is that mothers tend to want to hang on (speaking generally). For the company, and for the continuing role with respect to their adult children. Fathers more want to see the culmination of child-rearing, which is independence, and are more looking forward to enjoying an empty nest unfettered by the schedules and needs of adults not the ones they chose to marry to. Because that's what you have in a combined household—other adults, with their ins and outs, their preferences, their music tastes, their sleeping hours. Another layer of negotiation, fewer hours for that cherished hobby, more shifting around of cars in the driveway, fewer amorous opportunities.

Jack
Silver Spring, Maryland
I am also seeing a certain complacency creeping into the lifestyle of some of these returning adult children. Why hustle for job when you have a roof over your head and a warm meal? Yes, jobs are tight, but there is no reason some of these grown men and women can't take on part time work so they can help defray some of the home expenses. This leads to tensions within the family for their aging parents who should be planning their own retirements and building up a little nest egg to offset the losses on their 401Ks. Families should provide a temporary safety net for adult children in economic distress. However, our aging population cannot be expected to provide health care, food and clothing for adult children indefinitely.

Canku wicasa
Mid-South
Contemporary multigenerational families only extend adolescence. No real "savings" is realized as Little Johnny and Sissy simply spend a greater share of their own (and their

parent's) resources in juvenile pursuits. I reject the notion that boomerangs are returning home because they "can't afford to maintain their own household." They return home because they can't afford to maintain that profligate, financially over extended lifestyle to which Americans in general aspire. It is a mistake to compare the family structure of "years ago" (when it was "common" for multiple generations to live under one roof) with that of the post-modern, consumer driven family. Returning home broke and unemployed isn't the same as having first left at an older, more mature (emphasis on "more mature") age.

OakParker
Chicago
Many twenty-somethings, especially if they are not working or working only part-time, behave as if they are still in college, maintaining the life of very late hours, irregular meal times, chaotic social lives, loud music and minimal housekeeping. There's something about living at home again that turns semi-adults back into adolescents, and it's an effort to constantly negotiate your children to adulthood. Those of us who have enjoyed a few years of household quiet and personal freedom can find it a challenge to put our new-found peace and independence on the back burner.

Source: Online comments from "The Whole Family under One Roof?," Room for Debate, *New York Times*, December 26, 2011.

more of a mixed blessing? At least you'd gather such from some of the more recent headlines:

> "Boomerang Kids Don't Have to Be a Financial Drain"
> "Boomerang Kids: How Do Parents Deal with the Blessing of Children Who Move Back Home? Or, the Curse?"
> "Is It a Happy Nest the Second Time Around?"

Moreover, recall the Del Webb survey mentioned in chapter 10 by the Standard Pacific executives—only about 25 percent of boomers expect to be happier when their kids leave. The survey goes on to report that happiness seems to decline with the length of time the nest is actually empty:

- zero to five years since the children left: 27 percent feel happier
- six to ten years: 11 percent
- eleven or more years: 5 percent

Too bad the kids themselves haven't heard the news that they're missed.

Finally, we can even find a few headlines and associated articles and books that coincide with this reality:

Decorating for Boomerang Kids (our favorite)
Boomerang Joy
When a Child Returns Home: At Times, Freedom and Privacy Can't Hold a Candle to the Fullness of Family Life

---

Room for Thought 12.2.   Parents' Praise for Boomerang Kids

Karen Snyder
Dartmouth, Massachusetts
I have been surprised at how close in proximity and supportive we have all become in the last 5 years. I had assumed my sons would move to a distant state and live lives very independent of their parents, as my husband and I had done. Having grown up in a large extended family on Long Island I have often felt isolated in the community I live in. It has been a pleasant surprise to see our own small family develop the kind of connections I loved so much as a child.

Our transition to living together as adults, respecting each other's privacy and developing the ability to share household tasks was not always an easy one. It has been extremely gratifying to see our home become a communal residence. As a child of the 60s, had I not contemplated such a living arrangement?

proftom
Newberg Oregon
Our home is open, warm, friendly and genuinely welcoming. Its also a launch pad. Its mission control for everyone. It takes longer for younger people to launch into self sustainability these days, so we keep the place mission ready. These economic days young people need multiple lift offs and reentries. I am a boomer and needed one. I wished I had many, but the folks stood firm at one. My view is our culture is improving how we launch our youth. Instead of one giant blast off which often ended up in failed marriages, dead end jobs, and career disasters, our youth are provided a more stable platform to journey into the adult universe. They seem to be making better decisions than we did. They feel comfortable looking two or three times before they make the leap. It's a good thing.

Jen
Indiana
I am really starting to believe the isolation in our society is a big problem, responsible for a lot of the mental problems and depression people experience. I will welcome my kids living with me for as long as they want to and need to, providing they are trying to work and be productive citizens.

Katie

Portland, Oregon

I have three teenagers. There is a high probability that after college, one or more will move back in with us for a time. What's the problem with that? As I see it, nothing, as long as they're working or actively, truly, looking for a job. If they graduate with student loans or car loans, they can live rent free and in a year or two, knock off much, or all, of that loan. What a gift that is to them.

If they're cheerful, hard working, responsible, helpful around the house, pleasant to be around—hey, move back in, kiddo, for a year or so. Not forever—they need to build their own life. But we love our kids, and with us they can get some savings together and prepare for life in a, currently, brutal economic world. And now and then if they sit down and play Scrabble with me, or take me to the Cheesecake Factory, as I am getting old and need fun company, that would be lovely, too.

Rainy Day

Michigan

I've seen both success and disaster among my 50-something contemporaries.

If the family psychologically and culturally is supportive and respectful of all individuals and members do not constantly replay teen conflicts, then adult children can live successful lives with careers, dating, and adult responsibility, bringing welcome financial security and extra hands for housework and home maintenance.

We do not have children ourselves, but may, in the future, be welcoming adult nieces and nephews into our household. Already, my husband's many siblings are talking about ways to combine limited resources as we all age. There are many ways to create larger family households. I've loved my privacy, but seeing older relatives living alone in their 80s is bringing the disadvantages and loneliness to light.

Mary

Texas

My daughter asked to move back in for a year after college so that she could save some money before heading out on her own. One year and $12,000 richer, she got her own place. We loved having her and getting to know her as an adult. Her nest egg has meant that she has been able to handle her own financial emergencies, too. Seven years later, we're delighted to see her succeeding in life and on her own, but we certainly would welcome her back if need be, and we still kind of miss her.

Source: Online comments from "The Whole Family under One Roof?," Room for Debate, *New York Times*, December 26, 2011.

So despite the American popular press, the American population seems to recognize that boomerang kids are actually a good thing. Most folks writing in the area agree that things work out better if (1) the kid pays rent or contributes to the household in tangible ways, (2) it's a temporary and one-time situation, (3) the parents are in a long-term marriage, (4) it helps the kids with some sort of transition, and (5) the kid is good company. Most folks also agree on the causes of the return home: (1) economics/safety net, (2) the kid's divorce, (3) graduate school or other extended education, (4) drug/alcohol problems, and (5) temporary transitions. However, we actually don't agree with either list, particularly the notion of a "temporary transition" imbedded in both.

When you step back and look at the big picture, it's clear that boomerang kids are just another symptom of the cultural change affecting American society as we enter the twenty-first century. Indeed, most recently, based on a study of more than seven hundred so called boomerang kids, researchers at the University of Minnesota report,

> The fact that young people depend so heavily upon their parents well beyond the age when most people from earlier generations had already started families and had dependable jobs has triggered a great deal of public anxiety over whether these trends signal young adult immaturity and stunted development. The larger social trends in delaying family formation may be one reason for the extended dependence upon parents. Today, the road to adulthood is much longer and more arduous than it was thirty years ago.[1]

The last sentence above clearly describes a cultural shift. And as we mentioned in chapter 2, we see the current boomerang kid/baby boomer interaction as a very useful preparation for the fast approaching years of the boomers' retirement. We as a society are relearning how adult parents and children can live and work together cooperatively in extended-family arrangements.

Grandparents moving back is another symptom of the same cultural shift. The failing pension and health-care systems are also symptoms. The fundamental point is that people are moving back together again because the grand experiment of the World War II generation hasn't worked. Three generations belong together, and not just for financial or psychological reasons. Fundamentally and by nature, humans are built this way and have evolved this way. We've survived the millennia by living in such extended-family arrangements. We are happiest in such groups. And we are now

Room for Thought 12.3.   Boomerang Kids' Views

Kristina
Chicago, Illinois
There are many reasons that an adult would choose to live with his or her parents—not all of them are financial. I am a woman in my late 20s, and I live with my parents, older sibling, and my preschool-aged nephew. My other siblings live within walking distance. I have lived on my own—both with roommates and alone. Both experiences were lonely. I often wonder whether I should move out—but the primary thing that is keeping me here is that I enjoy spending time with my family. There are so many small moments that I would miss. This might change once I want to start a family with someone—but until I start my "own" family, THIS is my family.

some perspective
Boomerang children are not necessarily lazy and indifferent. I chose to move back home after my sophomore year in college because I thought it irresponsible to accrue debt just to live in an apartment. Now I don't have any school loans. I can start with a clean slate. I do work around the house—I cook, clean, re-paint rooms, troubleshoot the family computer, and more. Do I live at home so I can have access to cable or an iPhone? Absolutely not. That, in my opinion, is absolutely absurd. It simply makes more sense to save now and enjoy a mailbox free from a school loan bill later.

JM
San Diego, California
Parents and adult children can work well in a house together. I should know, I'm one of the children. My parents completely re-built their house a few years back, meanwhile I was getting evicted due to toxic mold and had some health issues that put quite a strain on my finances. So I negotiated a long term set-up with them. I pay some rent which helps to pay down their new home loan faster, but less than I'd be paying on my own so it helps me save faster. I buy my own groceries, make my own meals, do my own laundry, and pitch in with household tasks and projects. I've gotten the benefit of getting to know my parents as people, I go to plays with my mom (which my dad doesn't like), I build furniture and work on cars with my father. We even swap designated driving duty when we go out with our respective friends.

Skeptic
Boston, Massachusetts
Neither my parents nor I think there is anything wrong with it so long as I work as hard as I can, help out around the house, and help pay family expenses and my loans. Living

at home will also help me learn about managing finances/doing taxes/etc. from people who have been doing it for a long time, rather than figuring it out on my own and screwing up my potentially precarious economic situation. Sure, maybe I sound like a spoiled middle-class kid, but I think it's unfair to accuse boomerang kids of being lazy. Many of us simply can't afford to get our own places as we seek jobs, and engaging in a mutually beneficial living situation is our best bet.

RosaMimosa
East Coast
A co-worker, age 27, was at the beach with his friends. Over dinner with some lovely young ladies they had just met and the apparent attraction between him and one of the young ladies, his pals made a point loudly that "he lives at home with his mother." "Yes, I do," said Henry calmly. "I also have no debt, my car is paid for, and I also have over $22,000 in the bank for a house when I decide to get married." I received the wedding invitation 8 months later.

Stella
New Hampshire
For me it is not an opportunity to delay adult responsibilities. I work full-time, pay my student loans and all of my other bills each month. It has not only allowed me to save up a large amount of money on a marginal salary, but it has also given me precious time with my family that I wouldn't trade for anything. I have friends who weren't allowed to move home after college and to me that is just sad. There is nothing wrong with moving back in with parents or other family as long as responsibility is taken.

Heather
Canada
I'm in my early thirties, and I live with my parents: and together, we paid off the mortgage a good fifteen years early. I have a career and have been steadily employed since graduation. I'm also a single woman with MS, and the arrangement made sense: if I need help, my parents are around. And as they get older, I can help them . . . not just "in kind," but financially.

The trick is to quickly establish a new relationship that isn't based solely around the parent/child dynamic—in some ways, I'm still their daughter. But I'm also the third adult in the household, and treated as such. And I don't treat them as my 'rents—of course I regard them as my parents, with love. But I also don't treat them the way I did when I was a teenager (horrors!) or as a twenty-something. Our standard of living, collectively, is higher because we all contribute to the household budget and expenses.

pdxtran
Minneapolis, Minnesota
During the early 1980s, I was unemployed and unable to find a full-time job for three years. I worked at temporary and part-time jobs and lived with my parents and grandmother.

While on one level, I was grateful for the help, it was terribly stressful, because my mother and grandmother in particular could not get it through their heads that I was an adult, so they tried to micromanage my life. If I got a phone call, they would hang around asking, "Who is it? Who is it?" They ruined potential romantic relationships by making hints about marriage to anyone I brought home. When I went out the door to one of my jobs, they demanded that I stop so that they could critique my clothes. When I first moved in, they "worried" when I wanted to go to a movie by myself after dark . . . in a car, in the suburbs. They made social arrangements that I was supposed to be included in (mostly visiting their friends) without consulting me.

This was awfully hard to take after I'd been living in apartments with friends in other cities for nine years.

Finally getting a full-time job and spending that first night alone in my own apartment was one of the happiest events of my life up to that time.

Source: Online comments from "The Whole Family under One Roof?," Room for Debate, *New York Times*, December 26, 2011.

quickly learning that other institutions (companies, unions, governments, religious organizations, etc.) ultimately cannot take care of us; only our families can and will.

The growing numbers of boomerang kids bear this out. Estimates vary, but the numbers are huge. Almost 40 percent of all Americans twenty to thirty-four are now living with their parents according to the latest U.S. Census Bureau figures. For eighteen- to twenty-five-year-olds, the numbers were even higher: more than half live with one or both parents. Such living arrangements exist only because they work.

So given the natural tendency of humans to live in extended family groups, why did this strange experiment with separation occur in America during the latter half of the twentieth century? The explanations are several, intertwined, and crucial to understand if they are to be overcome. Indeed, the faster we "get over" the odd culture of relative familial isolation we have inherited from the World War II generation, the sooner we can begin to enjoy the benefits of extended-family living, the benefits of being together again.

Boomerang kids? What seems to be a curse is actually a societal blessing, albeit one well disguised by the popular press! Indeed, it's often easy to confuse blessings and curses. This is particularly so when abundance is involved. Think food, cars, oil, kids, and so on. You can be too thin, and some say you can be too rich.

Room for Thought 12.4.   A Little Humor about Boomerang Kids

JenofNJ
New Jersey
Am I the only person who would have preferred living in a cardboard box to living with my parents again?

ron shapley
New York City
Of course you saved alot of Cash . . . you were probably living rent free and mom put food on the table everynight. . . . I hope you can return the favor sometime when they might need your help. I'm not speaking as a bitter parent but as someone who is aghast at these living situations taken on by young adults who run to mommy when things get tough. . . . Man up!!

basine
Idaho
Having had kids move home I can honestly say that it is not easy. We did not raise our children to live at home. My husband, of 40 years, and I have enjoyed the empty nest. Each year we raise a huge garden and can for the kids. Our thought is it is cheaper to can for the kids than have them move home. Even now we enjoy the "tail lights."

Jeffrey Brown
Texas
The "Boomerang" situation is a good reason to have a small organic farm/garden. One can take incoming liabilities, i.e., unemployed family members, and turn them into productive assets, i.e., agricultural workers.

Michael Sousa
Dusseldorf, Germany
I am not convinced that it's the economy that is forcing grown children to live with their parents. In the 1980s the economy was booming—but if you ever saw "Dynasty" or "Dallas" or even "Falcon Crest," all the grown children lived in their parents house— and it did not seem to be a problem at all.

Source: Online comments from "The Whole Family under One Roof?," Room for Debate, *New York Times*, December 26, 2011.

We now turn to the four curses of American culture on multigenerational family living. All four have deep roots in American culture. Moreover, most Americans consider them blessings. And certainly these curses do have their positive attributes. But all four act to constrain the freedom of Americans to be inventive in designing appropriate households and living arrangements. The point is that we are victims of our own culture. Recognition of these constraints will give us freedom to think and act differently than the previous generation. And as the problems facing our generations are different from those of the past, we *really* need this new freedom.

1. The Curse of the Missing "ter"

America started with the Declaration of Independence. On July 4, 1776, the founding fathers broke from the tyranny of England to form a new country. That document and the idea of independence represent the essence of being American. Independence is literally the most celebrated notion of the nation. Indeed, the goal of mainstream American parenting is to inculcate this notion into the noggins of our kids. We make them make their own beds, make their own lunches, wash their own clothes, do their own homework, drive their own cars, etc., etc. How else can they be independent adults?

There are at least three problems with this approach: First, it stigmatizes both the boomerang kids and the grandparents living with their kids. Second, it doesn't work. Third, there is no such thing as independence. There is only inter*dependence, and thus the missing "ter" in the heading.

The Declaration of Independence was about politics and had little to do with interpersonal relationships. King George III of England was a terrible tyrant: denying our human rights, taxing us without representation, and perhaps worst of all, "cutting off Trade with all Parts of the World." That is, we had to pay more for the drugs of the day, tea from China and rum from Jamaica, because they were shipped through British ports. So the founding fathers declared "that as Free and Independent States, they have the full Power to levy War, conclude Peace, contract Alliances, establish Commerce, and to do all other Acts and Things which Independent States may of right do." Indeed, after we won the Revolutionary War some eleven years later, our ships started sailing directly to Canton and Kingston, rather than only to England. The Declaration of Independence was and is a wonderful and path-breaking document. But it says nothing about teaching your kids to wash their own clothes or to do their own homework. And even after we won the war, we still traded with England. Indeed, the United States is by any measure still interdependent with Great Britain. The Brits own more of America than any other country does, and the United Kingdom remains one of our most important trading partners. In fact, most recently we have depended on our British friends to go to war with us in the Middle East. And so it goes. One can make a good argument that political independence doesn't really exist either given the new globalization.

And this foolish notion of independence, originally applied only to politics, makes Americans feel incorrectly guilty about the clear interdependence that has always and will always exist across generations of family members. This American overemphasis on independence is now being recognized among the most independent-minded of all Americans, CEOs. In Bill George's wonderful book *Authentic Leadership*, he argues that the job of chief executive depends on six constituencies. Not surprisingly, the former CEO of Medtronic lists shareholders, employees, customers, vendors, and the larger community. What is unique on his list, even revolutionary, is his own family. He recognizes that his own success as a CEO in part depends on the quality of his family life. Thus, he organized his executive team and responsibilities such that he had time to attend kids' soccer matches and such. Remarkable![2]

There's also a final irony about American independence. We made a lot of tanks during World War II. Right after the war, the extra industrial capacity created during the war made cars cheap in this country. As indicated in exhibit 12.2, we have more cars per family than any other nation. And cheap cars created freeways and suburbia and shopping centers. With our cars we could load up at the grocery store and become independent of the daily shopping routine still facing households all around the world. Indeed, a car for every person in the family and everyone is independent. "See the USA in a Chevrolet" made road trips attractive and promised a new freedom and independence from public transportation. The latest incarnation of the "car = independence" argument has been the billions of dollars spent selling Americans on unsafe, gas-guzzling SUVs. "Go anywhere, any time in your Hummer. Your Hummer even gives you independence from roads (and traffic)." So now, while we are independent of our local grocery store, as a nation we Americans are completely dependent on our cars, big refrigerators, the continuous construction of new highways (for our sanity), and oil from foreign countries. The fuel burned in our cars is polluting the planet, changing global weather patterns, and given the recent drowning of New Orleans and the polar ice melting, reducing the amount of land to live on. Perhaps the greatest irony of all is that the space taken up by all our cars is limiting our freedom to build sensible housing. Granny flats are often built above garages, yielding the extra steps that will plague the coming elderly generation. And worst of all, providing the parking for our metal monsters subtracts living

Exhibit 12.2. Passenger Cars per One Thousand People in Selected Countries

United States	809
Germany	554
Mexico	264
Canada	605
Japan	593
France	598
Brazil	198
Italy	637
United Kingdom	526
South Korea	346
China	37
India	15

Source: World Bank, 2012.

space for American families, as noted in our discussion of constraining building and zoning codes in chapter 10.

Independence isn't just overrated. Most simply stated, *independence is a myth.* Human beings are social animals and are by our deepest nature interdependent on one another. Shouldn't the design of our homes, households, and communities recognize this fundamental fact? Perhaps the founding fathers should have held this truth to be self evident as well.[3] Had they done so, getting together again in multigenerational family arrangements would be much easier for all of us.

Both the elderly living with their kids and young adults living with their parents suffer from this cultural stigma of "dependence." Their own words provide testimony to the lack of recognition of their actual state of interdependence. They are missing what they are delivering in the interpersonal exchange of living together.

Stacie: I think the thing that affects me the most living here with my parents is it makes me be more dependent on them when I should be establishing my independence. That's hard for me because it's right there for me to grab. My parents want to give it to me, but they don't. Sometimes I grab it and sometimes I don't. Like, I depend on my parents for transportation, and I'm working for them for food. So I'm paying that back. I just sometimes feel like I take advantage of the things that are there for me, if I need them. They also want me to be independent. But at the same time, it's hard to establish that line.

Greg: There is an ego issue where you think that your peers might look down upon it or think that you are not out on your own or that you're strange for

Room for Thought 12.5.   "Independence" Gets in the Way

cschildknecht
Cincinnati, Ohio
Two of our four were home for Christmas. While we love our children dearly and having them come to visit, at this stage in our lives we enjoy the freedom to do as we please with no worry about meals and schedules that having adult children at home entails. Our children for their part enjoy visiting but like the lives that they have fashioned in the places they have chosen to live. We raised them to be independent and they relish that very independence.

One's children will always be one's children, no matter how old they are. It is difficult enough to realize that when they are living on their own—I think it would be next to impossible were they to come home permanently as residents. The parental imperative would, I think, make it difficult, if not impossible, to see one's children as anything other than young children.

madrona
Washington
I cannot conceive of a worse idea. I would not, under any circumstances, have lived with my parents one day past the day I could escape, even when it meant struggling and saving for five years before I had enough money to start college. I raised an independent, self-sufficient son who could earn a living before he married and had a child. As much as I love him, I would not ever live with him or vice versa. I too strongly value my own marriage and the intimacy that privacy allows, as well as my independent life and the freedom to do what I want when I want. Dreadful notion!

shawn
Pennsylvania
As a Gen-X'er, I do see the potential of having children living at home past high school/college, coupled with the fact that I will most likely need to support aged boomer parents (financially) at the same time. This just cannot happen. To expect our generation to pay out of both pockets for two overprivileged generations is insane. We just don't have it, and never had, maybe never will, the opportunities afforded to our parents. Good use of extra rooms? How about an unfinished basement. So I will encourage my kids to be independent as much as they can, while offering plenty of emotional support. Having them at home well into their 20s is not financial possible. "Kids these days" need to move in with friends with similar interests, and support each other within their means. I did it. For my boomer folks, I have no idea what to do.

Source: Online comments from the *New York Times*, Room for Debate, "The Whole Family under One Roof?," December 26, 2011.

living with your in-laws. Once we had Ryan, all of those concerns disappeared, because we could see how beneficial our living arrangement is to the whole family. When it's just yourself and a set of parents, you are all adults, and it might look a little strange. But as soon as you throw a child into the mix, the benefits are just so amazing. I talk to so many people and I'm almost embarrassed to tell them our situation if they have a similarly aged child. They just can't believe how lucky we are and how much help we have. I know so many people who have moved out here for a job and don't have any family in California. They have no support system and it's just incredibly hard to raise a child without having that support system, especially with both parents working.

So at least Greg is now seeing past the dependency stigma. Betsy also recognizes the reality of interdependence in her family's relationship with her mother:

Betsy: When my mom left San Diego, she was going to move in with my sister who is single. She owns a home in Valencia. My husband and I had been augmenting my mom's rent. So she was putting in $1,100 and we were doing the balance of it for her to live in San Diego. Bringing her here brought us something, the companionship and the family that my daughter needed and support that I needed, because all of my siblings are at a distance. She was a constant support that was missing for us. So that was how we justified the financial cost for us.

Therefore, my siblings did not help us with the San Diego residence because they said, "We didn't tell her to go over there." I think that's fair. Now they are saying that if she moves in with my sister, and my sister is going to be driving her to the doctors and all of those things and possibly having to upgrade her house to accommodate my mom, we should all help out. "Let's set up a Mom fund," where all of us contribute five hundred dollars a month. Then, at the end of this year, maybe our sister can take that money and redo her house with it. My sister protested, "Well, nobody helped you guys." We said, "Well hang on, the value we got was different. What you are doing will require you to make some changes since you are single and working. Maybe Mom can contribute what she might be paying if she lived in an apartment." So, as it worked out for the year, we decided to have my mom in an apartment.

Accessory-apartment advocate and housing expert Patrick Hare clearly sees the American independence idol as a major problem:

Pat: Here is one of the things that seems to be really important. Somehow through the single-family house, we have projected independence as a value. It has come to mean, I think without anybody intending it, "isolation." Because after the kids leave, statistically half of all the people live as couples. So what it means is that you are going to have two people at least living in a household by themselves. One of them is going to end up alone. But psychologically, the status of having that house is so important. The irony is that it is not really independence. What it means is that, when there is any crisis, you are going to be dependent on strangers. You're going to be dependent on home health aides, EMTs, all these strangers. And strangers that don't know how to deal with taking care of you. A person has to be there if you are going to the hospital. If your relatives live two hours away, they won't be able to help you there. In terms of quality of life, this whole independence in a single-family world is a disaster.

And, even the popular press is starting to come around. As Tamar Lewin reports,

> Perhaps because American culture places such emphasis on independence, many people express discomfort about discussing intergenerational help given or received. In dozens of interviews, grandparents said they did not want their names used because they worried that it would embarrass their children or did not want their grandchildren to know what they were paying for. "You'll have to ask my son whether he's comfortable having this in the newspaper," a Manhattan grandmother said. That son said, "No"; like many others in the middle generation, he did not want it known that he was not his family's sole support. "The near-taboo on the subject," Professor Bengston (University of Southern California professor of sociology and gerontology) said, "indicates a cultural lag, with the prevailing norms and attitudes trailing behind what is actually going on."[4]

When the *New York Times* reports it, it must be true!

2. The Curse of "I"

America is a strange place among nations. Americans generally don't notice this because we assume people everywhere think just like we do. Well, they don't. And the American difference is most prominent in the Individualism/Collectivism Index. Look at the numbers in exhibit 12.3. We're at the top of the list, the end of the scale. Americans place higher values on individualism than folks from any other country. These numbers are based on the research of a Dutch international management scholar, Geert Hofstede. In 1970 he surveyed IBM employees around the world about their work-related values. From those data he developed four dimensions of cultural differences, the most salient of which is his "Individualism/Collectivism Scale." John reports in his textbook,

> Individualism/Collectivism Index. The Individualism/Collectivism Index refers to the preference for behavior that promotes one's self-interest. Cultures that score high in IDV reflect an "I" mentality and tend to reward and accept individual initiative, whereas those low in individualism reflect a "we" mentality and generally subjugate the individual to the group. This does not mean that individuals fail to identify with groups when a culture scores high on IDV, but rather that personal initiative and independence are accepted and endorsed. Individualism pertains to societies in which the ties between individuals are loose; everyone is expected to look after himself or herself and his or her immediate family. Collectivism, as its opposite, pertains to societies in which people from birth onward are integrated into strong, cohesive groups, which throughout people's lifetimes continue to protect them in exchange for unquestioning loyalty.[5]

Individualism is, of course, directly related to and reinforces the notion of independence discussed above. But while independence is a myth, individualism is not. Moreover, individualism leads directly to competitiveness. Competitiveness can be a good thing. Our hugely successful American economic system is based upon the principle that competitiveness breeds efficiency. But competitiveness is not always a good thing. Think sibling rivalry as just the problem most pertinent to the topic of this book. In order to avoid suffering the negative consequences of our often-wonderful American individualism, it is important to understand its origins. Why are Americans the most individualistic people on the planet?

Reference to two books, one new and one old, provides us the answer. In the first, *The Geography of Thought*, University of Michigan psychologist Richard Nisbett tells us that the fundamental difference between Western (American and European) and Eastern (Asian) thinking is rooted in the geography of ancient Greece and China, respectively.[6] Simply summarized, 2,500 years ago, Greek culture grew up in an island geography where people weren't much affected by their neighbors. If you live on an island, you don't have to worry so much about your neighbors attacking you and you

Exhibit 12.3.   Individualism/Collectivism Index*

United States	91	Slovakia	52	Hong Kong	25
Australia	90	Spain	51	Serbia	25
Great Britain	89	India	48	Chile	23
Hungary	80	Surinam	47	Bangladesh	20
Netherlands	80	Argentina	46	China	20
New Zealand	79	Japan	46	Singapore	20
Italy	76	Morocco	46	Thailand	20
Belgium	75	Iran	41	Vietnam	20
Denmark	74	Jamaica	39	West Africa	20
France	71	Russia	39	Salvador	19
Sweden	71	Brazil	38	Korea (South)	18
Ireland	70	Arab countries	38	Taiwan	17
Norway	69	Turkey	37	Peru	16
Germany	67	Uruguay	36	Trinidad	16
South Africa	65	Greece	35	Costa Rica	15
Finland	63	Croatia	33	Indonesia	14
Estonia	60	Philippines	32	Pakistan	14
Luxembourg	60	Bulgaria	30	Colombia	13
Poland	60	Mexico	30	Venezuela	12
Malta	59	Romania	30	Panama	11
Czech Republic	58	Portugal	27	Ecuador	8
Switzerland	58	Slovenia	27	Guatemala	6
Austria	55	East Africa	27		
Israel	54	Malaysia	26		

Source: Geert Hofstede, *Cultural Consequences*, 2nd ed. (Thousand Oaks, CA: Sage, 2001).
*Higher numbers equal more individualistic cultural values.

cannot so much depend on them helping you either. In contrast, 2,500 years ago, if you lived in the crucible of Eastern culture, between the great rivers of China, you were literally surrounded by people. You had to pay attention to your neighbors because they could easily harm or help you. John Donne's 1624 declaration would never have come up in China or Japan, then or now, because folks from collectivistic cultures take the central notion for granted:

No man is an island, entire of itself; every man is a piece of the continent, a part of the main; if a clod be washed away by the sea, Europe is the less, as well as if a promontory were, as well as if a manor of thy friends or of thine own were; any man's death diminishes me, because I am involved in mankind; and therefore never send to know for whom the bell tolls; it tolls for thee.

We also understand the individualism imbedded in Northern European culture, including our own Anglo culture, with reference to the cold climate there and the Protestant Reformation. Harsh winters and snowdrifts prevent your neighbors from helping or hurting you, so folks from northern climes tend toward cultural values for individualism and independence. Indeed, the cold climes kept out the Romans and ultimately lead to the Protestant Reformation. That is, it was tough to be dependent on a priest through which to talk with God when a blizzard was blowing outside your door. Bad weather makes a direct, individual relationship with God more practical. It's no accident that Geert Hofstede noticed these differences. As a kid he grew up living on the north/south border of Europe demarked by the three great rivers of the region. The western-flowing Rhine, Waal, and Maas cut Europe in half, north to south, cold to warm, barbarian to Roman, Protestant to Catholic, and individualistic to collectivistic. These geographic influences can roughly be seen with reference to exhibit 12.3. But what puts Americans on the top of the individualism list? The answer lies in a question we have for you. Before reading on, we want you to sit back and ask yourself: What is the most influential sentence first written in English? Really, stop reading here, sit back, and contemplate our query.

Given up? Good guesses include something from the Magna Carta, John Locke, William Shakespeare, or perhaps our own Declaration of Independence. But we think the best answer is this: "By pursuing his own interest he frequently promotes that of society more effectually than when he really intended to promote it."

This is Adam Smith's "invisible hand" statement from his *Wealth of Nations*, published in 1776.[7] We paraphrase: individualism (and the often-associated selfishness, even greed) actually promotes competition, which, when healthy, promotes society by boosting overall productivity. The words of this Scottish philosopher were fundamental in the design of the American social, economic, and political system that so greatly influenced the rest of the world in the last half of the twentieth century. The date is important. All of our founding fathers would have read and been deeply influenced by his tome at the time. Perhaps even more important is the identity of his collaborator. Smith's arguments are in large part based on ideas about the American colonies, supplied by none other than our own Benjamin Franklin. The sage among the authors of our Constitution was very well acquainted with Adam Smith.

And Smith's epiphany solved the human conundrum of the ages. That is, "Do I worry about me or my group?" Smith advises folks, at least in the context of economic behavior, to simply worry about themselves and that will take care of your group. Individualism, even competition, are not simply justified, they're elevated as almost righteous. And Smith's philosophy writ large upon the blank slate of our new country. In Smith's own Great Britain, social hierarchy prevailed, thus limiting the impact of his ideas at home. So we Americans value individualism higher than even the United Kingdom, consistent with Hofstede's numbers in exhibit 12.3.

Finally, it is important to note that embedded in Smith's epiphany is a hedge. You may have gotten a glimpse of it in the Academy Award–winning movie *A Beautiful Mind*. Economist John Nash (played well by Russell Crowe) proved mathematically that it can be in one's self-interest to cooperate. But this would not have been news for Smith. Notice the latter's strategic use of the term *frequently*. Smith is clearly saying that there's room for cooperation in human society and economy. This is a notion often lost on Wall Street these days (think Gordon Gekko's "greed is good" diatribe in the movie *Wall Street*) and in our MBA programs around the country, where individualism, competition, even selfishness and greed are often exalted.

Long-winded perhaps we are. Our point here? We believe it's important for you to understand the depth of influence our culture of individualism has on our thinking. That knowledge frees you to consider the negative consequences of those cultural values. Indeed, even Adam Smith, the father of the philosophy of individualism, argued for cooperation. And there's no more sensible context for cooperation than your own extended family.

3. The Curse of Sameness

Little boxes on the hillside,
Little boxes made of ticky-tacky,
Little boxes on the hillside,
Little boxes all the same,
There's a green one and a pink one
And a blue one and a yellow one
And they're all made of ticky-tacky
And they all look the same.[8]

No one would argue about the importance of equality to society. That's one topic on which we even agree with the French! However, the high value we place on egalitarianism does cause problems when it comes to the design of communities. Edward T. Hall, anthropologist and father of the science of proxemics (the study of space), well describes the differences in community design he has observed:

In addition to positional value, the American pattern emphasizes equality and standardization of the segments which are used for measuring space or into which space is divided, be it a ruler or a suburban subdivision. We like our components to be standard and equal. American city blocks tend to have uniform dimensions whereas towns in many other parts of the world are laid out with unequal blocks. This suggests that it was no accident that mass production, made possible by the standardization of parts, had its origins in the United States.[9]

Our American value of equality serves us well when it comes to human relations, but not when it comes to community design. Home builders, consumers, and zoning officials tend to favor houses of equal value and size without mixing. Neighborhoods of mixed size, value, and use are disfavored. The current hue and cry against the so-called McMansions is the latest symptom of this downside to equality and, in this case, sameness. Or consider the recent report that PeopleSoft's billionaire founder, David Duffield, downsized his seventy-two-thousand-square-foot "castle" to only seventeen thousand square feet because his Alamo, California, neighbors protested its girth. His neighbors circulated a petition to limit houses to ten thousand square feet in the development where Duffield purchased a twenty-two-acre site. There is some humor here! Somehow we Americans have confused equality with sameness, and this has mightily deterred creativity in housing and community design.

Before we close this topic, we do want to make clear that egalitarianism and equality are important and pertinent in the discussion of multigenerational households in other respects. That is, egalitarianism promotes creativity by allowing all members of a group to table ideas—the more ideas the better. Moreover, egalitarianism is also important in negotiations. In chapter 6 we presented the decision to live together as a negotiation among adults. Once kids are eighteen, they are *legally independent*. According to the law of the land, no one owes anyone anything across the parent-child relationship at that point. And the negotiation about living together proceeds most efficiently by recognizing this fundamental equality, the fairest question being, "What resources do you have to offer in this relationship?"

4. The Curse of Wide-Open Spaces

The original colonizers of America came for the wide-open spaces. The appeal of the road trip goes back some five hundred years. Seeing new things and getting away from the crowds attracted our ancestors and still attracts people today. And this fundamental yearning for being in and particularly owning the wide-open spaces has a dramatic, if somewhat hidden, influence on our daily lives. Edward T. Hall puts it best when he explains how space speaks:

> Man has developed his territoriality to an almost unbelievable extent. Yet we treat space somewhat as we treat sex. It is there but we don't talk about it. And if we do, we certainly are not expected to get technical or serious about it. . . . The man of the house is always somewhat apologetic about "his chair." How many people have had the experience of coming into a room, seeing a big comfortable chair and heading for it, only to pull up short, or pause and turn to the man and say, "Oh, was I about to sit in your chair?" The reply, of course, is usually polite. Imagine the effect if the host were to give vent to his true feelings and say, "Hell, yes, you're sitting in my chair, and I don't like anybody sitting in my chair." For some unknown reason, our culture has tended to play down or cause us to repress and dissociate the feelings we have about space. We relegate it to the informal and are likely to feel guilty whenever we find ourselves getting angry because someone has taken our place. . . .
>
> Once while talking on this subject to a group of Americans who were going overseas, one very nice, exceedingly mild-mannered woman raised her hand and said, "You mean it's natural for me to feel irritated when another woman takes over my kitchen?" Answer: "Not only is it natural, but most American women have very strong feelings about their kitchens. Even a mother can't come in and wash the dishes in her daughter's kitchen without annoying her. The kitchen is the place where 'who will dominate' is settled. All women know this, and some can even talk about it. Daughters who can't keep control of their kitchen will be forever under the thumb of any women who can move into this area."
>
> The questioner continued: "You know that makes me feel so relieved. I have three older sisters and a mother, and every time they come to visit they march right into the kitchen and take over. I want to tell them to stay out of my kitchen, that they have their own kitchens and this is my kitchen, but I always thought I was having unkind thoughts about my mother and sisters, thoughts I wasn't supposed to have. This relieves me so much, because now I know I was right."
>
> Father's shop is, or course, another sacred territory and best kept that way. The same applies to his study, if he has one.[10]

The territoriality so well elucidated by Hall is of course related to the individualistic competitiveness described earlier. Indeed, individualism + territoriality = privacy. And privacy needs are the bane of most extended-family arrangements.

A related aspect of our wide-open spaces is the value we Americans place on size. Supersizing meals at restaurants is making Americans fat. How about our housing? It's clear that for mainstream Americans at the turn of the twenty-first century, size is equated with status. This has been so for some time—note Edward Hall's comments on this topic:

> Our pattern calls for the president or the chairman of the board to have the biggest office. The executive vice-president will have the next largest, and so on down the line until you end up in the "bull pen." More important offices are usually located at the corners of and on the upper floors of the building. Executive suites will be on the top floor. The relative rank of the vice-presidents will be reflected in where they are placed along "executive row." The French, on the other hand, are much more likely to lay out space as a network of connecting points of influence, activity, or interest. The French supervisor will ordinarily be found in the middle of his subordinates where he can control them.
>
> Americans who are crowded will often feel that their status in the organization is suffering. As one would expect in the Arab world, the location of an office and its size constitute a poor index of the importance of the man who occupies it. What we experience as crowded, the Arab will often regard as spacious. The same is true in Spanish culture. . . .
>
> The American will look at a Japanese room and remark how bare it is. Similarly, the Japanese will look at our rooms and comment, "How bare!" Furniture in the American home tends to be placed along the walls (around the edge). Japanese have their charcoal pit where the family gathers in the middle of the room. The top floor of Japanese department stores is not reserved for the chief executive—it is the bargain roof![11]

Like American offices, our housing reflects the value we place on view, elevation, and, of course, size. This is actually good news, because the girth of our houses allows for creativity in how we use the space inside. That is, if we can just suppress some of our values for individual privacy. Indeed, the size of new single-family homes has grown both in terms of square feet per house and the average number of rooms per house—see exhibits 12.4 and 12.5. Ann and Paul Ehrlich add that the size of the American house has nearly doubled in the last fifty years.[12]

Exhibit 12.4. Median Square Feet in New Single-Family Houses (1973–2010)

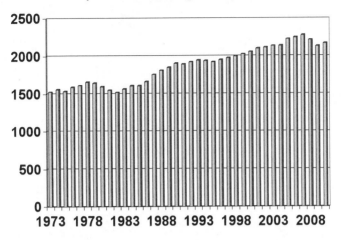

Source: U.S. Census Bureau.

Exhibit 12.5. Median Number of Rooms in Existing Single-Family Houses

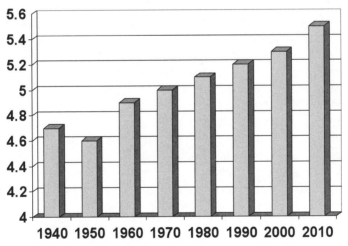

Source: U.S. Census Bureau.

Further, our houses remain among the most sparsely populated among nations around the world. See exhibit 12.6, although we must point out that this difference has abated some during the last five years. Among all the countries listed, only in the United States did the number of occupants between 2005 and 2010 actually increase, that is, from 2.58 to 2.62.

Exhibit 12.6. Occupants per Household

Germany	2.04
Sweden	2.04
Netherlands	2.27
United Kingdom	2.26
France	2.31
Italy	2.47
Japan	2.49
Canada	2.60
Spain	2.61
United States+	2.62
South Korea*	2.70
China*	3.39
Mexico*	3.85
Philippines*	4.82
India*	5.24

Source: Euromonitor, 2012.
* Top five countries of immigration to the United States.
+ The only country where household size increased from 2005 to 2010.

Folks from all around the world are astonished by how much room we Americans take up, how big our houses are. When a Dutch friend said about his first visit to an American home, "Your refrigerator is bigger than my closest," he was not only commenting on the size of the appliance. He was also commenting on the size of his closet back in the Netherlands! Yes, Europeans stop by the grocery store more often because the typical home only has one relatively small refrigerator, while many American homes have two big ones. Similarly, Europeans do own nice clothing, they just don't own as much as comparable Americans. They don't have walk-in closets, let alone ones with furniture in them as some new homes do now.

While American closets have been expanding, so have American garages. American men, of course, disparage the expanding closet, even if sometimes unintentionally. For example, John was even stupid enough to respond to his wife's question about a new pair of shoes with, "I thought you already had a pair of black shoes." But a man's garage is the home for his next best power drill. And while we are all making our closets and garages bigger to store the fruits of our consumerism, we are shrinking the space and time for our family interactions.

Recall the comments from Patrick Hare from the beginning of chapter 7: thirty-two percent of American homes have the potential for accommodating accessory apartments. Since he made his original calculations almost twenty years ago, American homes have become even larger, with fewer people under any one roof. All these figures suggest there is housing capacity available in the United States, if we can just be creative in our building and usage practices and adjust our basic values to allow for extended-family living. The "curse of wide-open spaces" can be transformed into a blessing of space for more generations as we progress into the twenty-first century.

The Blessing of Immigration

Many in the country today decry immigration as a major social problem for America—the curse of the unwashed knocking on our doors. We don't see it that way. Immigrants to the United States have always brought with them a bounty of new ideas. Now they are showing us new ways to live, or actually old ways, depending on how you look at multigenerational families and housing. As indicated in exhibits 12.7 and 12.8, most of the foreign-born folks in this country and most of the recent immigrants are from countries where multigenerational households have always worked and are still working well. Indeed, we get the term *casita* from our southern neighbors.

Exhibit 12.7. Foreign-Born Americans—Where They're From

Foreign-Born Population with Region of Birth Reported	40 million
Europe	4.8 million
Asia	11.3 million
Africa	1.6 million
Caribbean	3.7 million
Central America	14.8 million
South America	2.7 million

Source: U.S. Census Bureau, 2012.

Exhibit 12.8. Top Nine Countries of Origin of Immigrants to the United States, 2008–2010

Mexico	579,000
China	258,000
India	231,000
Philippines	124,000
Korea*	96,000
Cuba	84,000
Dominican Republic	81,000
Vietnam	72,000
El Salvador	60,000
Other	1,416,000

Source: U.S. Census Bureau, 2012.
*From both North and South Korea
Note: 2008–2010 total immigration to the U.S. was 2,998,000.

We close this chapter with excerpts from two of our interviews with immigrants to the United States who are thriving in three-generation households. You will notice they do not suffer from any of the four curses: the need for independence, individualism, sameness, or wide-open spaces. We can and should learn from them. We will need the blessings of their good ideas to help us manage the changing circumstances of twenty-first-century America.

As you may recall, in chapter 5, Lan, a first-generation immigrant from China, told us how she's imported the psychological advantages of three-generation living here to the United States. Her husband, their two children, and she live in a town house right next door to her parents. Lan said this housing arrangement works so well for all of them. Her parents can enjoy being with the grandkids every day, whenever they want. Likewise, the children love having the grandparents nearby. Her parents also help with babysitting, and since they don't drive or speak English very well, she is happy to take them shopping or to doctors' appointments. When asked whose idea it was to live together, she said:

Lan: It was my idea. I'm the one who brought them here. I'm responsible for them, and I wanted to make sure my parents are happy. If they lived far away in China, I would always be wondering if they were all right. They have retirement income in China, but no family there to take care of them when they get older. I think they take care of you after you are born. Then, by the time you grow up, you see things, you are learning. Those things in your mind are really strong. They are your parents; they give you life. Now that you're grown up it's time for you to do something nice for your parents. You have to welcome them and make sure your parents are happy and healthy. If your parents are happy and all right, you are happy.

Ironically, the worst of Western values seem to be seeping back in the direction of Lan's original home, aided by the new affluence delivered by the changing business system—at least as reported in the *Wall Street Journal*:

For thousands of years, Chinese have made the family paramount, with generations often living together, and younger members deferring to their elders. Fathers were the head of the household. But opportunities born of China's move to a market-based economy over the past two-dozen years are creating new wealth, new hierarchies and new strains. The scramble to keep up with neighbors, or one's own relatives, is testing family ties, contributing to a rise in social problems. . . .

Younger Chinese are opting for privacy over extended-family living and buying parents their own apartments. Others are putting their aging parents in nursing homes, as convenience trumps filial piety, an unheard-of violation of Confucian ethics. Over the past decade, the number of nursing-home residents has increased 40 percent to more than one million.[13]

Let's hope for the sake of the Chinese that this is another case of journalistic overstatement similar to the pejorative descriptions of the boomerang generation described at the beginning of this chapter. Indeed, twenty years of the new economy will change things for some, but we don't imagine most Chinese will give up on exchanging support across the generations as they've done across the millennia.

Finally and appropriately, let's go to where famed anthropologist Margaret Mead first learned about the power of culture and about how families work in other places. We've heard about Hawaiian *ohanas* and such. Paula comments here about the three-generation glue that traveled with her from the Pacific Islands that Mead first visited so long ago:

Paula: Well, we have Pacific Islanders and that's a really close network. There are two different types of Pacific Islanders. There are Samoans and then there are Tongans. They both have very close networks where the family lives together—the mother and the father and the children. Once the children get married, they come back into the family, preferably the father's family. It's a closer network. When the daughters get married, they come back with their husbands. They pool their money together and they purchase a home for the oldest sibling. That's how they get their homes. So then they start their own trickle-off, and then they get cousins and nephews and all come in together . . . pooling their funds together, resources together. You have the grandparents raising the children, while the daughters and sons are out working.

Conclusions

For some fifty years now, Americans have drifted away from family structures that have always before delivered happy and successful lives for most. Ignoring the importance of interdependence in favor of a mythical independence has hurt our interpersonal and familial relationships. While individualism and competitiveness often work well in the marketplace, they have no place in the context of a cooperative three-generation family arrangement. The sameness, often mistaken for equality, has lead to homogeneous neighborhoods that suffer from a lack of multigenerational participation. A culture of yearning for wide-open spaces has yielded a neglect of those close by. Luckily, new Americans are reminding us of the old ways that can work again now and in the coming years. Please pay attention to your culture. Recognize its many strengths, but at the same time resist its constraints.

Financial and Legal Considerations

Since the dawn of history, the family has been humankind's most efficient economic unit.

—RALPH WARNER[1]

HAT'S THE WORST THING that could happen? That's what an
attorney is paid to think about—the worst things that could happen. Indeed, for this chapter (and book) we have to include our
own disclaimer for fear of litigation. That is, the laws and tax
codes vary substantially across the fifty states and the District of
Columbia. We are neither attorneys nor tax experts. We have talked to some
of those. But what works in one state may not in another. What works for
one family may not for another. So we are not giving you specific advice
here. We are only trying to demonstrate how some folks in different places
around the country have handled the financial and legal aspects of living
together again in extended-family arrangements. At the end of this chapter,
you should know the right set of questions to ask financial and legal professionals, should you decide to consult them.

What's the worst thing that could happen? Family disagreements about
money and such can often destroy families. Good intentions are important.
But planning, anticipating, and writing things down can mitigate the potential conflicts that do erupt among family members. Talking to legal and

financial experts ahead of time can go a long way toward easing the friction, particularly when family agreements don't work out, key family members die suddenly, or economic circumstances deliver unpleasant surprises.

So you will still want to talk with a local attorney and tax consultant, particularly if you are planning to mix resources by living together with your adult kids or parents. Below we will try to cover some of the more important issues, but, of course, it will be your job to make your bed before you sleep in it, so to speak. We can only tell you where the sheets are. See exhibit 13.1 for the issues that demand your consideration and that you may wish to consult with the experts about. Heads up on these as you read this chapter and as you begin to think about and plan your multigenerational living arrangements.

Exhibit 13.1. Issues to Consider

Financial Issues	Legal Issues
Down payments and mortgage(s)	Ownership/control
Rent	Inheritance (trusts and wills)
Property taxes	Nonperformance
Transfer of wealth (estate/gift) taxes	—health crisis
Insurance (property, liability, health, life)	—employment crisis
Utilities	—pension crisis
Maintenance/repairs	Contracts
Remodeling	—Legal relationships
Goodwill of the siblings	—Caregiving contracts

Now, let's get to the good stuff. The folks we've interviewed have told us about all kinds of creative ways to conclude negotiated agreements with sons, daughters, sisters, brothers, mothers, and fathers that help make living together again a comfortable experience.

Household Finances

When living together again, how do you manage household finances? Simply put, who pays for what? In most cases, individuals living together pay for their own separate phone lines and groceries. Making agreements up front regarding rent, utility bills, mortgage, and taxes is an important step in keeping the peace.

Down Payments and Mortgages

As you will see below, a variety of approaches have been reported by the folks we've interviewed in arranging for the financing of their three-generation housing. Most of these substantial financial arrangements depend on the continuing goodwill of the family members, at least as described in the interviews. Just below are people's comments about down payments and mortgages.

Nancy: Since we owned our previous house, we had a great deal of money to put into the new place that we were buying with our daughter and her husband. But they had the money coming in monthly to take care of a great many of the expenses of the house. That part has worked out very, very well. Naturally, we don't make the kind of money that our son-in-law is making. So financially, from that standpoint, it has worked out beautifully, freeing us up. When you think about it, it makes a lot of sense. We do share in the mortgage. We both pay equally the mortgage. Our son-in-law and my husband got together and figured out what should be done.

Roger: We have all three of our kids living in separate quarters on our property now. One of them built his own house and is buying a fraction of our property. We have an arrangement where they are paying us what will amount to one-quarter of the appraised value. The downside is that the other two siblings aren't able to participate—they don't have the money. So we thought that we'll just do this because otherwise it just goes into our estate.

Leslie: A Realtor suggested I take the money from selling my house and build an apartment onto my daughter's home. She and her husband agreed to the idea but then ended up having to buy another house with enough property to do it. So they sold their house and moved into a bigger home with a lot. I helped them a little bit financially. Then after they were there for about a year, I put an addition on it. My apartment is about 1,200 square feet. I have my own private entrance, and it just works out very well.

Sharon: And financially, after you sold your house, you helped pay for the remodel yourself?

Leslie: Yes, I did. Also, they're paying me back the money I initially gave them to help with the down payment for their new house.

Sharon: So that's a form of income for you.

Leslie: They haven't started yet, but that is what they plan on doing. So I am on the title right now.

Sharon: So will that be a form of retirement income for you?

Leslie: It could be. But eventually, they would like for me to get off the title, which I would want to do. My unit I paid for. They said that if they ever sold the house, they would give me back the money I put into it. So that would include the money for the down payment to their house, as well as what I put into my addition. That was written in. I did agree that they would only have to pay back half of what I put into their house. The other half I'm giving to them as a gift because if ever I get old and feeble, they are going to have the brunt of taking care of me. So it was sort of a reward to them for taking this responsibility.

Sharon: You were saying that the Pacific Islander families will pool resources. Do they leave initially and then come back when they marry? Do they ever leave home?

Paula: They don't leave home until their resources are all together. I guess they have a situation where the older sibling is the first one to leave the house.

Sharon: So the family, including brothers, sisters, and parents, will come up with a little stash of cash to help the older kids get the down payment for a house and then leave home.

And, recall the story told in chapter 10 by Judy Richter of the *San Francisco Chronicle* about the creation of a family compound in Fairfield, California. We repeat the comments about financing here:

> Finding financing for construction was difficult. The family invited loan officers to lunch to explain the dream, but possible default was a worry. Finally a loan officer from First Northern Bank agreed to lend the money.
>
> "He caught the vision," she said. The project cost $1.4 million— the equivalent of $466,666 per family—for the land, design and construction except for the pool, landscaping and solar panels.
>
> The Shiltses used some of Joe's retirement money to buy the land, and all three family groups pitched in for the down payment after selling their houses. They own the house as joint tenants, and each family contributes to a joint account that pays for the 15-year mortgage and other shared costs. Although the new house is unique, Joe Shilts estimates that buying three new Fairfield houses suited to each family's needs would have cost "at least twice what we paid." New single-family

detached houses in Fairfield can cost anywhere from about $600,000 to more than $1 million.[2]

Finally, as we mentioned in previous chapters, in Hawaii there is a cultural history favoring *ohanas* (accessory apartments). Mike told us he plans to take advantage of these options in continuing to expand a family compound on the Big Island.

Mike: It was designed so there would be a central sort of communal area surrounded by the other houses. Most of the houses would have *ohanas*, actually just as places for visiting family and friends. Obviously, family members are invited to stay or participate in ownership. But one person would buy all the property, and as other people came in, he would basically sell the property to them at cost.

Sharon: So it would be maybe your older brother assuming the responsibility of buying the land and selling you a portion of it?

Mike: Right. And you could buy into it. It's mostly family, but they were also talking about having close friends, especially for the *ohanas*. Just having close friends come in for an extended stay. So we would have a mix of individual houses and *ohanas*.

Rent

We talked with Mark, a young college student living in Southern California who shares an accessory apartment in his parents' home with his friend. A part of the written agreement he has with his parents includes a nominal charge for rent to help with household finances. Other families we talked with do the same thing. In one case, the parents told us that they are quietly banking the so-called rent to later give to their child as a surprise down payment for a future home. In another instance, the son-in-law of a couple we know lived at home with his parents rent free for twenty years before he married their daughter. In doing so, he saved a lot of money himself and was able to put a very large down payment on his first home. Most parents know whether their children are the type who will save money or spend it. Accordingly, unless it's a financial necessity for themselves, they can decide whether or not to charge rent.

So a rental agreement is a part of many three-generation households where the property ownership is not split. Sometimes the kids and sometimes the parents are paying the rent. We start with Carol, a young woman who lives with her husband and two small children in a duplex next door to her parents.

Carol: At this point, we pay my parents five hundred dollars a month rent. When we first moved in, I was in law school and we were rent free. At some point, they offered to pay off all my law school loans. Then they said, "Well, how about, if you don't have that burden anymore, then you guys can start paying us rent." Obviously, five hundred dollars a month is below the market for anything around here. So that's something that we are contributing to them. Of course, by paying so little we are also saving money for our future home.

Lan: I own only my town house. The other one next door, my father-in-law owns. So for that one, where my parents live, I have to pay half the rent and my brother, who lives with them, the other half.

Mark: We wrote up a little lease. The rules I can remember are no smoking, we have to park on the street, no one else is allowed to move in with us. We normally have my parents call when they want to come. And it includes the rent. That's about it.

Frank: Even though our son owns his own home, he saves money by renting it out. He lives rent free with his grandmother and by doing so is better able to afford the mortgage on his place. When he gets married next year, he and his bride will move into his home. With both of them working and living together, their two incomes will make it easier for them to pay the mortgage.

Patrick Hare: Here is a story I use a lot in lectures. A woman sold her house to her daughter on the condition that the woman's mother, her daughter's grandmother, had a permanent lease for the rest of her life of the accessory apartment in the basement for a dollar a year. So things are fine. Both the parents worked, and the grandmother played a major role raising the kids. Then the grandmother suffered a stroke. She came back somewhat lethargic for a long time, and it seemed she didn't want to continue living. Both the daughter and her husband had a crisis in their work, and asked the grandmother to take back over at least some of the work she had been doing in taking care of the kids. That is when the grandmother came back to life!

Property Taxes

Most folks we talked to were just splitting the property taxes one way or another. The following is exemplary:

Norma: I get a copy of the tax bill on the lots here including this house. Being a mortgage broker, he [my son] calculates the amounts we both owe. So he figures out what he owes and he pays me, or I pay him my portion. So the tax bill gets paid.

Transfer of Wealth (Estate/Gift) Taxes

Many of the families we have talked to around the country see two primary purposes of three-generation household arrangements. The one we have discussed in great detail is the exchange of care services across the generations. Another important consideration is the transfer of wealth to the younger generations. The form of many of the agreements we've heard about reflect this latter purpose.

Eleanor: I think one of the greatest benefits, beyond the fact that you have your family close, is the financial benefit gained by making arrangements to reduce or eliminate many aspects of inheritance and estate taxes. The fact that the parent can come and say, "Look, we got this much out of our house and we want to do an addition on your house for us to live in. Then we can form a partnership or other type of legal arrangement." It's a wonderful way in which to give to your children this gift from you, without having to pay a lot of tax on it. It's something that you need to be aware of and that you can do. For example, I now have a 5,500-square-foot house because I've added five hundred square feet of garage and a thousand square feet onto it for my mother to live in. As the years come and go and we sell this, we're going to reap the benefits of that. I can turn around perhaps at that point and say to my children, "Let's build an addition on your house." That way, they will inherit this money, and it will keep surviving for many years to come after I'm gone.

Susan: I think there are two really important things about living together. One is the personal relationships that people have and how that is related to the physical layout of the shared space. The management of the costs and inheritance of the home are also very significant. It is important to get professional help with the latter. Just assuming that if you die the kids will take over the house, it's not that easy. The taxes could be terrible with our kinds of housing values. The government is very confusing about the rules on all of this. It's not nearly as simple as a lot of people think it is.

For instance, I'm involved with a revocable family trust. It means that I can change my mind. There is a point when it has to be made irrevocable for them to use it in some ways, but I think that's after I die, at which point maybe it becomes irrevocable. And I gift them thirteen thousand dollars a year (the legal limit of tax-free giving as of 2012) as part of the house equity. We have an attorney who does it. It is relatively complicated, because they actually do something called "fractiles," in which they say that a portion of a million dollar house is not really worth much, so they take a greater proportion to get up to thirteen thousand dollars. That makes quite a difference in proportion that you're giving or getting. And, of course, the houses here are so expensive, you have to wait a long time to give them a great deal of it. I don't really understand it, but we do what the lawyers and tax people tell us to do. Definitely get professional advice on how to get it managed.

Sharon: You also have a second child, so how does that get worked out?

Susan: In fact, my domestic attorney gave me good advice about that. What I try to do is give my other daughter, Margie, thirteen thousand dollars a year. She's in the will, so that when the house becomes available on my death, her sister, Julie, who lives here, may have to end up paying Margie an amount of money for some years to pay for her half of the house. They're not likely to have a lump sum to give her. That's something we should sit down and work out better. It's written down how it will be done, but the actual amounts have not been determined. Also, Julie and her husband should get some credit for the remodeling and house maintenance they're doing on the house. It's almost like they're beginning to pay part of the mortgage. By the way, if I were to die and they were living here, they could rent out this apartment where I'm now living. If they just paid the rent on this place to Margie, that would be a nice way to handle it.

Insurance (Property, Liability, Health, and Life)

The viability of the family partnership that we are recommending depends on hedging the risks of potential disasters related to both the property and the people living there. Fire, flood, accidents, and so on must be anticipated and insured against. Obviously, health and life insurance are associated with the individuals in the family, and the expenses are thus easy to assign. But property and the associated liability insurance will require thoughtful rules of division similar to property taxes and such. The key here is that all potential beneficiaries should be informed and consulted, given the intimate involvement and financial interdependence of the extended family unit.

Utilities

As for parents living in their adult children's home, we also found instances where rent is charged to help with household expenses. Caroline, a Northern California widow, will soon be living with her daughter, son-in-law, and two grandchildren in an apartment in their house. When asked how they plan to handle household expenses, such as utilities, she replied:

Caroline: Well we talked about that and came to the conclusion that rather than doing a percentage of what gas and electricity I use, I would pay them a flat rate for monthly expenses. Also, I would have my own phone line. It's just too complicated to figure out who uses what percent of what on the bills that come in.

Another couple we talked to in Washington take a different approach. They have a large lot with two accessory units where two sets of adult children are now living. In one case, a single daughter lives with her child in the unit attached to their home. Because of economic necessity, the parents pay the utilities for her and the grandchild. It's a different story for the other daughter. Using their own money, she and her husband built a small house on the property for themselves and their three children. Here's what Roger, the father of the married daughter, had to say about how they handle the utility bills:

Roger: We have a single lot, but they have a separate meter. So when I get the bill, I give a copy of it to my son-in-law, Charlie. He reads his meter, knows how much he has used, and makes that adjustment. We do the same with the water; we each pay our own share.

Of course, those who live in duplexes, houses, town houses, or condos in the same building have entirely separate meters for utilities and receive separate bills. This separation certainly makes their lives a lot easier, in most cases eliminating the need to make agreements about utilities. However, in many other cases, we found that families pay all the utility expenses for either parents or adult children who live with them in attached apartments or cottages in the backyard. They also tend to pay the mortgage, insurance, and property taxes themselves.

Maintenance and Repairs

Depending on the circumstances of home ownership, financial capabilities, and personal preferences, there are a number of ways that families can handle property maintenance. Susan lives in a converted garage in the backyard, while her daughter, son-in-law, and three grandchildren live in the main house on the property. Although Susan owns the house, she has made provisions for her daughter to eventually inherit it. Here's what she told us about how they pay for household repairs:

Susan: So far, I pay for every major repair on the house. I do have a home equity loan, which, of course, will be deducted from the value of the house when they take it over. And that, at least, reduces the taxes. Of course, they may inherit a loan that they'll have to pay. But for them to live here is a lot less than they would ever have to pay for a house anywhere around here. Meanwhile, I have this great advantage of having a son-in-law who will do most of the fix-it work. Before they came, when I was here by myself, I used to have to hire someone to come in to do things.

Gardening and other maintenance issues also came up with another family we talked to. Elena shares a duplex with her daughter, her son-in-law, and grandchildren. Here's what she had to say:

Elena: At first, I didn't always agree with what their yard should look like. I would offer to go in and help. On my way in or out of their house, I would pull weeds along the way in and just dump them. They were both working and they didn't have time to do that. Now we both have gardeners and things look a lot better. Also, even though I have the smaller of the two units, I own 50 percent of the whole property. So whenever we put a new roof on, we will share half and half in the costs.

Remodeling

Remodeling can also be a source of angst, particularly when long-term and short-term views collide:

Paula: My mother had about two more years before she retired. She decided to sell her home. My sister and her three children were living with her at the time. My mom decided, "I've got to make a move. I've got to go on." She realized that staying in Silicon Valley with the high cost of living wouldn't work for her as a retired person. So she decided to put the house up for sale and it sold within thirty days. Since she had to stay at her job to get the full benefits of retirement, she thought she would purchase a mobile home, which was a couple of blocks away. At the last minute, she said, "Well, you have a garage and it's detached with a bathroom in it. Why don't I fix it up, and I'll stay there until I retire?" My husband and I were already thinking about doing that anyway, so we agreed. We wanted a little hideaway place for us away from our three kids.

The only problem that I saw was with my husband and my mom. Since Mom's paying for it, I thought we should let her make all of the decisions on the remodel. But my husband as the head of the house had his own way of thinking of how he wanted it done. I had to pull his coattail and say, "Did we put any money in this?" There were times he said, "I want this type of toilet." I'd say, "Well, then pay for it." That happened a lot. He knew that my mom had money but also wanted to let her know that he could pay for some things too.

Contracts

Several of the folks we talked with provided their insights into the importance of writing things down in signed contracts, particularly when arrangements are complicated. A bit later in the chapter we include an interview with a legal expert on several of the topics mentioned here. But the fundamental point is best made by Tony:

Tony: You really have to treat it like a business deal, like a business transaction. Because if you do it on a personal level, it is easier to hurt up front than it is down the road.

Helen, a knowledgeable real estate agent, told us about how complex things can get.

Helen: It depends on how you hold title on a property when one party dies, if parts need to be sold or it can be deeded to the other person. So you want to make sure that doesn't put your children in jeopardy financially or force them to move out of their housing situation. Who gets the tax benefits for the property and what is the percentage? What happens if one party decides to leave? There needs to be a mechanism on how that part can be sold or if both parties decide to sell. When two parties own a property and one party chooses to sell, the value of that parcel is devalued perhaps 20 to 30 percent, because no one in the market wants to buy into a family situation.

Sharon: I am just wondering if what you are talking about is a shared piece of property? With your situation with the house next door to your daughter, there is no concern about that because you own it outright. I guess what we have been talking about is really the idea of the guest cottage or two families investing together in the same property. Do you have a recommendation if you were going in on a piece of property with your children, how would you set it up for yourself?

Helen: I would make sure that it was a big enough piece of dirt that we could subdivide and put it in separate ownership. My experience is that when you mix money and emotions and family it can get really messy.

Sharon: What is happening these days are situations where families just can't make it unless they combine resources. So if parents offer to buy a house and tell their adult children they can live in it while they will live in the cottage in the backyard, is there a way that you would suggest structuring that?

Helen: I guess you have to have a good understanding of who your kids are and how they work. It is probably cleaner if you own the property, and you might want to sublet. There are a lot of ways to do it. If your children rent, a lot of parents would put that money in an account for the children later on and not even tell them about it. You need to talk to a very sophisticated accountant. This is particularly so because the pertinent tax laws are complex and they change substantially from year to year.

Sharon: What happens if you want to loan your kids money for a down payment on a house?

Helen: One option is to make the loan and then gift it back to them over time. If you do choose to forgive the loan by gifting it to them, you can gift up to thirteen thousand dollars per year. What I do is gift my children a portion of the loan I gave them for their house every year in January; it is on paper. I send them a letter stating that I've done this; they sign and return it to me. That way I have a paper trail that I've lent them this money, but in reality I gifted it to them.

Many folks also have questions about contracts and legal and financial options. Here are some of those:

Dan: When it comes to financial matters and combining resources, are advantages gone and flexibility reduced because you are intermingling? What will that look like? What have other people done? What would the lawyer say? That would be helpful. We are going to have to find information ourselves, so if you could give us examples of what other people are getting into, that would be great. Because regardless of the specifics, if there is any intermingling going on, what are the dos and don'ts?

Mary: I guess you also have to consider the other siblings involved.

Dan: That is a tough one too, because my daughter has a family and she is so very much on the outside, not included in this. She sees us doing things for them that she would like to be involved in and stuff like that. We haven't worked that out yet, but we will.

Here Todd and Lynne ponder the issues associated with building a casita on their property for her mother, and Eleanor talks about what she did:

Todd: For the utilities and phone, we will probably be able to run separate lines. We will be able to get two services for the power so that it can be completely separate. We will run into problems when it comes to the mortgage. If there are two separate mortgages, then we run into subdivision restrictions. So we will be kind of playing with that. Technically, it will be our house. Either she is listed on our property title as a tenant, or she gets to gift us the money for *x* number of years for the house, and we make the payments. We can get it to the point where we both own the mortgage, are paying a percentage, and can take the deductions. Essentially, we've talked about this being our inheritance up front.

Lynne: I think it would be nice to have a section in the book regarding tax and estate planning and what ways to get around issues. . . . But just the whole idea of how to prepare your estate and how to prepare yourself financially is complicated, especially when there are other siblings involved that are not involved in this housing situation. So how do we do it clean and fair? Those are questions that we still don't have answered.

Eleanor: I think there are a lot of questions that people don't think to ask. I have consulted with some families who are considering doing this. There are a lot of issues that come up about "Mom or Dad has their own home and we need to sell that and we're going to use the funds from that to build this addition." That's all well and good; however, there are tax situations to be dealt with. There are inheritance situations. If Mom or Dad is in a nursing home, there are other situations to get into there. If they have certain types of problems, you have to think ahead when you are going to do the construction. Are they ill? Do they have a special situation? What are the tax problems? What are the inheritance problems? How are you going to handle the money issue? What are you going to cover? Also, if there are health considerations, it's much less expensive to prepare the house for that when you build than it is to go back and retrofit. Retrofitting is very difficult sometimes.

A Model of How to Do Things

One of our families has been particularly conscientious in organizing the financial and legal affairs associated with their special three-generation household. Their case touches on many of the questions described just above. They live in a big home, in a nice neighborhood, with three kids and the mom and dad in the main house and the grandparents in the spacious pool house out back. It's a perfect setting, but it took a while for them to get settled. Let's let them describe it in their own words:

Janet: When we first moved in here it was crazy. We didn't know whose responsibility was what. Four adults managing a home is hard. The gardener would come. We didn't know who would instruct the gardener. The pool guy would come. Who was in charge of that? Something would break down. I felt like with four adults someone should be in charge. It took a while to delineate responsibility.

Craig: We did set up ground rules for household finances and bills. We just kind of sat down and figured out who pays what. It probably only took us forty-five minutes. Certain things were split 50/50 like the gardener. Initially, the property taxes were also 50/50, because when we started, we had equal shares of the whole place. Other things we use more of, so we should pay more. Since we have three-quarters of the total square footage of the house and cottage combined, we pay three-quarters of the power bill. We each have our own telephone. We don't get too detailed; we either say it's 50/50 or 75/25. Then whatever the bill is that month, we'll each pay our respective percentage.

Sharon: So you had a democratic meeting it sounds like?

Craig: Right. When we bought this place together, it worked out perfectly. It worked out because an older generation usually has either equity in a property already, or they have cash savings. But they don't have a lot of income if they're retired. Whereas the younger generation doesn't have the savings and equity, but they are at or entering a peak earning capacity. So when you look at a normal mortgage, you have typically 20 percent down and a high monthly payment. In our circumstances, Janet's parents didn't even have a mortgage on their previous home. They owned a nice piece of property outright. We were kind of a typical younger family with young kids, doing fine in our second or third home. But we were outgrowing our house. Although to find a bigger one to buy, we could afford a larger monthly payment, it would have been difficult to scrape together a down payment large enough to keep the monthly payment reasonable.

So the way we approached this is 50/50. They actually were able to spend less than they would have if they had found another house. Fifty percent of this property at the time was less expensive than a smaller property would have been for them. We put our home equity in too, but we took roughly the

80/20 rule. We contributed 20 percent of the down payment, and we pay about 80 percent of the monthly mortgage. They were responsible for 80 percent of the down payment, and they pay 20 percent of the monthly mortgage. So it solves both things, because they didn't want to have a large mortgage payment, and they shouldn't. And we're completely comfortable with it, because we wouldn't have been able to come up with such a large down payment by ourselves.

Sharon: So in terms of ownership, are you 50/50?

Craig: Exactly. We have agreed that it is a 50/50 ownership. At the present time, they actually have contributed more than we have, because their down payment was so large. Since our monthly payments are so much greater than their payments, the ratio of cash each of us has in the home reduces each month. At a certain point in time, the sum of our monthly payments will equal their total cash contribution. From that time on, we'll have put more cash in the house than them. Nevertheless, we agreed on a 50/50 ownership, regardless of the amount of time we'll live here together.

Sharon: Ultimately, then, say they should pass away, how would you work that out with your siblings?

Craig: Their 50 percent interest would go into a family trust and be divided up between the beneficiaries. After they pass away, and when that equity is requested by other siblings, we would refinance the house. We would convert their interest into cash to pay them off, so we could still remain in the house. It has to be fair for everybody.

Goodwill of the Siblings

Consideration of their siblings was mentioned by several of the folks we interviewed. We are not really surprised by such consideration expressed by our sample because they are all cooperative family members, in a sense defined as such by their extended-family living circumstances. Our point here is that the best care for the elderly is delivered by all their kids' combined efforts. Obviously, in most cases only one child will carry the burden of cohabitation, that is, if and when it becomes a burden. But all the kids should pitch in as they can. And the goodwill of one's siblings becomes an important family asset in both the interpersonal and financial senses. It is an asset that should be invested in, particularly in the context of any extended-family agreement.

Perspectives from a Legal Expert

As you know, we've interviewed more than one hundred Americans involved in extended-family living arrangements, and with the exception of this chapter, we have primarily focused on the interpersonal aspects of this wonderful institution. The interpersonal aspects are our area of expertise. When it comes to the rich mix of legal and financial issues described above, we've called in a relief pitcher so to speak. Tom Peterson, a partner of the Orange County, California, firm of O'Brien and Peterson, has practiced law, specializing in general business, real estate, and estate planning, for thirty-two years. John's interview with him, on what Mr. Peterson calls a "new area" of law, is both interesting and informative. So we've included it here in its entirety.

John: What I tried to do is make up this case and talk about a specific example. Let's take the example of our "model" family as just described in the previous section. Recall that a daughter and her husband decided to move in with the daughter's parents. They decided to buy one home that has a large pool house. So the parents are living in the pool house and the daughter, son-in-law, and three kids are living in the main house. The younger folks are paying 80 percent of the mortgage and they put up 20 percent of the down payment on this piece of property. The older folks put up 80 percent of the down payment and are paying 20 percent of the mortgage. They share the ownership of the property 50/50. So the question is what are the different legal instruments that might be applied in such a case? Let's also assume that the daughter (and parents) is worried about how her brother will react to this substantial blending of his sister's and his parents' resources? One of the things I would like to do is make a list of the concerns and a list of the instruments. By instruments, I mean things like a living trust and a will. Are there family partnerships and prenuptial or cohabitation agreements? What other legal instruments might be pertinent to this?

Tom: Well another one would just be the method of holding title to the property. So we just refer to *title holding documents*. Another could be just a straight *contractual agreement*. That's a pretty good list because otherwise you get pretty exotic. I don't think you need to be talking about *corporations* or *LLCs*. They are just forms of business entities. But the latter two are still possibilities. I would just lump them all together.

John: Would there be specialists that would handle these different things?

Tom: Yes. The *living trust* and the *will* would be done by an estate-planning attorney. The *family partnership* would be done by either an estate-planning attorney or a family law attorney. The *title holding documents* would be a real estate attorney primarily. The *contractual agreements* would be the business attorney. If you find somebody who does all of that, just let me know. I'm probably one of the closest. The only ones I don't do are the *nuptial agreements*. You need a family law attorney for these.

John: So if we go back to my example, I'm moving in with one of my kids and we're co-buying a house. One of my questions is, "How complicated do we want to make this?" The purpose would be to give our readers an example, saying, "See how complicated this actually is? You need to seek professional advice."

Tom: Well, I'm just shooting off ideas. There is sort of the simple way and the complex way. Just on your example of you and your wife moving in with one of your children or another relative, a simple approach would be to adjust how you hold the title to the property. So you could just say, assuming your daughter or son is married, that each of the four of you now hold the title one quarter each as tenants in common or as joint tenants, however you want to do it. That's so simple. It's just one title document and it's recorded. That's the ultimate simplicity. But the trade-off for that ultimate simplicity is that all of your rights, including determinations and survivorship, set according to law by how you set it up. So if you set it up as a joint tenancy among the four of you, then whoever is last standing gets the whole thing. If your son and his wife get killed in an automobile accident, the whole thing goes to you if you are the last standing, and their kids don't get anything, so it's a very simple thing to set up, but it probably doesn't meet your intentions because it's all done by rules of law that you don't control. It's the same if you do it as a tenancy in common. That means it's not the last standing. But it means that each quarter interest goes by law to whoever your heirs are. So if you have a will and direct who your heirs are going to be, you can do it that way. So that would take two documents: a *tenancy in common deed* and *wills*. If you didn't have wills or any estate-planning documents, the tenancy in common would just say it goes to whoever your heirs are by the succession law. So again it's very simple, but you may not accomplish what you wanted to accomplish.

John: So the other issues that need to be considered are (1) inheritance and (2) tax laws. We haven't even talked about tax implications. I wonder what else there is to worry about. Inheritance I realize is a very complex issue by itself. But what would be the tax implications of all of that? If we are thinking about the middle of the country, let's say it is a five hundred thousand dollar piece of property. Does the size of the property make a difference?

Tom: Sure, because there are currently a two million dollar estate tax and a one million dollar gift tax lifetime exemptions. So let's say this piece of property was worth two million dollars and there was a tenancy in common, then if something happens to you, you are going to be now dividing one quarter of that two million, so five hundred thousand dollars. So you would have been using five hundred thousand dollars of your exemptions based on this one piece of property. If you did it by joint tenancy, it automatically goes to the survivor, so you don't have to worry about doing any court probate, but the decedent's portion would still be included in his or her exemption. So there are all sorts of tax consequences that are going on there. On each one of these—the trust, will, partnerships, nuptial agreements, title contract, or business entity—the tax implications are very important and very tricky.

John: Do you think most folks do this by some kind of verbal agreement?

Tom: Without knowing them, that would be my guess. There are a lot of people that do these things just verbally. It's just not mothers and fathers and children and grandchildren. I've had a lot of cases of the father being the surviving parent and the mother passing away. The surviving parent is getting older and lonely, so he has somebody move in with him. So they have an agreement orally that they'll do this and do that if something happens to him. That gets to be real messy. Nine times out of ten it's just some oral agreement. People always say, "Well, it's just my family, or it's just my girlfriend. I trust them." It's not really a question of trust; it becomes a question of proof. How do you prove this was their agreement? And if you don't prove it, then it's going to go under inheritance law or some other state-mandated method. And especially having to prove it to the IRS. They are not going to say, "Well, that was your father, so we trust that you did it that way." The IRS doesn't care. They will say, "Well, prove that was the agreement that you had with your father or girlfriend."

John: Then what do you suggest?

Tom: Well, for the example you gave initially about the 80/20 down payment/mortgage split, I guess I would most recommend a *family partnership*. That's literally what they are doing, setting up a partnership among the four of them setting out who has what responsibility, getting what share of what. It really is a family partnership. You could do it by all the other different kinds of instruments, but boiling it down, it really is a family partnership. The problem with calling it a family partnership is that, from the IRS point of view, this implies that there is a business, a partnership business that's being conducted. In this case it's really not a business; it's really a method of dividing property and dividing the benefits or the burdens of that property as opposed to running a business. So either a family partnership or just a *straight contractual agreement* would be the simplest way for them to do that.

John: Then you would have a separate will for each person or a living trust to handle the inheritance issues?

Tom: Yes.

John: The tax implications would be managed through the living trust?

Tom: Yes, the living trust or in the will, that's pretty straightforward. The contractual agreement would need to be set up based on how it's being operated while they are all alive and . . . I'm trying to think of a way . . . you couldn't really control it upon death because the contract wouldn't be an estate-planning document. It wouldn't qualify as a will. It wouldn't qualify as a trust, although you could modify it to make it do those kinds of things, at least the trust part of it. So you have more of the contract governing how they deal with their property while they are alive, and you have an estate-planning document to take care of what happens if they pass. You could do very exotic things and have a contract that says, "We are all in this, but if something happens to one of us . . . we have a buy/sell agreement, so my share gets bought by the other three." For purposes of this, the purchase price is *x*, *y*, or *z*. So in effect you can keep that piece of property in the survivor's control, but you get a little more exotic at that point.

John: Now let's say I'm the father in this "model" arrangement described above. My wife and I are moving in with my daughter and her family, but at the same time I'm worried about the goodwill of my son. My son would have no legal recourse. But from my point of view, I want all my kids to feel like they are being treated fairly. So I need to specify for them what the kid that I'm living with is providing to me and my wife. One way to handle that would be an annual report of this family partnership agreement. I don't know if you have ever heard of such a thing.

Tom: Yes. It is a good idea even without worrying about nonparticipating siblings. It would also be useful for tax purposes as well.

John: So that's something you would recommend? It does two things: It's recording what's happening, and also it is informing the other family members who have an inheritance stake.

Tom: I would recommend it. I guess the question is who should get it or what is the purpose of doing it? One purpose is just to inform the participants, so you, your daughter, her husband, and your wife, everybody, knows the tax implications. You would almost have to do it for your housemates, but do you want to inform your son or other children so they know what's going on? That's not necessary, and they don't have any tax interest in this, so that would sort of be a bonus to them.

John: It's hard to avoid the problem that you were talking about. . . . I think that you said that very often the first time you hear from potential clients is when they are trying to figure out what to do about some cohabitation deal their parents and siblings are cooking up. So the idea would be to avoid that and to keep peace in the family. Sharon talked with a woman in San Diego whose mother moved close to them and they paid her housing costs for a five-year period. Now their youngest kid is going off to college. So the elderly mother is going to move next to the home of another sibling with another financial arrangement. So the question is, "How do you allocate credit for the help that everybody is giving?" The main thing would be just to inform everybody. If somebody has a complaint, then let them voice it.

Tom: But what is it that you are concerned about if they have a complaint? Let's say the brother who isn't part of this deal . . . I'm just talking from strictly a legal point of view. He doesn't have any legal complaint or any legal right or any legal say-so to this deal. But from a family point of view, just to know what's going on is different. Nonlegal issues are more significant in that situation. So let's assume that the nonparticipant son says, "Well how come Dad is only getting half of this even though he is putting up 80 percent of the money?" Suppose he gets upset about this? There is nothing legally he can do about it. Should he have some family right to say, "You guys need to modify this." I suppose that is what you are looking at.

John: I'm actually more worried about this arrangement. Let's say after five years or for whatever reason it dissolves and then the parents want to move in with another kid. You want their goodwill. You want to keep goodwill in the family. So it's not so much what recourse they might have; it's maintaining the goodwill so everybody continues pitching in.

Tom: Trusts are required to have an annual report. So this partnership or this family arrangement could have an *annual accounting* in the same way.

John: Okay. And then that would also document . . . as you said it would keep the tax implications updated.

Tom: Right.

John: How lengthy is a family partnership document? Are we talking about five pages, twenty-five pages?

Tom: It could be anywhere from two pages to thirty pages. It just depends on what you want covered in it. If all you are intending to cover is something like, "It's our intention to buy this piece of property together, and this is how we are going to do it, and this is who is contributing what," you could probably do it in two pages. If you are saying, "Well, this is what we are buying and this is when we are going to do it; and if something happens to one of us, this is what happens; and if something happens to somebody else, this is what happens." You can go on for thirty pages.

John: You must be amazed sometimes at what people have done to themselves by not planning and documenting their agreements. We are talking big amounts of money.

Tom: Big amounts of money and people who should know better.

John: Those are the cases that end up in court?

Tom: Yes, they are the ones that end up in court. A mess gets left behind because legal documents were not prepared. Thus, the whole family ends up coming apart at the seams because everybody is at cross-purposes at that point. The person who set it up, who everybody could look to and say, "Well Dad wanted it this way," but then you get, "Dad didn't want it this way; we're going to do it this way." They are all doing it in Dad's name. But, Dad is not around. So everybody starts arguing about what Dad wanted and nobody knows.

Please see exhibit 13.2 for an example of a very simple family partnership agreement that captures the essence of the "model" arrangement described earlier. For such a simple two-page document, you will need to invest about five hundred dollars in legal fees. The thirty-page document will require an investment of about one thousand dollars. The return on these investments will be invaluable.

Exhibit 13.2.   Example of Family Partnership Contract

This Partnership Agreement ("Agreement") is entered into by and between John L. Smith, _____ and _____ , ("Smith Children") on one hand; Jack Smith, _____ and ("Smith Grandparents") on the other hand; and Becky Smith, _____ and _____ , and _____ ("Smith Grandchildren") on the final hand, effective the day of June 2007 regarding the following interests:

Recitals

A. The Smith Children currently own an interest in real property identified as (address) ("Real Property"), which they desire to share with the Smith Grandparents on an equitable sharing arrangement and pass on thereafter to the Smith Grandchildren.

B. The Smith Grandparents desire to contribute to the shared living arrangements in exchange for a life estate and certain tax benefits.

C. The Smith Grandchildren agree to share their family residence in exchange for a remainder interest, love, comfort, and support.

Agreement

Now therefore, the parties each agree to form this Smith Family Partnership on the following terms and conditions.

1. The Smith Children agree to contribute the Real Property to this Partnership at its current fair market value of $ _____ together with all mortgages, liens, and other encumbrances against said Real Property in the amount of $ _____. The Smith Children further agree to manage, supervise, and direct this Family Partnership, including the responsibility for preparing all income tax returns, real estate tax returns, gift tax returns, estate tax returns, and other documentation related hereto. In return for this consideration the Smith Children will receive a 50% interest in the Family Partnership and a share life estate in the Real Property

2. The Smith Grandparents agree to pay to the Partnership $ _____ total cash and/or $ _____ monthly toward their uses, repairs, support, taxes, and maintenance obligations. In return for this consideration the Smith Grandparents do hereby receive a shared life estate in the Real Property and 50% of the Partnership tax benefits therefrom for as long as said financial contributions continue or are hereafter waived. The Smith Grandparents will receive their Real Property interests and 50% Family Partnership interests by means of a Partnership Deed and/or Life Estate Deed as the parties shall determine.

3. The Smith Grandchildren agree to share the Real Property with the Smith Grandparents and fully participate in all Family Partnership activities. In return for this consideration the Smith Grandchildren will receive a remainder interest in the Real Property to be disbursed upon conclusion of the life estates and this Partnership.

4. The Partners each agree that all tax benefits and burdens of this Partnership will fall solely upon the Smith Children and the Smith Grandparents in proportion to their financial interests as determined from time to time by their tax accountant and/or attorney, but intended to be 50% each. Partnership deeds, life estate deeds, and other real property recording documents will be prepared as required. A Partnership bank account will be established to collect all payments received hereunder and disburse all fund required hereunder, including Partnership mortgages, taxes, maintenance, repairs, reserves, and otherwise as determined by the Partners. It is *specifically* agreed that the Real Property can be sold, exchanged, or otherwise disbursed solely as determined by the Smith Children as Managing Partners and upon such disbursement the Partners will each receive reimbursements according to their financial investments hereunder.

5. This partnership will terminate upon the death of the last partner, bankruptcy, assignment to creditors, attachment, move-away, termination of payments, or other breach of this Agreement by any Partner as determined by a majority of the other non-breaching Partners.

IN WITNESS WHEREOF, all of the Partners of the "Smith" Family Partnership Agreement, have executed the Agreement, effective on the date set forth.

"Smith Children"

(signature) _____

(signature) _____

"Smith Grandparents"

(signature) _____

(signature) _____

"Smith Grandchildren"

(signature) _____

(signature) _____

(signature) _____

Questions to Ask Your Own Experts

You will need to talk with you own local legal and financial experts. Recall that the pertinent laws vary substantially around the country. You will want to ask (1) which of the following instruments apply to your specific case, (2) which do not, and (3) why.

- Title holding documents
- Joint titles
- Tenancies-in-common
- Shared equity mortgages (a relative, etc., provides the down payment as a co-investor)
- Sale of house to child (at a deep discount)
- Reverse mortgages (the bank provides a stream of tax-free cash subtracting from your home equity)
- Private mortgages (you pay tax-deductible interest on a loan from a relative, etc.)
- Trusts (revocable/irrevocable)
- Living trusts
- Wills
- Corporations
- LLCs (limited liability companies)
- Contractual agreements
- Nuptial agreements (pre- and post-)
- Cohabitation agreements
- Local government subsidies for provision of low-cost housing— low-cost mortgages for the creation of casitas (Boston is an example)
- Tax deductions and other government assistance for elderly care and dependence—call (800) 829-1040 or go to www.irs.gov
- Family partnership agreements (including an annual accounting)

Family Partnerships Defined

Because the best answer to most of these questions will be a family partnership agreement, we have included a definition of that instrument: Family partnerships (FPs) reduce estate taxes and protect assets from creditors' claims. They allow a person to retain control over assets without having them eroded by estate taxes. FPs are structured as either limited partnerships (Georgia being the most favorable state) or limited liability companies (Virginia being the most favorable state).

Parents can establish an FP by transferring assets such as real estate, marketable securities, or an interest in a family business without adverse tax consequences. The parents retain exclusive control over the partnership, such as the power to make management decisions, to sell assets, and to determine the time and amount of distribution to the partners. The FP has the following features:

- The parents may receive compensation for the reasonable value of their services.
- The parents can give interests to their children, either outright or in trust, over a period of time at discounted values of 20 to 40 percent.
- The children are taxed on their proportionate share of the income, which provides an effective income-tax-shifting device.
- The assets owned by the FP are not generally subject to an individual partner's creditors' claims.
- After the interests are transferred to the children, any appreciation in the FP's assets attributable to those interests will escape taxation in the parents' estates, and the parents' retained interest are entitled to valuation discounts.
- The business can be passed to the younger generation without losing it to a forced tax sale or liquidity crisis.[3]

Caregiving Contracts

Finally, we are happy to report a new form of family contract that seems to be growing in popularity and is completely consistent with our advice in this book. The *Wall Street Journal* well summarizes this innovative and timely option:

A small but growing number of families are setting up caregiver contracts, in which adult children or other relatives are hired, for modest salaries, to take care of elderly or disabled family members. These arrangements, which are also called personal-service or personal-care agreements, can help reduce the size of a parent's estate and thereby improve their chances of becoming eligible for long-term-care coverage under Medicaid. They can also minimize battles between siblings and other family members. For many other families, the contracts simply help reward the significant amounts of time, effort, and money that family members often spend watching over and taking care of an elderly relative.[4]

For more information on caregiving contracts, please see the websites listed in the Resources section of our book beginning on page 337.

Looking into the Baby Boomers' (and Their Kids') Future

The agreement that makes sense this year may look pretty silly five or ten years from now, depending on the state of the general economy and, in particular, the state of your own extended family's economy. The latter is hard to predict, but the former is not. Quite common circa 2013 are a variety of plans for transferring wealth from the World War II generation to their kids—instruments such as living trusts, shared equity mortgages, discounted sales of real estate, investments in casitas, and so on. However, circa 2020 all this will change with the probable demise of Social Security, Medicare, and most private pension funds. Prominent in any long-term family partnership agreement should be consideration of this darkness on the far horizon. That is, what happens when your elderly family partners can't produce the current or expected income stream they've promised? Planning for it now will reduce its impact a decade from now.

At the beginning of this chapter, the family was described as "humankind's most efficient economic unit." Prudence, planning, and communication across the generations will keep it so!

14

Making Agreements
for Living Together

Peace, like charity, begins at home.

—FRANKLIN D. ROOSEVELT

Get out of my chair, Meathead!

—ARCHIE BUNKER

 OW DO YOU keep the peace when you're living together again? That's the bottom-line question. The answer lies in one key word—*communication*. When creating an extended-family living arrangement, it is advisable to set up democratically determined ground rules that are fair for all and allow for both communication and privacy. As we mentioned in chapter 6, we recommend an egalitarian family meeting among adults to talk about expectations up front. It helps to have a formal chat to make some agreements. That way, you are all clear about what's what—what they expect from you and also what you expect from them. One young man we spoke to did just that. Mark is a young college student living in Southern California who shares an accessory apartment in his parents' home with his friend. Here's what he had to say about the ground rules that he and his parents have established to facilitate positive relations.

Mark: For making up ground rules, I think the most important thing is to get everyone together and see what bothers people and what doesn't. Just common courtesy. We had a meeting and wrote up a little lease; my mom typed it up. The rules I can remember are no smoking, we have to park on the street, no one else is allowed to move in with us. We normally have my parents call when they want to come over or if they need help with anything. That's about it. It's a pretty laid-back situation. If I'm not happy with something, I will just talk to them about it.

Sharon: How do you handle expenses such as heat, gas and water, and the telephone?

Mark: We have separate electricity and pay our own bills. Also, we are responsible for our own phone and cable bills. We share the utility bill for gas and the hot-water heater. We pay a tiny little rent that goes toward those expenses. I pay one hundred dollars and my roommate pays two hundred. It's still dirt cheap; you can't find anything cheaper than that around here.

Family Meetings

One way to encourage positive relations within extended-family living arrangements is to conduct family meetings on a regular basis. A friend of ours told us how worthwhile her weekly family meetings are. She said that they conduct what is called "family home evening" on Monday nights. It is an evening dedicated to the family where group decisions are made and responsibilities are assigned. It also provides a forum for sharing positive feelings and choosing activities for family fun. To keep order and be productive, she said these gatherings often include a printed agenda and someone designated as the facilitator to run the meeting.

In another case, a couple told us about their current and future plans for family meetings. Mary and Dan moved to Colorado to help babysit their two grandchildren. They've been living in their own separate house nearby but are planning to move into a cottage in the backyard of their son and daughter-in-law's property. They look forward to the convenience of being closer to the grandchildren and having the ability to just pitch in and help out when needed. Also, both families have good communication skills and like being together. Here's what they had to say about the possibility of ground rules being established with their new living arrangement.

Dan: I am sure there will be some. I feel very flexible right now because I have felt so very comfortable with them. I trust them and I am not worried about boundaries. However, we will, as we see a need for them, create clear boundaries.

Mary: What we do is have family meetings. Dan and I have marriage meetings; they have their own family meetings every week. Sometimes we will just mix the meetings. We talk about everything—chores, responsibilities, and also fun things. We plan our dates and look at our calendars, that kind of thing. When we live on the same property with them, I'm sure we will continue having joint family meetings there.

Meeting Guidelines

On the *Parenting Toolbox* website, Ron Huxley lists the following steps for a family meeting:

1. Meet on a regular basis.
2. Everyone gets a chance to talk.
3. Everyone gets treated with respect and has an equal say.
4. Stay with the real issues and don't get sidetracked.
5. Keep the meetings short and stick to a schedule.
6. Focus on members' strengths and not their weaknesses.
7. Keep a record of the family meeting and post it where everyone can see it.
8. Remember to plan to have fun.[1]

When establishing households in close proximity, it is important to talk both before and shortly after the move takes place to make agreements on how to live together. Regular follow-up meetings to see how things are going are also recommended. Step one for your own family would be to sit down and decide who is going to act as the meeting organizer and facilitator. That role could be alternated among family members, depending on your preferences. Then you need to determine when, where, how often, and how long to meet. If a time cannot be found that works for everyone, try rotating the meetings to accommodate other members' schedules.

The meeting organizer can prepare an agenda for the meeting. If someone can't make it, then ask for their input on any known agenda items. Also, invite people to bring topics to discuss. If an agenda is not copied ahead of time, those topics could be listed on a large sheet of paper (a flip chart) for all to see. You could even make the list at the beginning of the meeting.

When meeting, it is helpful to sit around a table or in a circle of some sort. Then the facilitator can go around and give everyone an equal chance to speak. Family members can be encouraged to listen to others, not interrupt, and be supportive, not critical. They should try to keep their comments to the topic at hand and not dominate the conversation space. They can use humor, when appropriate, to keep it light. Above all, they need to respect and listen to each other.

At the start of a meeting, it is a good idea to agree on an ending time. Then, if someone needs to leave early, his or her business can be addressed beforehand. One way to begin on a positive note is to ask each individual what he or she thinks is working well in the living arrangement. Next, you could switch to what issues need to be worked out. The facilitator can ask questions to clarify what the problems are, then brainstorm solutions with the family. During the negotiations, it may become necessary for people to compromise. Ultimately, try to make decisions by consensus, where most agree. At some point, make your plans for family fun. At the end of a meeting, establish the next meeting date, time, and place, as well as who will be in charge.

You may want to have someone take notes to recap what was said. A good follow-up to any family meeting is to distribute a written summary of what was discussed, including who has agreed to do what by when. These notes could be sent out by e-mail. Also, the report can include information about the next meeting.

The Casual Approach

For those who prefer a more casual approach to family meetings, certainly issues, along with outings and vacations, could be discussed informally around a dinner table either at home or in a restaurant. One family we know has a tradition of getting together on Saturday mornings for coffee and doughnuts, so if there is a problem, it can be aired at that time. Other families prefer less structure and like to call meetings on an as-needed basis, sometimes incorporating them into driving time. On the other hand, if the extended-family living arrangement includes only two or three adults, a walk-and-talk approach could be used for family meetings. That way, you get a two-for-one. You're getting family business accomplished and exercising—both at the same time. Regardless of how they are set up, family meetings are an essential step in helping families help themselves to create unity and love in the home, heal resentments, and avoid serious problems.[2]

Discussion Topics

A number of topics lend themselves to discussion at family meetings. All of these broad subjects came up with the people we interviewed:

- Length of stay
- Communication preferences
- Relationship issues
- Privacy issues
- Household finances (covered in the previous chapter)
- Shared responsibilities
- Personal preferences
- Child care
- Family fun

Specific examples within these general topics follow as we tell the stories of how families have made agreements for living together that work.

Length of Stay

In making agreements for living together, we suggest you also talk beforehand about when *not* to live together. In the case of adult children moving home, you may want to set up time lines for them to move out. Sharon and her husband told each of their five children that, after they graduated from college, they were welcome to live at home rent free for six months until they could find a job and save enough money to rent an apartment. That was during the 1990s, when the economy in California was more robust and housing was not as expensive. Today, they would probably extend that time period to one year or longer if need be. So many of their friends with younger children are doing that now. As we stated earlier, over half of eighteen- to twenty-five-year-olds nationwide are currently living at home.

Likewise, another friend has a daughter in her early thirties who has just moved back home. Although the single daughter is employed, she had run into financial difficulties. Her mother agreed to let her live at home rent free for a year so she could pay off her credit card debt. As we said earlier, 30 percent of adult children between the ages of eighteen and thirty-four are now living at home in the United States. Certainly, these statistics represent further evidence of the growing trend for more Americans to live together again.

Moreover, there can be other benefits with this type of arrangement. In fact, many young people are living at home to save money for a down payment on a place of their own. One young couple we spoke with in Utah said just that. Brenda and Joe have an agreement to live rent free with her parents in a separate apartment above their garage for six months to a year. Here is their story:

Brenda: We're looking at houses right now. In the next couple of months, we think we'll be into a home of our own. Although we considered other living choices, in the end, we realized we wanted to buy a home sooner without having to rent a place first. Renting would have prolonged our inability to buy a house.

Joe: We had to take care of some financial issues, and living here allows us to do that. We did look at other apartments, but it just seemed like Brenda's parents were very open and willing to let us use their apartment. In the end, we realized it's a better situation not only for financial reasons but also to have them nearby to help or to just spend time with. She has a large family and it's very enjoyable. We have Sunday dinners over there and also get together on special occasions. It's really nice to have them close by.

In the case of elderly parents who live near their children, a question that often comes up is when is it appropriate to move them into a caregiving facility? At some point, it may simply become too much work and responsibility for the family caregivers to continue to have an elderly parent or disabled relative live with them and have any kind of decent life for themselves. When mobility, safety, and incontinence become major issues, then it may be necessary to seek alternative housing for the family member. It helps to talk this over ahead of time, particularly to see if the individual has any special preferences as to where he or she would like to be. Eleanor, whose in-laws used to live in an apartment in their backyard, told us how she and her husband handled the predicament that developed with her disabled mother-in-law.

Eleanor: The biggest problem we had was when my mother-in-law got to the point where she was not able to bathe or feed herself. Even though my father-in-law was a very large man and strong, she was dead weight and he could not lift her. We did try having a nurse there on eight-hour shifts for a short time but found that did not work. We ended up having to place her in a nursing home. Explaining it to them was so difficult. Even though we had agreed, when they came to live with us, that when it became necessary, she would have to go to a nursing home, they still didn't get it. They couldn't accept that we were not a nursing home, that I could not lift her and do those things. She begged to stay home. She also got to a point where she didn't think anybody was doing anything for her, when, in fact, everything was being done for her. Her husband was just turning himself inside out for her, and she was starting to treat him very badly. Finally, we did have to put my mother-in-law into a skilled-nursing facility.

Even though Eleanor and her husband had a tough time moving his mother to a nursing home, at least they had the comfort of knowing they had communicated ahead of time what would need to be done. Indeed, making agreements up front for when not to live together can give all family members peace of mind in the long run.

Communication Preferences

Daily interaction with family members can involve a myriad of different ways to communicate with one another. From making contact to giving advice to handling disputes, it's up to you to let family members know your communication preferences.

Making Contact

When living so close to each other, how do you want family members to contact you? Most of the people we talked to prefer a "call first" means of communication. Instead of dropping by, they want people to call them first to see if it's a good time for a visit. That way, they would not be interrupted if they were doing something. Certainly, that method would allow for more privacy for both sides as well. In other words, treat your family with the same respect and consideration you would show your friends.

Caroline, a Northern California widow, would agree. She will soon be living with her daughter, son-in-law, and two grandchildren in an apartment in their house. When asked about what type of ground rules might be established in her new living arrangement, she replied:

Caroline: We've always maintained a certain respect for each other's privacy. So we decided that we are not just going to drop in whenever we feel like it. We are going to call first and say, "Is it convenient?" I think it is a very good rule because, you know, they could be having a family argument or something, and I could burst right into the middle of it. And the same way in reverse. I may be having a nap, and not only that, I do have friends who come and stay with me too.

In another case, Tracy told us, when she wants to see her mother-in-law, who lives in a cottage in their backyard, she will call first most of the time. She also said that they will occasionally use an intercom to communicate with her. In fact, several other families mentioned using intercoms as a way to make contact with extended family members. Still others use e-mail instead of the phone to make plans or put in requests for help on certain dates. That way, there are no interruptions.

One family told us about the "no-fly" buffer zone they installed in their home when they built an attached apartment for his elderly parents. It is a fifteen-foot-long hallway with doors on each end "to separate them from us." The door on his parents' end has a mail slot, so they don't have to interrupt each other to deliver mail. They use a white board that hangs on one of the walls to leave messages for each other. Importantly, when one or the other of them wants privacy, the door is shut. An open door says, "Come on in."

So far, we've talked about making contact between adult members of a family. What about young grandchildren making contact with their grandparents? Here's what Helen had to say about her preferences when she stayed at her daughter's place in her RV.

Helen: One of the most important ground rules was that the grandchildren could not come over without permission. At first there were no ground rules with the RV, and then I felt my grandchildren needed ground rules. I needed to be present in the RV when they came. The other understanding I had with my daughter was that when I was tired I would excuse myself and return in two hours. The other strategic thing I figured out was to start the day by saying, "This is what I can do to help you today." That makes it so much easier.

On the other hand, some individuals prefer a more casual, free-flow approach. A woman who lives with her husband and four children in the house next door to her in-laws told us how both she and her children make contact with their grandparents.

Linda: If the kids want to go over to Nanny's house, I'll say, "Why don't you give her a call and see if she's there." But oftentimes, we'll be out in our yard and Nanny and Papa will be in their yard, and we'll have this over-the-fence communication. "Mom, could I go over to Nanny's house?" There is that verbal invitation. So I would say it's fairly loose. We've never sat down and established firm ground rules; we haven't had to. It's interesting, my father-in-law is a very private person. My mother-in-law is much more casual. She will knock on the door and say, "Hello, I'm here. I need to ask you a question." I don't necessarily call when I go over there either. I will just knock on the door and say, "Are you there? I need to talk to you about something." I think it's just comfortable for both of us. We probably interact with each other this way about four times a week.

An adult grandchild whose grandmother lives next door to her, her husband, and three children said that she and her grandmother do not have a "call first" rule. When asked why she didn't, Dana replied:

Dana: Because I think her having to call me to say, "I'm coming over," would make her feel like a guest, and she's not. She is part of our family.

As it is, Dana receives more than enough calls every day from her grandmother. She told us how she has handled that communication dilemma.

Dana: She calls constantly. I mean, the telephone rings twenty times a day. So I now have caller ID so that I can see when she is calling. The times that I won't pick up the phone are the times when I've just dropped her off after lunch. If the weather is bad and I've just dropped her off, she'll call. I know it's over nothing. I know it's over, "Did you watch the news? There is an epidemic in China, so don't let the children out."

Karen, who lives in a family compound of four houses with her mother and six siblings with families, told us about her family's different styles of making contact.

Karen: If I want to go over to my mom's house, I just show up. Like I said, everybody is different. I have a sister-in-law who is from the South, and she is very formal. At her house, you know, you respond differently or behave differently. Whereas at my house, the doors are never locked. Cousins come and go all the time. Everybody has their own rules, but there's no specific code of conduct. Everybody just respects everybody else.

However, as this next story shows, failure to talk about ground rules for making contact ahead of time can also produce negative results. One woman spoke about a communication pitfall that occurred when her parents moved into an apartment attached to her house. Gail and her husband had decided to build this addition as separate living quarters so that they would have to walk outside if they wanted to visit each other. As they were to find out, this helped with the privacy issue but didn't entirely take care of it. They had not discussed ground rules ahead of time for making contact with each other. As a consequence, here's what she said happened.

Gail: Dad had a copy machine in his condo that he wanted to keep, but there really wasn't room for it in the apartment. We had room for it in our house.

We were, of course, thrilled with the idea of having use of the copier in our house, but it made for a sticky privacy issue. It's their copier, and they should be able to use it whenever they need to, but it's our home, and we cherish our privacy just like everyone else.

In addition, Mom enjoyed just popping over for a visit. Sometimes this was great because the timing was perfect. At other times it was an inconvenience and I or my husband were kept from something we needed to be doing. As the months went by, my husband and I both found a bit of resentment building up, yet were at a loss as to how to handle this. My folks were, after all, being incredibly helpful with child care, errands, and countless other things. I felt guilty being resentful of the frequency of the drop-in visits, but I knew it had to be dealt with because we were all in this for the long haul.

Luckily, I didn't have to be the one to bring this up. My father, bless his soul, was commenting to someone else about our new living situation, and then, as an aside, said to me, "By the way, we're not stopping in too often are we? I've been meaning to ask you about that. We don't want to intrude."

That was my opening, and we ended up having a very good, frank discussion about the problem. We decided that Mom and Dad could come into the downstairs area anytime they needed to use the copier, but that they would just make their copies and leave. If they wanted to visit or needed help with something, they would call first (as we would), and we could arrange a time that was good for everyone. Having this discussion was such a relief. Now I thoroughly enjoy my visits with my parents because I don't have other things demanding my attention at the same time. Also, my husband can arrange helping Dad with a project when it's convenient for him, rather than feeling that he has to drop everything because Dad is standing right there in the kitchen waiting for him.[3]

Giving Advice

How tempting it is to offer unsolicited advice on raising children, especially when you see a situation where you think you know the right way. Gail talked about yet another example of a communication problem with her parents.

Gail: One day, I was out raking some piles of grass from the previous afternoon's mowing. While I was out there, I overheard Mom in the apartment saying to Dad, "What is she doing that for? She has boys who can do that for her. Do you think I should say something?" I was glad to have warning of what was to come, because after a moment or two, out came Mom who asked me why I was doing the raking. "Because I want to," I replied. "But,

you have enough to do," she said. "You have boys who could do that for you."
I took a deep breath, put on my best "Mom, I love you" smile, and said,
"Mom, I'm going to say this as nicely as I possibly can. It's none of your business." With a look of surprise (because I had probably not spoken to my
mother this way since I was an argumentative 13-year-old), she went back
into the apartment and complained to Dad about what I had said. Then Dad
came out and made a peace offering of some freshly sautéed Portobello
mushrooms. While I was munching, he said, "Just for the record, I don't
think you should be doing the raking either." "Well, it's none of your business either," I said, with that same endearing smile on my face. When I told
this story to a friend, she said, "Wow, it just strikes me how much worse this
would be if your parents were actually living in the same house with you.
This kind of loving interference could be happening on a daily basis." She
definitely had a point.[4]

Later, while on a walk/talk with her dad, Gail continued the discussion
about the unwanted advice on parenting. She explains how she was able to
clarify her position and indicate her communication preferences.

Gail: Dad and I take exercise walks together, and on one of these walks, the
raking incident came up. I was able to say, "You have to trust that whenever
I do something, it's because it's something that I really want to do, or I've
decided that it's most efficient for me to do it. My children are not wanting
for chores. They help out a lot around the house, and are very good about
doing what is asked of them. I know you don't see everything that goes on,
but please trust me on this. If I have to explain or justify every decision I make
to you and Mom, I will grow to resent it very quickly." Although I am not sure
Dad and Mom really believe that my kids have enough chores, they have
respected my request not to interfere in these matters. I, in turn, do not make
a fuss when they tell the kids, "We're the Grandparents, and we can spoil you
if we want. You can stay up late and have extra cookies when we're in charge."

The most important thing we have all done is to take the risk to speak
about things that might hurt the other's feelings. We have grown closer
because of it. I think that keeping silent on the difficult issues would have
pushed us apart.[5]

Handling Disputes

With any family, occasionally disagreements will surface that need to be
attended to on the spot. It's important to come up with ways to fight fairly.
Registered nurse Susan Miller suggests the following:

Agree to fight constructively. This means setting out ground rules for fair fighting such as taking turns to say what you want to say, agreeing to follow up on issues raised, and finishing the fight so that bad feelings do not go on forever.

Honesty in communication is generally good but sometimes too much honesty can really hurt and damage a relationship. Remember that you want to nurture the relationship and some things are better left unsaid. Pick your battles carefully.[6]

One difficulty of living with the elderly can be dealing with their negative attitudes. George, whose wife's grandmother lives next door, told us how he feels about having daily contact with her. He uses a "stone wall" approach to handling the grandmother's complaints.

George: [laughter] It's difficult living with an older person because I get home from work, open the door, and want to relax. The first thing I see is Grandma sitting there, because she's always over for dinner every night. So the first person I see when I walk in the door is Grandma. Instead of "Hey, George, how are you doing?" It's "The TV is not working." From my experience, if you ask someone who is elderly how they feel, the glass is always half empty. "Oh, I don't feel good." I've even said to her, "The day I walk in the door and ask you how you feel and you say, 'Great!' or 'I had a nice day,' I'm going to think I'm in the wrong house." My own grandmother is ninety-seven and she is ten years older than Gram, yet she's got more of a positive perspective. Things are always bright and shiny, whereas with Grandma things are "my aches and pains." It can get tiring.

Sharon: Some of that is just how the family dynamic is and what they are used to. Good for you, though. I like to emphasize the positive myself.

George: Yes. It makes life a lot better if you come from the positive side. We had a choice when Gram wanted to move in with us—move into our house or move in next door. When we bought the place next door, there was a stone wall between the two houses. I took the stone wall out and made it all into one big yard. So I told Grandma when she moved in, "I took the stone wall down, but every time you complain, I'm going to put one stone back on the wall." The wall should be about twenty feet high by now. But so far we haven't put any stones back in there [laughter].

George has a great sense of humor, which undoubtedly helps him get through a not-so-perfect lifestyle. Indeed, we've found that using humor and looking at the positives in life can be helpful in most relationships.

Relationship Issues

Sometimes relationship issues can be associated with generational differences or the position of someone in a family, that is, a parent or in-law versus an adult child. Problems can also arise out of personality conflicts between individuals. In all these instances, it is advisable to establish ground rules for communication.

In-law Issues

In some cases, we found the in-law factor did not seem to make a difference in how people got along. In others, it did. Leslie lives in an apartment attached to the main house of her daughter, son-in-law, and two grandchildren. She talked about the easy relationship she has with her daughter.

Leslie: I think it's easier to live with a daughter, and I love my daughter-in-laws completely, but it's just a lot different. My daughter, if she doesn't like something, she can say it to me; I can say it to her. But you would be a little bit more hesitant to say something to a daughter-in-law and vice versa. I think it would be harder.

Another mother, who lives across the street from her daughter, issued a warning about potential problems with a son-in-law, stemming from the close relationship she has with her daughter.

Jean: I think the only thing that you might be careful about is the other partner. My daughter and I are very close, but how does her husband feel about that? The spouse needs to be truthful about how he really feels about living across the street from his mother-in-law. How is that relationship? It could be difficult. My daughter and I, we don't overdo it. If you are really close and spend all of your time communicating with your mom, that might be hard on your husband. There could be some jealously.

A young woman told us about difficulties she encountered with her husband when her mom helped pay for their garage to be remodeled into an apartment where her mother now lives.

Paula: The problem that came up was between my husband and my mom. My idea was, since Mom's paying for it, let her make all of the decisions on the remodel thing. But my husband had his own way of thinking of how he wanted it structured. There were times when he said, "I want this type of toilet." I said, "Well, then pay for it." That happened a lot. He knew that my mom had money but also wanted to let her know that he could pay for some things too. Of course, my mom felt she was being helpful. She is not expecting us to pay her back, because in the long run she knows it will help us. Later, if we wanted to rent it out, we could. If we wanted to live there ourselves and fix the other portion of the house up just for the kids, we could. We could even have that as a second house if we wanted to for the kids when they get older.

On the other hand, some people told us they get along fine with their in-laws but couldn't live with their own parents. Individual personalities and lifestyle preferences can make a huge difference in the ease of making agreements to live together. A young woman we spoke with will soon be living in a cottage on the same property with her in-laws. When asked whether she would recommend this type of living arrangement to others, she responded:

Marge: I don't think it is for everybody. I think you need to have the same kind of values and priorities in life, pretty much the same lifestyle or close, and really open communication. It would be very difficult for people who are closed minded or someone who was brought up in an authoritarian household. I couldn't do this with my parents, as much as I absolutely adore them. There is no way that I could live with them or even move this close to them. The other issue would be the whole wife/mother-in-law or husband/mother-in-law situation. My mother-in-law and I have bonded uniquely, but there are some people who would not be able to live with their mother-in-law.

Personality Differences

Along with in-law issues that need to be worked out, personality differences can also lead to problems with living together. When such problems do occur, it is worthwhile to make agreements on how to deal with them. Vicky, whose parents live in a guesthouse in the backyard, told us how she and her "controlling" mother have learned how to compromise with each other.

Vicky: In terms of ground rules, my husband and I feel honesty is the best policy. If something is bugging you, you need to speak up, because if you shelve it, that can lead to a problem. But there are differences in communication styles between generations and also people. My family used to be really closed about most stuff. We couldn't say, "Hey, this is bugging me." It's really more the communication between my mother and me. That has changed over the years. My mom is very controlling, but she is also very, very sensitive. If I say stuff that hurts her feelings, she just crumbles. I tend to be more direct than she is. She's always been upset with me for being that way; she wants me to be softer. But over time she's realized the importance of being a little tougher, and I've understood that I need to couch things in different terms to really get my point across.

Overall, close relationships do play a key role in successful extended-family living arrangements. A family we spoke with in Utah concurred. Paul and Charlotte live on the ground level of their home, while their daughter Stacie and two of her friends share a basement apartment right below. Here's what they had to say about recommending their living arrangement to others:

Paul: I think people whose relationships are very close and open would stand a much greater chance of making it work than people who may be more distant or not tolerate one another as well.

Stacie: I would definitely recommend it to other people. I get to be close to my family. If I need the privacy, I get it. That closeness does need to be there because, although there is a locked door, we are very close in proximity.

Charlotte: I think it's important to have family counsel often. That's where you get together and you talk out problems. Rather than waiting for conflicts to get into crisis-like states, we deal with them right away so they don't get run up the flagpole and become major issues. No matter what, I think that active communication is really essential for sustaining positive relationships.

Privacy Issues

Privacy is another important topic that comes up at family meetings of those who live together. How do people get away from each other and have time to themselves? Certainly, we all need to have seclusion, solitude, or emotional space in our lives. Earlier in this chapter, we discussed making agreements on how and when to make contact with family members. Other privacy issues include shutting or locking doors and accessing each other's cupboards.

Giving Space

One woman we spoke with made reference to knowing when to "give space." Nancy and her husband live in a guesthouse in the backyard of their daughter and son-in-law's home. She talked about how they manage privacy.

Nancy: We haven't had any friction. It's been absolutely amazing. I think we know when not to get too involved over there. We just give them their space.

How much easier it is when the grandmother lives full-time in the self-contained house in the garden with its own separate entrance, kitchen, and bathroom. Then there is little call for either party to have to move somewhere when the other needs more psychological space. Each person is able to live an independent life, without intruding on other members of the family. Certainly, their lives can flow more smoothly with this luxury of more privacy.

A family we talked to in Oregon has already tested this idea. A young couple live in the larger house on their property with their six-year-old daughter. Since they both work at jobs that required travel, his mother was invited to come from Florida to live with them and help babysit. Initially, Madeline lived with them in a wing of their house, with the understanding that a cottage would be built in the backyard as soon as possible. She now lives in that cottage and had this to say about her newfound privacy:

Madeline: Well, I finally have my privacy. Before coming here, I had lived alone for so many years and gotten used to that. I don't think we ever had any issues while I lived with them. But when they had guests over, I was always concerned about how visible I should be. I didn't want to act like I was ignoring their guests, especially if it's people that I knew. But on the other hand, I didn't want to be in the middle of their conversations. So this way, I think we each have been able to enjoy our guests more.

Madeline's son, Jim, also commented on their mutual need for privacy.

Jim: We put a lot of thought into what we did, before we did it. The cottage has enabled us to give Madeline her own space and privacy. We can enjoy our privacy as well, and still have a family between us. I think the key thing is to give the women in the family some privacy. Even though we may not see each other every day, we are only seventy-five feet apart and know that we're there for each other.

In another case, a woman's mother lives in a guesthouse attached to the main house. Joan told us why and how she established ground rules for privacy during the dinner hour.

Joan: Our friend who does marriage counseling said, "I think it's important that you do establish some ground rules." One is "Whose turf is where?

When do you cross that turf, and when is it appropriate?" We didn't come up with any written ground rules. But we did discuss some issues in terms of privacy. In particular, we talked about when we could all come together as a family. My husband and I had not been married that long before we did this addition to the house for my mother. We both got married later in life, and then had our daughter. The dinner hour for us, especially since we are both working, is really the main time that we can come together as a couple. So we don't invite my mother over for dinner during the week. She is also on a schedule. My mother likes to have her dinner at noontime or go out with friends for lunch and have a heavy meal. She would just prefer a sandwich and soup or something like that for dinner.

So that is one of our understandings, that we as a family need time together. Especially when my daughter was young, it was the "bewitching hour" or another friend of mine called it the "arsenic hour." It was that period between 4:30 and 6:00 or 5:30 and 6:30 where children are getting maxed out, and they are not on their best behavior. They want their food as quickly as possible. They want to eat it as quickly as possible. Having a parent there, even though she's like a close friend of yours, is not the best idea.

A young couple live with their two small children in a duplex next door to her parents. Greg and Carol told us about what they have encountered with privacy. As you'll see, they actually benefited from a negative experience Carol's mother had previously had with Carol's grandmother.

Greg: Carol's parents were in a similar situation as we are in now with them. Her grandmother lived next door to them in this same house. I think Carol's grandmother was not as respectful of their privacy. She would barge in on them unannounced. So they've had a lot of experience with what that's like. That's why I think they've been so respectful of our privacy, and I'd love to think that we have done the same for them.

Carol: For us, from the beginning, my parents really left us alone, unless we wanted to be with them. I'm sure that comes from their experience with my grandmother imposing on them so much. So we have our privacy. We don't have to see them if we don't want to. If we come home and we're tired . . . it's not like, "Hello, I made you cookies." But whenever we do want to be with them, they always seem just happy to see us.

Locking Doors

In contrast to the informal arrangement regarding privacy just discussed, Charlotte and Paul use a locked door as a formal vehicle for privacy. Again,

Paul and Charlotte are the couple from Utah who live on the ground level of their home while their daughter Stacie and two of her college friends share a basement apartment right below. Here's what they had to say about their ground rules for privacy, including how they handle all females living with one male in the house.

Stacie: One of our ground rules is they don't come down without notifying us first. I think it has to do with the tenant situation, where they have two people renting from them. Most of the time they will just knock and call down the stairs to say that they are coming. Also, the door is locked and I'm the only one from downstairs who has the key. Normally, I'll just come up and knock and use the key.

Paul: I like having the run of the entire house, and I do when it's just our children that are here. But when we have other people here that are formally renting, then there are courtesies that we extend to them for us to be able to access our food storage room downstairs. The other thing is that there is a gender difference. They are all females that are here, and I'm the only male. So my wife might ask me to get five potatoes out of the food storage and bring them up. I know one particular girl is a little bit more sensitive to me being down there than the other, so I will ask my wife, "No, I think this girl is home. Would you go down and get it or can you wait, and then I'll go down and get it later?" So there are those kinds of contingencies you have to think through in order to make the thing work.

Charlotte: The locked door does give us a sense of privacy, both entities— the children downstairs and Paul and myself up here. It's very important we have that privacy.

Stacie: I like the fact that I can be close to my family, but also I can have some privacy when I need it too. I can just go downstairs and be with my roommates.

Accessing Cupboards

Charlotte: Another thing I need to say is that we did set a limit on Stacie's ability to be able to take whatever she wants. We feel when they graduate from high school, they need to be responsible for themselves. We've raised them like that. We don't go out and buy our children cars. We don't buy them their clothes; they buy their own clothes. They get a job; they support themselves. Since Stacie has been living in this house downstairs, if she uses food out of our kitchen cupboards in our part of the house, she is expected to ask us first. The very fact that she has to ask for it makes her feel responsible. I think that's really important.

Shared Responsibilities

When living together, there are numerous responsibilities that need to be shared. General responsibilities include household chores, along with safety and security questions. Also, issues around pet care, the mail, and parking need to be figured out.

Household Chores

The basic questions are who does what household chores, and when and how do they do them. The subjects that came up in our interviews were the garbage, ironing, and mail. Most families living in separate households took care of their own laundry and housecleaning.

Only one family we spoke with talked specifically about taking out the garbage. Madeline lives in a cottage in the backyard of her son and daughter-in-law's home in a small town in Georgia. She helps babysit their daughter when both of them travel. Taking out the heavy garbage cans to the street would be difficult for either Madeline or her young granddaughter, Katie. She told us about the unique way they handle taking out the garbage at their house.

Madeline: Jim works as a volunteer with the local fire department. When he and Christine go away for work or are on vacation, the fire department guys always tell Jim, "Leave Madeline our list of names and phone numbers. If she needs anything, have her call." If Jim and Christine are out of town, they will come by, take the trash cans out, and bring them back in. They're just wonderful.

Her granddaughter, Katie, told us how her grandmother helps them out by living so close.

Katie: Neither one of my parents know how to iron, so Grandma does the ironing for us.

And recall from chapter 3 that Madeline's daughter-in-law told us how they handle the mail:

Christine: It is important to me for Katie to have easy access to Madeline because she is the only grandparent that lives nearby. I want their relationship to grow and develop. The mail sits on our counter until Katie comes home from school every day. I have Katie take it out to Madeline, so that they can visit with each other, even if it is only a two-minute exchange.

We found that picking up the mail can present all sorts of challenges, especially if families share the same box. Roger, who lives with his wife in Washington on a large rural lot with two accessory units and two sets of adult children, told us how they came up with a process for mail delivery with only one box for so many people.

Roger: The mail is in a lockbox up there with another group of boxes. So whoever drives up the hill first in the afternoon can stop for it. The person who picks up the mail will put the flag up. So when the next guy comes by and sees the flag up, he won't stop. If the flag isn't up and it's late in the afternoon, they know the mail is still in the box and will stop and get it. Here at home, Charlie's mail goes in the top box and ours goes in the yellow box right outside our front door. Whoever gets the mail sorts it and puts it in the appropriate boxes.

In another case, a family with a guest cottage in the backyard spoke about the difficulty they have had with mail delivery. It seems that their cottage has become like a revolving door, with different family members and friends living there for several months at a time. Tony gave us suggestions on how to handle the mail for long-term guests.

Tony: Instead of letting them use your address, have the guest get a P.O. box. That way you won't get all their junk mail later that you can't get rid of. Also, after they've left, you won't have the challenge of arranging for their mail to be redelivered to them.

How much easier it is to live in close proximity in completely separate residences. Linda, a young woman who lives with her husband and four children in a house next door to her in-laws, talked to us about the mutually beneficial system they've worked out for mail pickup.

Linda: When they're gone, we pick up their mail and water the plants. And they do the same for us. That's a real plus. We go to Hawaii for one week out of the year together as a family. Then there is one week in the summer when we piggyback with them to the cabin. But other than that, our vacations typically don't overlap. So there is that "neighborhood watch," close-up and personal, that goes on.

Elena, who shares a duplex with her daughter, son-in-law, and grand-children, told us the benefits of living so close when it comes to the mail.

Elena: We do have separate mailboxes—"A" and "B." If she has a delivery, I go over and get it and vice versa. It's fun because we can trade magazines, and if I am not home or vice versa, we can easily pick up each other's mail.

Nancy, who lives in a cottage in the backyard of her daughter's home, talked about how she will pitch in and help with household chores when needed.

Nancy: I will go over when Janet is busy and unload the dishwasher and pick things up. She is always so grateful. I love being able to do that.

Sharon: So it sounds like a pitch-in family. That is what I did raising my daughters. Everybody pitched in. It wasn't so much that I had to make a list for them; if something needed to be done, we all worked together.

Pets

We heard a number of stories about the benefits of living nearby when it came to sharing responsibilities for pet care, especially when people are away on vacations. One man who lives with his wife in a cottage in the backyard of their daughter, son-in-law, and grandchildren's home helps out by walking the dog every day. An invalid woman who lives with her son and daughter-in-law feels good about assisting with their dogs. She lets them sit in her room at her feet while she watches television. Another woman who lives with her daughter and son-in-law feels useful by looking after their cats while they're away. In other cases, family pets both keep people company and also provide security. Madeline, who lives in a cottage in the backyard of her son and daughter-in-law's home, had this to say about how they share the family dog.

Madeline: The dog stays between both houses. So I can watch it, like I watch my granddaughter. If they're away for the weekend, the dog spends the weekend with me. I take care of the dog and the dog takes care of me. It's the best of both worlds.

Jane, whose mother lives in a house nearby on a family compound, had a similar story.

Jane: We realized as the years went by that this really was the best situation, because when we were gone on vacation, my mother would keep an eye on the house and our animals. We've always had dogs. They knew when we were gone they would be able to go down to my mother's house and stay there. It was good for her because she had a dog there and she felt safer, rather than being all alone in the house.

It helps to make agreements for acquiring pets too. Leslie, who lives in an apartment attached to her daughter's house, now babysits the family dog when her daughter and grandchildren are out-of-town. She also told us about wanting to get her own dog when she retires. She has talked to her daughter about this, and they've set up ground rules already for the future dog.

Parking

Parking cars can be a huge issue in neighborhoods with limited parking. Tony, who has the revolving-door guest cottage in the backyard where family members and friends stay for months at a time, spoke about the importance of determining how many cars will accompany your house guests. From his own experience, he warned:

Tony: At first, it is cars. Then all of a sudden, it is motorcycles and RVs and all sorts of things that show up. The problem is where do you put them all?

Mark, a college student who lives with his parents in an apartment attached to the main house, talked about his problems with not enough places for parking. When asked what he disliked about his living arrangement, he said:

Mark: Parking. In our neighborhood there are a lot of situations like this. Everybody has at least two cars; there is never any parking. That's the only downside of this whole situation. There is a family on the other side of us that has their grandparents and brother-in-law living with them. Across the street, they rent out the garage. They just put a triplex in there. Nobody has extra parking; you have to park on the street.

The other thing that came up in talking with people is the inconvenience of having to park outside a garage. It's much harder to bring in groceries in the rain with no garage to park in. Also, what can be done about excess cars when entertaining? Leslie, who lives with her daughter, son-in-law, and grandchildren in an apartment attached to their house, had this to say:

Leslie: I like to entertain. I like to cook. The street is wide, so there is no problem with parking on the street. My guests can't park in the driveway because my son-in-law can't get out. So that has worked out well.

In another case, Joe, who lives with his wife in an apartment over the garage of his in-laws, told us how he handles parking there with such a large family and so many cars. Fortunately, the home site is a large one. He said that he just always parks outside on the street to be considerate.

Safety and Security

We heard several stories regarding safety and security issues with living together in close proximity. Many families told us how nice it was to have family nearby to look after things if they were away and to help out in emergencies related to health issues. Also, the personal security of having someone else around, even the shared dog, made many folks more at ease. Additionally, we discussed in some detail safety issues for seniors in chapter 11, "Making Your Home Accessible to Seniors." Of course, avoiding stairs altogether by using ground-level housing or installing an elevator, along with putting grab bars and stall showers with seats in bathrooms, are key safety issues for seniors.

In addition, a number of people told us stories about safety issues for children. In one case, Jean, who lives across the street from her daughter, son-in-law, and two grandchildren, explained how they have handled their proximity problem.

Jean: It is a very busy street, which is a concern because of the children. I have two little ones. I have a seven-year-old grandchild and a three-year-old. So, of course, we had to be careful of them crossing the street to come and see me. What they decided to do is put a lock on their front door way up high where neither boy could reach it. They keep that door locked at all times.

A swimming pool was a concern for another family with young children. Susan, the grandmother who lives in an apartment in the backyard, told us how they manage that situation and still allow the grandkids to come by when they want to.

Susan: The swimming pool is between the house and the front of my apartment. We fenced it off, so the little kids can't get to it. Also, one of my doors was childproofed. We did that, not so much for my privacy, but mostly so they couldn't be wandering around my place when I wasn't there.

Personal Preferences

When living together, it is important to consider and discuss how to accommodate personal preferences at family meetings. Lifestyle differences between people and generations can and do come up. In particular, we heard numerous stories about issues around neatness, decor, noise, house temperature, laundry, pets, and smoking. Once again, it helps to bring things up and try to resolve differences.

Lifestyle Differences

In chapter 6 we told you about Helen, a Northern California Realtor, and her quest for privacy when visiting her daughter and three grandchildren in Arizona. She has tried a number of housing arrangements, including staying at a hotel, staying in their house, and renting an RV. Here's what she had to say about those experiences:

Helen: When I stayed at their home, the two boys were in a bunker across the hall, and I had the other guest bedroom next to the bath. But our lifestyles are different. The kids are active in the middle of the night, crying from nightmares and things like that. I would be awakened and then have to try to go back to sleep. For me, it was hard to live in their house, meet my own physical rhythms, and have some privacy.

On the other hand, lifestyle similarities were what led one woman we spoke with to decide to build a house together with her adult daughter that would include her own separate two-room wing. Carla is a retired widow, and her daughter needed help with babysitting her ten-year-old daughter. Originally, Carla had planned to live by herself in a home in Monterey, California. However, she changed her mind about living so far away from her children and decided to move to Southern California to be with her daughter instead. Here's her story:

Carla: Since I was not going to move to Monterey, I thought that maybe I should move in with one of the children. The question was which one. Well, with the three of us having such different lifestyles, I thought perhaps I was far more compatible with my daughter. Plus, she had just gone through a difficult divorce and has a ten-year-old. So she said to me, "Well, with my work at the college and having to be gone, and since you are going to be writing and consulting, maybe we can build you an office. We could buy a house together." It was her idea to purchase this property in Southern California and decorate it together. It's a new house in a subdivision, so we've had a chance to select the flooring, walls, and carpeting. We have similar tastes and it's been a good experience.

Neatness Issues

In our interviews with people about personal preferences, the one topic that came up the most often was neatness. Of course there are lifestyle differences when it comes to being neat and tidy. In many cases, we also found generational differences, with the older generations being more concerned with neatness. The question is how do you make agreements regarding this issue. Caroline, who plans to live with her daughter and son-in-law in an apartment in their house, told us how they have already handled this issue.

Caroline: They are very laid-back, and that could be a problem in the house. In being very laid-back, they don't care if there is stuff lying around. They clean up once in a while, but they don't clean up every day. On the other hand, I like to have everything straight and neat all the time. That's not the way they live. So she said, "Mom, the only thing that you have to promise us is that you won't come and clean up after us." Before, I had always thought that, since they're so busy all the time, I could help them. In fact, as I found out, they don't want the help; they want to do it themselves. I'm so glad they thought to tell me that up front.

The next story illustrates what happens when families don't communicate about lifestyle preferences. Dan lived with his wife for a time in the home of her parents in order to save money to buy their own place. They did not have a separate apartment with their own entrance and kitchen. He told us how privacy and boundaries related to neatness became an issue for him.

Dan: My mother-in-law is very neat and tidy and doesn't do well with untidy places. At one point, my wife and I had separate closets. In my closet above the hanging clothes were shelves of sweaters. It was just not that important to me to keep them neat and organized. At one point, she went in and pulled out all of my sweaters, folded them, rearranged them, and put them back up there neatly. After that, I wondered, "If she feels comfortable going into my closet and rearranging my clothing, does she feel comfortable going in and looking at other things like finances, just out of curiosity?" I have no reason to believe that she did, but it still was a concern. I couldn't say, "Stop doing that," because then it would seem like I wasn't grateful to them for giving us a place to live.

That would be a concern if we did move close together again. If for some reason they moved into the guesthouse that we have on our new property, what are the boundaries going to be? Is Grandma going to be coming over and cleaning our house because it's not vacuumed to her standards? Those sorts of things. From that experience, we would now set up ahead of time what the expectations would be for living together with other people. That's the most important thing.

So Dan has learned from experience the importance of making agreements up front about living together. He is also in the sometimes difficult position of being the "in-law." He needs to learn ways to overcome his hesitancy to communicate his preferences to his wife's parents.

In yet another case where two families share the same house, neatness has become a major problem. Tim and his wife invited his daughter and her three children to come and live with them after the daughter was divorced. Even though they have their own separate kitchens, they do share a common entrance. The daughter's apartment is downstairs and they live upstairs. Here's what Tim said about the problem they have with neatness and how they've managed it:

Tim: Our greatest area of conflict is that of neatness. It's gotten so bad that we don't go downstairs to their place, because our standards are so different from theirs. We just can't stand the mess and the chaos. Fortunately, they are more in our space than we need to be in theirs. We eat together a lot at night up here.

When given a choice of whether to live together or not, neatness can be a criterion for making that decision. Although Paul and Charlotte are happy to share their home with their daughter Stacie and her college friends, Charlotte told us why they would not do so again with one of their sons.

Charlotte: Paul and I have high expectations about keeping the house nice. Most of our children do that, but we have one child that does not. He is a catastrophe. He is living in an apartment now because we don't want him to live in our house anymore. He's just horrendously messy. I think it's really important that you talk before you do this with people and find out what kind of expectations they have about keeping the place nice. Since Paul and I have high expectations, and Robert didn't, that caused a problem for us. Stacie does. We like our home taken care of. Even though we don't go down there, we know that it's okay, that there is not grease on the floor.

Over time, Vicky and her mother have worked things out regarding their neatness differences. Even though they have separate living quarters, with her mother and father living in the guest cottage in the backyard, her parents are often in their home. Vicky explained to us how they've come to terms with the tidy issue.

Vicky: When we first moved in here, I remember it was hard because my mom had a real high standard for how this place should look. Even in our house, she used to come in and freak out when the kid's rooms were a little bit disarrayed. Well, over time she mellowed because she realized we needed to live here too. She had to back down from her expectations, and we had to raise ours a little in terms of how everything looked. She used to come in here and say, "The windows need to be cleaned. Oh, your rug needs to be cleaned." Now she doesn't do that anymore.

Surely, learning to compromise has been a key to the successful merger of this extended family.

Decor Issues

Of course, there are personal preferences when it comes to decorating a home. Whether it be an attached or detached apartment on the same property, ideally the people living there should have their own choice of wall colors and placement of furniture. Several families we spoke with have done this. In one instance, Jim and Christine, who live in Oregon, gave his mother, Madeline, the freedom to make most such choices in the cottage they built for her in their backyard. However, Jim and Christine picked out the cabinets and other permanent fixtures as all recognized that eventually it would be turned into an office.

Joan would agree with the importance of utilizing an aging parent's belongings in planning housing for them. She told us that many friends have asked to see what she and her husband have done in creating an apartment attached to their home for her mother.

Joan: They've come and they've looked. I've talked to them about how to care for an aging parent and how you plan for it. In terms of planning, since my mother had her own house, we tried to plan it so that some of her furniture would fit into her new surroundings. Since she wasn't completely selling everything and starting over, she was able to pull from her past. That has worked quite well.

In yet another situation, Leslie paid for the remodeling done to her daughter's house to create an apartment for her to live in. Although the house belongs to her daughter, Leslie was given free rein to design it and pick out all the wall colors and floor coverings.

House Temperature

The temperature of rooms in a house can become a problem for some, especially for older people. Jane, whose mother-in-law lives with her and her husband, told us how they have handled the room temperature issue.

Jane: My mother-in-law likes it very warm because she does not have very good circulation. I like it very cold. Actually, having my office upstairs helps. I have control over my own heat up there. Downstairs we've put an extra portable heater next to my mother-in-law.

In fact, when possible, we recommend separate thermostats for those living in two-story houses. That way, if there is a separate apartment downstairs, residents then have choices regarding room temperature. Of course, the advantage of people having separate, detached housing is that the heating problem doesn't come up.

Noise Issues

If you're considering making a move to live together, do think about the type of neighborhood where you'd like to be. Carla told us how her experience of living in a noisy condominium influenced where she and her daughter decided to build their home. When asked what criteria were used to make the decision, she replied:

Carla: I wanted to know what kind of neighborhood it would be, whether there would be lots of children, lots of noise, and all of that. Would it be a place where I'd be comfortable? If you are in a planned community, the house shouldn't be next to the swimming pool, where everybody is there swimming all the time and making noise until late at night. That's how it is in our complex. My condo is right over the swimming pool. I wanted to know the location and what kind of community it was. Were there a lot of teenagers with loud cars? I was very anxious to help my daughter select a place where we didn't have to live far out in the suburbs or have all the nuisances of the city, such as motorcycles and loud cars.

Fortunately, in this day and age, there are a number of ways you can get around noise issues. Using earplugs is an obvious solution. With all the electronics available to us, you can also find headsets for listening to radio or television. In Sharon's kitchen, she has a TV that she likes to watch while cooking dinner. So she doesn't bother her husband with the noise of the TV while he's reading the newspaper, she'll frequently put on a lightweight, cordless headset. He gets a quiet room, and she gets to hear the news on TV.

Hearing loss can cause all sorts of problems for multigenerational families. We often heard in our interviews about "negotiations" over the volume of the television. There is a special device called TV Ears available to the hearing impaired whereby they can listen to a TV program at a higher noise level than others, who may want the volume turned down. Again, there are headsets available that allow you to listen to television programs or the radio without disturbing others. People in the same room can be sleeping, reading, or studying, while someone else is enjoying television or music on the radio.

Folks living directly below and above each other is another common noise problem. Adding insulation between floors can help. Also, the Japanese approach of leaving the shoes at the door instantly cuts down on the noise of walking.

The noise of crying kids also came up when we spoke with a grandmother. Susan initially lived with her daughter and son and their children together in the main house while her apartment in the backyard was being remodeled. She told us how difficult it was for her to sleep at night with the crying babies and how relieved she was when she was able to move into her own separate place. She can now play her own music loud at night and appreciates the separation sound-wise.

In another case, a teenage granddaughter told us how she and her sisters try to be quiet for their grandparents, who live in a cottage in their backyard. When they use the hot tub near the swimming pool, they know they can't be very loud, otherwise they would wake them up.

A friend told us the story about yet another noise issue for a family of six adult children all living at home with their parents in a large house. The problem is, with so many people who work, when can people do their laundry without disturbing others? One daughter's bedroom is right next to the laundry room. There are times when her sister, who works odd hours, will throw a load of wash in at midnight. The noise from the machine will wake up the sister sleeping in the room next to the laundry room. Certainly, the noise at that time of night would wake up others as well. This family needs to meet and set up a plan for doing laundry that does not interfere with someone's sleep.

Laundry

We found that most families we spoke with prefer to have separate washers and dryers for doing their laundry. For example, if someone needs to walk through a family member's kitchen to use their laundry facilates, privacy can be an issue. One couple told us how they came up with a solution to this problem. Both of them work and her mother does not. The mother lives in an apartment in their home and only uses their washer and dryer when they are both at work.

Another family uses the laundry room in the main house as the connecting junction for both the separate apartment for their son above the garage as well as the attached cottage for her in-laws. The laundry room serves as a hallway that goes from the garage to the kitchen of the main house. Through it, they also can go upstairs into the addition that is above the garage or into her in-laws unit. This design feature allows all of them to share the laundry room without infringing on each other's privacy.

Different families have different needs. If space is a problem, in this day and age we have the benefit of so-called stackable appliances. In the space the size of a small closet, one can have a washing machine on the bottom with a clothes dryer on top. Ultimately, it seems to work better for all parties to have separate laundry facilities.

As for who does the laundry, one individual we talked with learned from experience that it is important to talk that issue over ahead of time. Dan and his wife lived for a time with her parents. He told us about the problem he had with the way his mother-in-law did his laundry.

Dan: It was great that my laundry was done. Yet my mother-in-law would fold my jeans, put them away in a drawer, and they came out all wrinkled. So I had to iron them, and it would drive me nuts. But I couldn't say, "Stop doing my laundry." Because then it would seem like I was not grateful to them for giving us a place to live.

Dan's story illustrates the problem that some families have with communication. How much easier it might have been for all concerned if family meetings were held in his household.

Smoking

Making agreements for where and when people smoke when living together can be a huge issue. One man shared the difficulties that he and his wife have had in establishing ground rules about smoking with his mother, who lives in the same house with them. Now, after years of debate, she has made the decision that, if she wants to smoke, she has to smoke in her own bedroom, not in their family room where everybody sits together. In another case, the mother-in-law agreed to smoke outside the house. An elderly, wheelchair-bound, Alzheimer's mother who smokes required a different solution. She lives with her son and his wife in their home now. The only places she can smoke are in the kitchen corner or outside the house. They put a giant fan right over her chair in the kitchen so it can suck the smoke out of there.

Child Care

In chapters 4 and 5, we already talked about the many benefits of having grandparents and siblings around to help with child care. For everyone's sake, it helps to have agreements about when, where, how often, and how long people are expected to look after the kids. Some families prefer a flexible, on-call system. Others like to have specific days of the week set aside for babysitting so they can schedule around it. Still others don't want to babysit at all or will do so on a limited basis, especially if the grandparent is still working outside the home. The main thing we recommend is that you talk things over ahead of time so people don't feel encumbered by being expected to do what they hadn't planned for.

In addition, a marriage and family counselor offered some advice to us on the topic of child care. Mary lives near her son, daughter-in-law, and two grandchildren, and frequently babysits.

Mary: I think it really helps if you agree on ways to raise children. I think that is part of the reason that we have gotten along so well. We are all on the same page regarding expectations and discipline. I think that is a big piece of it, because it is about respecting other people and respecting yourself.

For those who don't mind being called on at the last minute to babysit, several people gave us examples of when this might be done. Joan, whose mother lives in an apartment attached to the main house, told us about her mother acting as a backup to day care.

Joan: We decided to live together because, at that time, I was still working. My daughter was a very young baby. We had a nanny come in while I was at work. From my perspective, my mother provided an extra set of eyes around the home environment during the day. Even though we had a caregiver for my daughter, if that person wasn't able to come or was coming an hour late, there was just another person around. We did it for that reason, and also so my daughter could have a relationship with her grandmother.

Others told stories about their reasons for requesting or providing help with child care on an as-needed basis.

Todd (whose parents live nearby): We can call up one of the grandparents and ask them to look after the kids while they take their nap so we can go do something else.

Linda (whose in-laws live next door): Well, probably on a selfish note, it's so nice to have Nanna there if I need to park a kid somewhere and run out with another child. She is more than happy to do that for me.

Jean (who lives across the street from her daughter and son-in-law): Whenever they have to go out by themselves, my daughter will call and ask if I'm available to look after the grandkids. Of course, I always jump at the chance to babysit and be with them.

Jean's enthusiasm for being with her grandkids reminds us of hearing from people that one major advantage of such activities is "keeping people young." Craig, whose in-laws live in a cottage in the backyard, told us about the benefits to his in-laws for being flexible in helping him and his wife with their child-care needs.

Craig: I think it's great for them having us here, because they have so much fun following the kids' basketball and water polo games. Our calendars get synched and they go to every single game. I think it takes the older generation and keeps them young longer. It plugs them into our day-to-day activities. "Can you pick up so-and-so from school?" or "Can you take them to the dentist?" We are so lucky they live so close to us. By staying engaged and active, they are bound to live longer too.

Tim, whose daughter and three grandchildren live in an apartment in the same house with him and his wife, Dorrie, talked about ways they've agreed to help out with the grandchildren on a regular basis.

Tim: Right now, between us, we spend six hours a day in the car driving three children around to school and after-school activities such as ballet, gymnastics, and baseball. We really devote a lot of our time to just being chauffeurs. In fact, we don't know how a single working mother does it. It is unbelievable the amount of time necessary just to take them around to their various activities. That to me was a huge revelation in terms of generational shifts. When I was a child, my parents took me nowhere. I went on my own; I biked or did not go. So this whole concept of chauffeuring and taking children somewhere has been an extraordinary learning experience about different generations doing things differently.

Living so far out in the country leaves Dorrie and Tim little choice other than to drive their grandchildren everywhere. These days, with so many youngsters being chauffeured and with the problem of obese children nationwide, we were especially glad to hear the following story about a grandmother who has a schedule of walking with her grandchild to school. Jean, who lives in her own home across the street from her daughter, described how she does it.

Jean: I run across the street about 8:05 in the morning, and we walk up to school, which is a short walk. In September, my daughter went back to school. She wants to be a nursery school teacher. So she goes to class and also takes her little one to nursery school on Tuesdays and Thursdays. My oldest grandchild didn't really have a way of getting to school safely, so I walk with him to school two days a week, which is wonderful because it gives us a little quality time to be together. It's a win-win situation.

Perhaps one of the most favorite scheduled activities we heard about is that of grandparents giving their adult children a regular night off for what now is commonly called a "date night." Kristi, whose parents live in a cottage in the backyard, told us how they set it up.

Kristi: Yes, we will set it up in advance. When they moved in, I did ask if maybe Tony and I could take one night a week for a date night, and they were perfectly happy with that. They are always willing to pitch in that way.

For those who prefer a more scheduled routine in caring for the grandkids, we heard about a number of options for families where both parents and grandparents work outside the home. Gail, who works part-time as an accountant and lives with her husband in a duplex next door to her daughter, son-in-law, and grandsons, told us about the babysitting schedule they've set up.

Gail: I babysit all the time. They have no day care outside of us. Don watches them in the morning, and I only work half a day. So I come home at noon and I have them with me in the afternoon. They do have a sitter, but she only gets them once a week. So I do have a day off. I just love having that close relationship with my grandsons. I feel like I'm almost a second mother, rather than a distant grandmother.

Another working grandmother told us she plans to help babysit her grandson, who attends a year-round school, during his intercessions. Carla, who writes and works part time as a consultant, has the flexibility to help out. She will soon be living in a house with her divorced daughter and ten-year-old grandson and will have her own separate wing with an office there.

For so many families with both parents working, the question of who is going to care for the children is a huge concern. In one case, a young woman gets collective help from a number of different sources, including her mother, her mother's housekeeper, siblings, and a nanny that she shares with her brother. She and her brother each have two children. Fortunately for her, her mother lives nearby and her brother lives next door. Kathleen's story is told in detail in chapter 4 under the section "Siblings Help Out."

Family Fun

In the beginning of this chapter, we made reference to Ron Huxley's steps for a family meeting from the *Parenting Toolbox* website. The last of the eight steps listed is "Remember to plan to have fun."[7] Consequently, we decided to end this chapter with a discussion about making agreements for family fun. Certainly, making arrangements for fun both together and apart are important. We've already given an example of grandparents and siblings providing time off for adult children to have date nights, weekends, or vacations by themselves. In addition, we heard a number of stories about families taking joint vacations, sharing meals, attending kids' activities, as well as going to movies, zoos, and parks. Playing board games such as Monopoly or dominoes was also mentioned, along with playing tennis, swimming, and walking. In other cases, families have fun cooking and gardening or even playing musical instruments together.

Actually, multigenerational family vacations (some folks call them "togethering") can be not only fun but also a useful way to experiment with living with your adult family members again. Indeed, a vacation with relatives, with the associated tight quarters and group schedules, can bring out the worst in some and the best in others. And the travel industry is happy to help out in your experiments. Several cruise lines offer lower rates for large family groups, actively encouraging entire family reunions. Nickelodeon Family Suites by Holiday Inn in Orlando has what they call extended-family suites that include four beds for children and two private rooms for adults with king-size beds. A variety of travel websites promote multigenerational trips as a growing family-bonding trend.

Women typically are the key contacts for families. They set up kin gatherings, keep track of relatives, and promote intergenerational contact. We've found that women in the middle generation are the most involved with these relationships. The mother-daughter link is central for both maintaining family contacts and the flow of support across generations.[8] One woman we spoke with whose in-laws live next door had this to say about inviting them over for family fun.

Linda: One worry I have is that I'm taking advantage or overstepping my bounds as far as the children go. If I lean on my mother-in-law too much, I would like to think that she would just say no. I brought it up with her, and she has assured me that she would. They end up doing a lot for me as far as watching the kids goes. Specifically, when my husband and I go on vacation, just the two of us, they have been able to actually live in our home and watch the kids. It's so much easier. One thing I like to do to show my thanks is have them over here for dinner every couple of weeks. It's a way I can reciprocate and show appreciation. By the way, my twelve-year-old son is extremely sensitive. If a week or two goes by without Nanna and Papa coming over for dinner, he'll ask me, "When are they coming for dinner?" It's a special event for all of us.

Linda also told us about arrangements for her mother-in-law to give the children music lessons.

Linda: The fact that my kids have such a close relationship with their grandparents is wonderful. Just as an example, my mother-in-law is instructing my seven-year-old on how to play the flute. He and my twelve-year-old, who will be playing the ukulele that she taught him how to play, will both be in the school talent show. When it's time to rehearse, they go over to Nanna's. Also, my daughter has been playing piano since third grade. Before she had formal instruction from her piano teacher, my mother-in-law started her on the piano for a six-month period. Anna was able to walk right next door and get her beginning experience on the piano. It's the older generation passing on skills and talent to the younger ones.

Next, she talked about the fun they have together in the communal garden between their houses.

Linda: My in-laws had the foresight to buy the empty lot between their home and ours. Before we moved here, they knew that they just wanted a physical buffer between their neighbors and themselves. Papa has always gardened that patch of yard, but he's older now. I would say in the last two or three years, his interest in laying all the crops has dwindled. My husband is the main gardener now. When my father-in-law is out in the yard, that usually induces the kids to go out. "What are you doing? Can I help?" They have a lot of fun in the garden together. They help clear the land and with weeding. We had a family day when all of us including Nanna and Papa got out and did a lot of clearing. The following week, we all planted seeds. Also, we have a huge snail problem. My sons will go out and bring me back a bucket of snails. I pay them five cents a snail.

Nancy, who lives with her husband in a cottage in the backyard, told us how she and her husband enjoy attending their three granddaughters' sports events. They end up going to most of their games and will often pick the girls up from school and take them to their basketball and water polo games. In turn, the three granddaughters were very enthusiastic when they told us how lucky they are to have their grandparents around to give them support at their games.

I (Sharon) have had a lot of experience in making agreements for family fun, including treasure hunts, shopping, and travel. One time I had my grandson John over for the weekend while his mom, dad, and sisters went out of town. I was concerned about how I would keep him busy since his sisters are usually over when he is and they play with him. Fortunately, I planned ahead. His birthday was just a few weeks before he came. Instead of giving him all three gifts he had requested, I only gave him one and saved the other two for him to open during his stay with us. I knew he would receive so many presents on his actual birthday and wouldn't miss them. By the way, for all the grandkids' birthday and Christmas gifts, I give them toy catalogues and let them make their own selections. They have a budget to work with. That way they get what they want, and I'm not buying them something they already have.

One of the gifts John opened at our house was a bug and butterfly collecting kit. It included bug-scooper forceps. Instead of collecting bugs with it, I sent John on a Tom Sawyer (paint-the-fence) treasure hunt to gather acorns for me. He and a neighbor child took turns using it to fill their respective buckets with acorns. It was a win-win activity for them and me. They had fun playing together, and I didn't have to weed out so many little oak tree seedlings that spring!

Also, I had this idea that it would be fun to take the grandkids on a special trip with us by themselves when they turned ten. So I brought this up with my daughter before Tori's tenth birthday last July. She agreed to ask Tori where she would like to go. With no hesitation, her answer was "Paris!" Tori went on to tell her mom that she would have to learn French before she went. Was I ever surprised! I had no idea that ten-year-olds even knew where Paris was. On her actual birthday, we gave her a travel book on Paris along with forty French lessons on CDs. We ended up having a fantastic nine-day trip to Paris and the Brittany coast the following summer.

We found that traveling with a preteen can be a great experience, if you plan ahead. We made a number of agreements on how we would manage the trip. Tori loves to read, so she brought several books with her. We also let her select all the places she wanted to visit in Paris. We made sure that our museum visits were no more than two hours long, and that she had plenty of free time to run around to work off excess energy at parks. Whenever possible, we walked from our hotel to visit places like the Eiffel Tower. During the trip she did endure one three-hour meal at a restaurant in Paris with our French friends. Afterward, when we met up with them at their home in Brittany, she asked ahead if she could be excused from the table to go and read when she was finished with her dinner. Then, at the end of each day, Tori helped me edit photos I had taken of our activities on my digital camera. After we returned home, I let her select the prints she wanted for her own travel photo album.

In addition, I keep a history of family fun through photos, and I do an annual biographical letter for each of the grandkids. I love to take pictures at family gatherings. What I do is make copies not only for us and our adult children, but also for the grandchildren. My daughters have memento boxes for each of their children, so that's where they go for now.

Also, when each grandchild turns three, I give them a "first reader" with him or her in it as a birthday gift. I work with their mother to produce this special biographical book. What we do is take pictures of the child between two and a half and three years old while engaged in his or her favorite activities. Then we make up a list of questions that relate to the photographs. Some of the fifteen questions we used for Christopher's book were

Do you want to build a planter box with Dad?
Do you want to ride your bike at Vasona Park?
Do you want to play in the sand at Pajaro Dunes?
Do you want to read the *Bob the Builder* book?
Do you want to sleep with your teddy bear?

Next, I make up a separate page on the computer in large print where each question is used, Mom asks, "Do you want to sleep with your teddy bear?" Christopher says, "Yes!" These pages are placed in a five-by-seven-inch album on the left side, with the corresponding four-by-six-inch photos to the right of each page. In Christopher's case, the title of his book is *Christopher Says "Yes!"* The title of Tori's book is *Tori Says "I Do!"* The title of Miranda's book is *Randi Says "Sure!"* The title of John's book is *John Says "Yes!"* Each indicator of agreement, "Yes," "I Do," and "Sure," was the child's favorite way of expressing the affirmative at age three.

Finally, I include with each child's birthday card a letter to them outlining their activities for the year, including family fun. It's an annual biographical letter I do for them, which my daughters place in each of their memento boxes. I plan to continue that until they turn eighteen, when they're old enough to write up their own memoirs.

Conclusions

As we've said throughout this chapter, *communication* is the key word to success in making agreements for living together. Whether or not you have a happy and satisfying family life is determined by how well you communicate with each other. Certainly, the use of compromise, affection, and respect are all key ingredients essential for keeping the peace. Also, it is very important for all participants in the housing arrangement to meet on a regular basis to talk about what's working, what's not working, and how to fix things. General topics of discussion that come up during family meetings are length of stay, communication preferences, relationship issues, privacy issues, household finances, shared responsibilities, personal preferences, child care, and family fun. As for length of stay, it helps to talk ahead about what events might precipitate a change in your arrangement. Regarding communication preferences, most families prefer a "call ahead" policy for interaction. As for relationship issues, try to determine compatibility before living together. When it comes to privacy issues, giving each other space was mentioned frequently. Regarding household finances, shared responsibilities, and child care, talk ahead about needs and expectations. As for personal preferences, be aware that lifestyle differences, decor, neatness, noise, house temperature, pets, and smoking may all need to be addressed. Finally, be sure to take the time to make agreements for family fun. Having fun together can help nurture positive relationships. Indeed, living together again with good communication can add balance to your life, giving you more contentment, peace, and freedom.

Finally, we want to close the book with our favorite quote of all, reprised here from chapter 5:

Bill: My wife and I enjoyed a few short years of three-generational living in a two-flat house in Chicago. We occupied the first floor. Our daughter and her husband and our two grandchildren lived above us. We sat around the same dinner table every night. Those were the happiest, richest, and most rewarding years of our lives.

We wish such days for you!

Back in 1997, John was asked by his business school dean to write about the economy of 2020, then twenty-three years in the future. In retrospect, he now admits he missed the mark on Tiger Woods' success. But, looking at the "easy to see demographics" unfolding in the decades to come, the economic doldrums beginning in 2008 were quite easy to see coming.

2020 Is 23 Years from Now

REDICTIONS ABOUT 2020? Two are easy. First, Tiger Woods will have won more green blazers and more green in general than any athlete in history. Second, we'll all be about 23 years older. Both things will rivet the attention of the nation. Woods will make us happy. Retirement-age baby boomers will not.

The math is pretty simple. In 1953 there weren't enough 1st grade teachers. 1956 brought us the Schwinn shortage. 1964 it was college classrooms, 1960 jobs, 1978 houses, and now in 1997 we have the shortage of sure investment opportunities. Baby boomers' fear of the future is now driving the current boom in stock market investment. Fast approaching their fifties, retirement planning is now the rage.

The problem is, even the best investments only produce money. And money is nothing. I'm not saying it isn't important. Like motor oil is to your car engine, money is the lubricant of society. You don't trade your 70 hours a week and/or your creativity for money. Rather, your hard work and good ideas are actually traded for a nice place to live, nice schools for your kids, and nice vacations. The money just makes the trade a little more efficient. Now I know this isn't what you learned in your finance classes. Money can actually disappear—in a stock market crash or in hyper-inflation, for example. Remember

1987? Or, just ask your Japanese friends about the relationship between money, stocks, and real estate. Simply stated, money isn't stronger than demographics. That's why in trying to understand the past and the future, cultural anthropologists focus on people, not money.

Culture's primary impact is that it makes us all imitate our parents, the generation ahead of us. As strange as the Generation-Xers' behavior (tattoos and cigars) looks to their parents today, the Xers will be driving minivans in the next millennium, too. And boomers' parents are now showing us all how to party. In most cultures, throughout history, old folks have lived with and been supported by their kids. Not our folks. They've all had their babies paying into social security and such. And that boom crop can afford a lot; 3.5 kids can support a nice house and nice vacations for 1.5 parents pretty easily. Boomers' parents are enjoying the biggest binge in history.

But, in 2020 it will be 1.5 kids supporting 2.0 parents. That simple ratio will be far more salient than any P/E ration. The breakthroughs in bio-tech (info tech will be passé) will serve to lengthen life. Cancer, AIDS, and heart disease won't kill, bodies and minds will just wear down. And the costs of the worn-down baby-boom generation of 2020 will simply not be supported by their 1990s investments in stocks, no matter how red-hot or blue-chip.

I guess I can see three ways to defeat this destined demographic demon. First, of course, culture can change. For example, think how profoundly birth control has changed our values and everyday lives. In 2020, when baby boomers are forced back into the homes and care of their kids, everyone may see it as a positive thing. Indeed, haven't we all decried the decline in family strength? In 2020 we may see the rejoining of young and old in the household as the best kind of family reunion. When old and young are living together again, the fierce independence and political power of the AARP will have gone the same way as other vestiges of culture like communism and cabbage-patch dolls.

Globalism is the second way out. While we share this nationwide graying with places like Japan and Western Europe, things are much different in places like Mexico and the Mekong River Valley. The question is can we invest in the legions of young people in the latter lands fast enough now, so they will be willing to return the favor in 2020? Let's for a moment focus on the example of our NAFTA neighbors to the south. The free trade agreement with Mexico passed in 1995 was more than Ross Perot's Waterloo. It was the single most important event in U.S./Mexico relations since the U.S. Marines marched into the Halls of Montezuma (in Mexico City) in the 1840s. For the first time in history we have treated Mexico as an equal. Most Americans have missed this significance, but no Mexican did.

Yes, American jobs have migrated south. But, isn't that better than Mexican workers migrating north? Yes, the peso crash landed. But, now in 1997, the key part of the term is "landed." Indeed, this year they repaid us the billions we loaned them, and they did it early! Yes, cocaine corruption is king in places like Tijuana. But, whose fault is that? The trade in illicit drugs is, and always will be, demand driven. The Latin American drug lords supply, but they don't advertise.

If we manage our Mexican marriage right, the fruits of the relationship will be a wonderful wealth for both countries in 2020. We need to focus our cross-border investments now in factories and young people' brains. That will enable them to make the cars, televisions, computers, and medical equipment for us. And we'll supply the engineering, financial, healthcare, consulting, and management services and software to them. Immigration won't be an issue. Economic integration will mean open borders in the 2020s like we had in the 1920s, like the Europeans have now. If we can genuinely embrace globalism, the young people of Mexico and the other developing countries we support will help to abate the baby-boomer bomb of the next millennium. Indeed, this is the best of the three approaches to the crisis of gray coming in 2020.

Finally, as I mentioned, there is a third solution, a xenophobic one. You've heard the story of the two hikers who ran into a grizzly bear. One hiker stopped to slip on his running shoes. The other asked, "What are you doing, you can't outrun a grizzly?" His friend replied, "I don't need to outrun the bear, I just need to outrun you!" Yes, a short-sighted Adam Smithian selfishness may lead to better stock-market gambling than your "friends." But, even the biggest fish, with 20-20 vision, can't see very far in a putrid pond.

Source: John L. Graham, "2020 Is 23 Years from Now," *UCInsight Magazine,* Spring 1997, pp. 4 and 23.

A P P E N D I X

An Important Book Review of *Together Again*
(the precursor to this book, published in 2007)

TOGETHER AGAIN: A CREATIVE GUIDE TO SUCCESSFUL MULTIGENERA-
TIONAL LIVING, by Sharon Graham Niederhaus and John L. Graham. M. Evans
(An imprint of the Rowman & Littlefield Publishing Group) (2007).
C.307 p.illu.index. ISBN 10-59077-122-2. Paperback, $16.95

HIS BOOK is a particularly valuable resource for those in the
field in Intergenerational Relations. The authors (siblings themselves) have combined their expertise to produce a guide for families and professionals who are dealing with multigenerational
households, e.g., living in a single home or living nearby. They
provide some helpful background and historical perspective since multigenerational living arrangements were so common in earlier times. The authors
note research documenting the more than 6 million such living arrangements in the United States and provide an insightful analysis of the ration-
ale as well as issues that must be faced. While some are fairly obvious (such
as interior design and remodeling to ensure safety, access, and privacy), others (such as financial and legal considerations) are less obvious and more
complex.

The book has received accolades and notoriety in the media through a
feature story on ABC Television News "Good Morning America" (04-20-2007)

and a special segment in "USA Weekend" magazine (08-26-2007). The focus of these stories has been on the many benefits to young and old living in multi-generational households.

One of the most creative chapters deals with the pairing of younger and older generations to work together towards mutually beneficial common goals. This is the epitome of excellence in intergenerational programming. Rather than viewing the generations in conflict or competing for scarce resources (e.g., generational stake), the authors skillfully emphasize the many benefits that emerge from intergenerational living. The authors are among the first to embrace multigenerational families as a potential positive and significant trend.

Despite their optimism, the authors also recognize the many tensions that can develop in multigenerational households. They identify these challenges so that families and professionals can anticipate the difficulties that may arise. One key to success described in the book is developing a clear and precise "contract" or agreement that spells out the expectations and responsibilities of each member of the multigenerational family. The contract is a dynamic document, subject to change based on agreements by those who participate. However, the real value may lie more in the process of establishing the areas of concern and the identifying potential solutions.

These documents do not avoid all stress and conflict. As the authors note, personality differences and unique family priorities/values may supersede "rational" attempts at mediation and resolution. Knowing first hand the pitfalls of making room for adult children who have completed college, many families will appreciate the sensitivity and understand the structure developed by the authors to bring underlying tensions to the surface. For example, what are appropriate expectations to establish for recent graduates living at home with their parents? Are the tasks that they can assist with similar to those they undertook at younger ages? Should new expectations emerge such as meal preparation, laundry, shopping, transportation, or elder care?

The book is impressive for its recognition of the variety of multigenerational family situations. No one is left out. There is ample attention, of course, on living with aging family members as well as attention on the boomerang generation of young adults moving back to the family nest for financial and emotional reasons. There is recognition of the adult child and grandchildren moving in following divorce as well as the same need among single parents with children who have never married. What is particularly commendable is the emphasis on providing readers with a context in which these changes are occurring. The context can be emotional, historical, economic, sociological, or demographic, but readers are always recognized in these presentations. The authors even anticipate the negative cultural bias in having people of vastly different ages "living together." The inability to live independently is itself a social stigma that adds significant stress to the multigenerational household.

The writing style is down to earth and easy to understand. The concepts and principles of successful multigenerational families come to life with the many first person accounts from different generations. More than 100 families participated in interviews and shared their individual challenges in negotiating among three generational families. In one section the authors offer schematics of homes for those interested in designing household arrangements for multigenerational living. There is sufficient variety in topic coverage and helpful suggestions that make this book a particularly valuable resource for families facing the challenge of living together with multiple generations. The importance of family dynamics, family structure, and family economics is part of the framework. Ideally families will use this resource *before* establishing multigenerational households.

Readers from any discipline will find great value in this book, particularly those professionals who assist families with the transition to multigenerational living arrangements. In summary this is a practical book that fulfills the promise of its title: "a creative guide to successful multigenerational living."

Dr. Paul Roodin
SUNY Oswego
Oswego, New York
Journal of Intergenerational Relationships 6, no. 2 (2008): 237–39

Notes

Chapter 1: Dodging the Nursing Home

1. To be precise, the "stereotactic resection of his left frontal temporal lesion was complicated by postoperative bleeding in the right occipitoparietal region; perhaps in the hypothalamus; and pulmonary edema."

2. "Proposition 13, War by Initiative," Special Report on Democracy in California, *Economist*, April 23, 2011, 8–10.

3. "Why One Economist Predicts Slow Growth," *Economist*, October 4, 2010.

Chapter 2: Two Decades of Change for American Families Have Already Begun

1. E. S. Browning, "Debt Hobbles Older Americans," *Wall Street Journal*, September 7, 2011; Catey Hill, "Coming Soon: Smaller Raises for Seniors?," *SmartMoney.com*, July 13, 2011; Mark Whitehouse, "Another Threat to the Economy: Boomers Cutting Back," *Wall Street Journal*, August 16, 2010; and "Demand for Equities May Drop," *Economist*, January 9, 2012.

2. Kathleen McGarry and Robert F. Schoeni, "Social Security, Economic Growth, and the Rise of Independence of Elderly Widows in the 20th Century," NBER Working Paper No. 6511, April 1998.

3. As far as we know, Seth Crone invented the use of the term *moving picture* in this context, as it connotes that seeing the big picture is not good enough. You also need to see how things change through time, as well, for true enlightenment.

Chapter 3: Why Living Together Again Makes Sense

1. Harold T. Christensen, "Family," *World Book Encyclopedia*, 1976.

2. Karen A. Franck and Sherry Aherntzen, eds., *New Households, New Housing* (New York: Van Nostrand Reinhold, 1989).

3. Elizabeth Arias, "United States Life Tables, 2000," *National Vital Statistics Reports* 51(3), December 19, 2002, 1–38.

4. Michael Muskal, "Americans Are Living Longer, Need More Services," *San Francisco Chronicle*, November 18, 2011.

5. Daniel Callahan, *Setting Limits: Medical Goals in an Aging Society* (New York: Simon & Schuster, 1987).

6. Ibid.

7. Nancy Hooyman and H. Asuman Kiyak, *Social Gerontology: A Multidisciplinary Perspective* (Boston: Allyn & Bacon, 1999).

8. "National Report: 1 in 5 Kids Alone after School," *San Francisco Chronicle*, September 11, 2000, A4.

9. Patrick H. Hare, personal interviews, 2000.

10. Nivein Behairy, "Children's Use of Technology, in Their Own Words" (Ph.D. dissertation, Graduate School of Management, University of California, Irvine, 2003).

11. Sherry Turkel, *Alone Together: Why We Expect More from Technology and Less from Each Other* (New York: Basic Books, 2011).

12. Robert D. Putnam, *Bowling Alone* (New York: Simon & Schuster, 2000).

Chapter 4: Stories about Caregiving Benefits for the Young and Old

1. Jean Hanff Korelitz, "All in the Family," *Real Simple*, August 2003.

2. Ellen Graham, "Two Generations, One Nursing Home," *Wall Street Journal*, May 13, 1998, B1.

3. Barbara Lovenheim, "Child's Support," *AARP Magazine*, March/April 2006, 17–18.

Chapter 5: Stories about Grand Relationships

1. Neale Donald Walsch, *Conversations with God: An Uncommon Dialogue*, bk. 3 (Charlottsville, VA: Hampton Roads, 1998), 28.

2. Nancy Hooyman and H. Asuman Kiyak, *Social Gerontology: A Multidisciplinary Perspective* (Boston: Allyn & Bacon, 1999), 268.

3. Ibid., 269.

Chapter 6: Deciding to Live Together: Inventive Negotiations

1. "Car Plows through Market, Killing 9," *CNN.com*, July 16, 2003.

2. That is, if it already hasn't!

3. In chapter 12 we'll go into some detail about how "mainstream" American culture is really kind of an odd notion. But please bear with our simplification of things for this chapter.

4. Phil Moeller, "How to Make Multigenerational Living Work," *U.S. News & World Report*, January 14, 2011.

5. Mary Pipher, *Another Country* (New York: Riverhead Books, 1999).

6. Ibid.

7. Kathleen A. Hughes, "He Says Maine, She Says Florida," *Wall Street Journal*, March 21, 2011.

Chapter 7: Proximity and Privacy: Living Together in Helpful Ways

1. Pat Curry, "Make Room for Everyone," *Builder*, December 2005, 63–64.
2. Andres Duany, Elizabeth Plater-Zyberg, and Jeff Speck, *Suburban Nation: The Rise of Sprawl and the Decline of the American Dream* (New York: North Point Press, 2000), 52.
3. "Home, Sweet Manufactured Home," *Reader's Digest*, September 2005, 30.
4. Ben Brown, "Communes for Grownups," *AARP Bulletin*, October 2004.

Chapter 8: Other Times, Other Places

1. Margaret Mead and Ken Heyman, *Family* (New York: Macmillan, 1965), 80.
2. www.contemporaryfamilies.org/public/families.php, March 2004.
3. William Strauss and Neil Howe, *Generations* (William Morrow: New York, 1991), 36–37.
4. James A. Michener, *The Covenant* (New York: Fawcett Crest, 1980), 22–25.
5. Barbara Ehrenreich, "The Real Truth about the Female," *Time*, March 8, 1999, 57–68.
6. James A. Michener, *Chesapeake* (New York: Fawcett Books, 1978), 286–287.
7. Ibid., 602–603.
8. Laura Esquivel, *Like Water for Chocolate* (New York: Anchor Books, 1989), 10–12.
9. Blanche Weisen Cook, *Eleanor Roosevelt: Volume One, 1884–1933* (New York: Viking, 1992), 183.
10. Sean Mitchell, "The Interior Landscape—Space," *Los Angeles Times*, April 28, 2005, F1. Used with permission.
11. *Parade Magazine*, December 28, 2003, 12.
12. Adam Gopnik, *Paris to the Moon* (New York: Random House, 2000), 71–73.
13. Peter Hessler, *River Town: Two Years on the Yangtze* (New York: HarperCollins, 2001), 90.
14. Edward T. Hall, *The Hidden Dimension* (Garden City, NY: Anchor/DoubleDay, 1966), 103–104.
15. Constance Hilliard, "Take a Closer Look at the Nuclear Family Norm," *USA Today*, July 12, 2001.

Chapter 9: Designing and Remodeling Your Home for Privacy

1. Patrick H. Hare, *Survey of Installations of Accessory Units*, report 4 of *Accessory Units: The State of the Art* (Washington, DC: Patrick J. Hare Planning and Design, 1989), 6.
2. Some say 40 percent, see James R. Barth, Long Li, and Rich Palacios Jr., "McMansion Economics," *Los Angeles Times*, November 21, 2010.
3. Hare, *Survey*.

4. Bert Verrips, *Second Units: An Emerging Housing Resource*, POS Housing/Greenbelt Program, Technical Report #2-E (San Francisco: People for Open Space, 1983), 4.

5. Patrick H. Hare and Jolene N. Ostler, *Creating an Accessory Apartment* (New York: McGraw-Hill, 1987), 30–31.

6. Jeannie Matteucci, "Backyard Cottage Industry," *San Francisco Chronicle*, October 9, 2011.

7. Norma J. Shattuck, "Behind the Big Door," *San Francisco Chronicle*, October 20, 2004, G1.

8. Charles Smith, "Family Hopes to Add a Room When Rebuilding 1920s Two-Car Garage," *San Francisco Chronicle*, October 12, 2005, G3.

9. Shattuck, "Behind the Big Door."

10. Smith, "Family Hopes."

11. Ibid.

12. Charles Smith, "Please, Don't Park Guests in the Garage," *San Francisco Chronicle*, May 11, 2005, G5.

13. Hare and Ostler, *Creating an Accessory Apartment*, 34, 35.

14. Lou Manfredini, "Going the Rental Route," *USA Weekend*, September 19–21, 2003, 17.

15. Available at www.diydoctor.org.uk/projects/barn_conversion.htm.

16. Patricia Bass, "Show Me the Green," *Palo Alto Weekly, Home and Real Estate*, October 14, 2005, 1.

17. Bass, "Show Me."

18. Carolyn Said, "White House Picks Up Conservation Mantra," *San Francisco Chronicle*, October 9, 2005, A13.

19. Bass, "Show Me."

20. Ibid.

21. Jane Knoerle, "Affordable Green: Sunset's Idea House Is Rich with Energy-Saving Innovations," *Almanac*, October 19. 2005, 16.

22. Ibid.

23. Penny Doherty, "When Adding a Second Unit, Consider These Factors," *Wall Street Journal, Real Estate Journal*, 2004.

24. Lynn Comeskey, "Experience Counts," *Palo Alto Weekly, Home and Real Estate*, October 21, 2005, 17.

25. Leo L. Cram, "Accessory Apartments," GG14, Missouri Gerontology Institute, University of Missouri–Columbia, October 1993, http://extension.missouri.edu/p/GG14.

26. Courtney Rosen, *How to Do Everything* (New York: Free Press, 2000), #252, "Hire a Builder."

27. Molly Tanenbaum, "Get It in Writing," *Almanac, Fall Real Estate 2005*, October 10, 2005, 26, 28.

28. Rosen, *How to Do Everything*, "Hire a Builder."

Chapter 10: How to Find, Buy, or Build Housing

1. This estimate is based on the fact that nationwide circa 2005 approximately 6 percent of existing housing units are sold in a given year.

2. Andrea Coombes, "Relative Proximity," *CBS MarketWatch*, October 7, 2004.

3. William Strauss and Neil Howe, *Generations* (New York: Perennial, 1991), 391.

4. Andrea Gross, "Making a Big Move," *Time*, October 12, 2003.

5. Richard Paoli, "Americans Favor Family as Neighbors," *San Francisco Chronicle*, October 5, 2003, G3.

6. Pat Curry, "Make Room for Everyone," *Builder*, December 2005, 63–64.

7. "House Party," *San Francisco Chronicle*, August 5, 2001, 23.

8. Excerpted Jamboree Housing Corporation, "Jamboree Housing Corporation Breaks Ground on Courier Place Apartment Homes in Calremont, CA," news release, December 3, 2010, www.jamboreehousing.com/images/documents/news_articles/courierplacemediarelease.pdf.

9. Ryan Chittum, "Smart Development Plans," *Wall Street Journal*, March 12, 2003. Used with permission.

10. Carol Lloyd, "The Fab New World of Prefab Houses," *SFGate.com*, May, 11, 2004.

11. Judy Ricter, "A Full Table," *San Francisco Chronicle*, September 10, 2005, sec. F. Used with permission.

12. The information in this section is based on Martin Gellen, *Accessory Apartments in Single-Family Housing* (New Brunswick, NJ: Rutgers CUPR Press, 1986), 1034–4.

13. San Francisco Development Fund, "Small Solutions: Second Units as Affordable Housing: The Evaluation of the Double Unit Opportunity Program of San Francisco Development Fund, 1985–1988," The Fund, San Francisco, 1988.

14. Jim Berson, personal interview, August 22, 2000.

15. Marion Softky, "Woodside Tackles New Rules for Extra Living Units," *Almanac*, September 27, 2000, 6.

16. Julie Harris, personal interview, September 12, 2006.

Chapter 11: Making Your Home Accessible to Seniors

1. Patrick H. Hare, "The Suburban Frailty Boom," *Aging Network News*, August 1991, 10.

2. Iris Harrell and Lisa Sten, "Universal Design," *San Jose Magazine*, June 2003, supplement "San Jose Home and Garden Program."

3. Ronald L. Mace, Graeme J. Hardie, and Jaine P. Place, "Accessible Environments: Toward Universal Design," in *Design Intervention: Toward a More Humane Architecture* (New York: Van Norstrand Reinhold, 1991).

4. Mitra Kalita, "Blueprint for a New American Home," *Wall Street Journal*, November 2, 2011.

5. Jerrine Barrett, personal interview, January 23, 2001.

6. Mace, Hardie, and Place, "Accessible Environments.

7. National Association of Homebuilders, "Certified Aging-In-Place Specialist (CAPS)," www.nahb.org/page.aspx/category/sectionID=686/fromGSA=1.

8. Roseann Henry, "6 Ideas for Elder-Friendly Design," *This Old House*, www.thisoldhouse.com/toh/article/0,,519817,00.html.

9. "Helping Older Homeowners," *San Francisco Chronicle*, March 13, 2004, sec. F.

10. Henry, "6 Ideas."

11. Cindy Gackle, "Home Accessibility = Greater Independence," www.mscare.org/cmsc/images/pdf/HomeAccessibility-Gackle.pdf.

12. Ibid.
13. Cheryl Lu-Lien Tan, "Going UP? Elevators Invade Suburban Homes," *Wall Street Journal*, April 28, 2005.
14. AARP, "Grab Bars à la Mode," February 1, 2004, www.aarp.org/home-garden/home-improvement/info-02-2004/bathroom_grabbars.html.
15. Ibid.
16. Gackle, "Home Accessibility."
17. Lew Sichelman, "House for All Ages," *San Francisco Chronicle*, January 5, 2003, sec. H.
18. Gackle, "Home Accessibility."
19. Leslie Haggin Geary, "5 Steps to an Elder-Friendly Home," *CNN Money*, October 22, 2002, http://money.cnn.com/2002/10/22/pf/yourhome/q_seniorfriendly/index.htm.
20. Gackle, "Home Accessibility."
21. Geary, "5 Steps."
22. Gackle, "Home Accessibility."
23. Ibid.
24. Henry, "6 Ideas."
25. Premier Bathrooms advertisement, AARP Bulletin, 47 no. 5 (2006), 31.
26. Gackle, "Home Accessibility."
27. Ibid.
28. Ibid.
29. Henry, "6 Ideas."
30. Geary, "5 Steps."
31. Ibid.
32. Henry, "6 Ideas."
33. Gackle, "Home Accessibility."
34. Ibid.
35. Paul J. Donio, "Tailor-Fit Kitchens," *This Old House*, www.thisoldhouse.com/toh/article/0,,214601,00.html.
36. Ibid.
37. Gackle, "Home Accessibility."
38. Harrell and Sten, "Universal Design."
39. Donio, "Tailor-Fit."
40. Gackle, "Home Accessibility."
41. Harrell and Sten, "Universal Design."
42. American Occupational Therapy Association, "Making the Home Senior-Friendly," *About.com*, http://seniorhealth.about.com/library/eldercare/bl_apact3.htm.
43. Geary, "5 Steps."
44. Gackle, "Home Accessibility."
45. Henry, "6 Ideas."
46. Gackle, "Home Accessibility."
47. Geary, "5 Steps."
48. Gackle, "Home Accessibility."
49. Ibid.

50. Susan Fornoff, "Making Room for Mom and Dad," *San Francisco Chronicle*, September 18, 2004, sec. F.

51. Gackle, "Home Accessibility."

52. Amazing Phones advertisement, *San Francisco Chronicle*, October 12, 2004.

53. Benny Evangelista, "Public Gets Firsthand View of the Future," *San Francisco Chronicle*, May 17, 2004, sec. D.

54. James Brooke, "Robotic Elder-Care Products Gaining in Popularity in Japan," *San Francisco Chronicle*, March 5, 2004.

55. Ibid.

56. Ibid.

57. Ibid.

58. Virginia Division for the Aging, "Elder Cottage Housing Opportunities (ECHO)," www.vda.virginia.gov/echo.asp.

59. Gail Hand, "The Joys and Pitfalls of Inter-Generational Living: One Family's Success Story with Building an In-Law Addition," June 12, 2004, www.the-homestore .com/about-us/in-the-news/aarp-joys/.

Chapter 12: Overcoming Cultural Stigmas: Four Curses and a Blessing

1. Teresa Toguchi Swartz, Minzee Kim, Mayumi Uno, Jeylan Mortimer, and Kirsten Bengtson O'Brien, "Safety Nets and Scaffolds: Parental Support in the Transition to Adulthood," *Journal of Marriage and Family* 73(2): 414–29.

2. Bill George, *Authentic Leadership* (San Francisco: Jossey-Bass, 2003).

3. Perhaps the French noticed our omission when after their own revolution they based the design of their new government on "liberty, fraternity, and equality." The "fraternity" recognizes the missing "ter."

4. Tamar Lewin, "Financially Set, Grandparents Help Keep Families Afloat, Too," *New York Times*, July 14, 2005.

5. Philip R. Cateora, Mary C. Gilly, and John L. Graham, *International Marketing*, 16th ed. (New York: McGraw-Hill, 2013), 111–12.

6. Richard E. Nisbett, *The Geography of Thought: How Asians and Westerners Think Differently . . . and Why* (New York: Free Press, 2003).

7. Adam Smith, *The Wealth of Nations*, bk. 4 (1776; New York: Modern Library, 1994), 485.

8. Lyrics of "Little Boxes," words and music by Malvina Reynolds. © 1926 Schroder Music Co. (ASCAP), renewed 1990. Used with permission.

9. Edward T. Hall, *The Silent Language* (New York: Anchor Books, 1981), 179.

10. Ibid., 163–65.

11. Edward T. Hall, "The Silent Language of Overseas Business," *Harvard Business Review* (May–June 1960): 92–96.

12. Paul and Ann Ehrlich, *One with Nineveh: Politics, Consumption, and the Human Future* (Washington, DC: Shearwater Books, 2004), 109.

13. Kathy Chen, "China's Growth Places Strains on a Family's Ties," *Wall Street Journal*, April 13, 2005, A1.

Chapter 13: Financial and Legal Considerations

1. Ralph Warner, *Get a Life*, 3rd ed. (Berkeley, CA: Nolo, 2000), 76.

2. Judy Richter, "A Full Table," *San Francisco Chronicle*, September 10, 2005, sec. F.

3. See LegalZoom.com's guide to setting up a family limited partnership at www.legalzoom.com/lp-guide/form-family-limited-partnership.html.

4. Rachel Emma Silverman, "Who Will Mind Mom? Check Her Contract," *Wall Street Journal*, September 7, 2006, D1–2.

Chapter 14: Making Agreements for Living Together

1. Ron Huxley, "Steps to Running a Family Meeting," *Parenting Toolbox*, June 26, 2004, http://parentingtoolbox.com.

2. See Kimberly K. Money and R. Bruce Money, *Creating a Functional Family in a Dysfunctional World* (Dallas: Taylor, 1999), 169.

3. Gail Hand, "The Joys and Pitfalls of Inter-generational Living: One Family's Success Story with Building an In-Law Addition," June 12, 2004, www.the-homestore .com/about-us/in-the-news/aarp-joys/.

4. Ibid.

5. Ibid.

6. Susan Miller, www.islandparent.ca.

7. Huxley, "Steps to Running a Family Meeting."

8. See George L. Maddox, ed., *The Encyclopedia of Aging* (New York: Singer, 1987), 248.

Resources

Please see www.allinthefamilybook.us for the latest information on multi-generational family living.

We have mentioned a number of resources in our book related to elder care, family communication, household aids/products and organizations for seniors, remodeling, and other helpful contact ideas. Following is a list of these categorized alphabetically by the need they fill or the service they perform.

Elder Care

Baby Boomer's Guide to Caring for Your Aging Parents by Gene B. Williams, Patie Kay, and David Williams. Lanham, MD: Taylor, 2005.
Caring for Your Parents: The Complete AARP Guide by Hugh Delehanty and Elinor Ginzler. New York: Sterling, 2005.
Family Caregiver Alliance: www.caregiver.org.
How to Care for Aging Parents by Virginia Morris. New York: Workman, 1996.
National Alliance for Caregiving: www.caregiving.org.
National Family Caregivers Association: www.thefamilycaregiver.org.
Tax deductions and other government assistance for elderly care and dependence: call (800) 829-1040 or go to www.irs.gov.

Family Communication

Another Country: Navigating the Emotional Terrain of Our Elders by Mary Pipher. New York: Riverhead, 1999.
Generations: The History of America's Future, 1584–2069 by William Strauss and Neil Howe. New York: Quill, 1991.

Household Aids/Products for Seniors

Bruno Stairlifts: (800) 462-0664, operator #10, or go to www.bruno.com.
First Street: To order a catalog with "helpful innovations for baby boomers and beyond," call (800) 704-1210 or go to www.firststreetonline.com.

Flexible Beds:

- Flex-A-Bed: (800) 787-1337 or go to www.flexabed.com.
- Sleep Comfort: (800) 675-5231 or go to www.sleep-comfort.com.
- Joerns Ultracare 770 Bed (adjustable height bed): (800) 826-0270 or go to www.joerns.com.

Grab Bars:

- For information, go to the AARP website at www.aarp.org.
- Port-A-Bar portable grab bar: (800) 542-5076 or go to www.grabitonline.com.

Lift Chairs: For information, go to the Pride Mobility Products website at www.pride mobility.com.

Medical Alarms: For a free brochure about the Life Alert alarm, call (800) 404-5474.

Medication Reminders: For information about the E-pill Medication Reminder, go to www.epill.com/ind.html.

Power Magnification: For information, call Video Eye at (800) 909-4948 or go to www.videoeye.com.

Sinks: For information about adjustable sinks, go to www.ad-as.com.

Toilet Seats: For information about the Guardian model #30270 elevated toilet seat with handles, go to www.qualitymedicalsupplies.com.

Walk-in Tubs: For information, call Premier Bathrooms at (888) 777-2209 or go to www.premier-bathrooms.com.

Organizations for Seniors

American Association of Retired Persons (AARP): www.aarp.org.

American Bar Association Commission on Law and Aging: www.abanet.org/aging.

Elder Cottage Housing Opportunity (ECHO): To find out if there is a program in your area, contact your local HUD (Housing and Urban Development) office.

Generations United (a national organization focused on promoting intergenerational strategies, programs, and policies): www.gu.org.

National Academy of Elder Law Attorneys: www.naela.com.

Remodeling

Certified Aging-in-Place Specialists (CAPS) is an NAHB training program for remodelers to do the kinds of home modifications homeowners require as they grow older in their homes: www.nahb.org.

Creating an Accessory Apartment by Patrick H. Hare and Jolene N. Ostler. New York: McGraw-Hill, 1987.

Directory of Accessible Building Products by National Association of Home Builders (NAHB): (800) 638-8556 or go to www.nahbrc.org/bookstore and click on "Seniors' Housing."

Green Building: For information about using environmentally responsible products when remodeling, call the Green Resource.

Harrell Remodeling: For information about remodeling with certified-green building professionals, call (650) 230-9000 or go to www.harrell-remodeling.com.

Home and Garden Television (HGTV): Lists 21,000 house plans you can explore, including 26 for accessory units and 615 for duplex units. For details, go to www.hgtvpro.com.

Lind Interiors: Deborah Lind, ASID, has two creative examples of granny flat additions to single-family homes. For details, go to www.lindinteriors.com.

Roll-Out Shelves: Call (415) 681-1655 or go to www.rolloutshelves.com.

Other

Therese M. Maloney, Ph.D.
Clinical Psychology (PSY 16981)
1617 Westcliff Drive, #105
Newport Beach, CA 92660
(949) 640-9144
tmaloney@mednet.ucla.edu

R. Thomas Peterson
Attorney at Law
2424 S.E. Bristol Street, Suite 300
Newport Beach, CA 92660-0757
(714) 662-7740

Visit the website for our book: www.allinthefamilybook.us.

Index

Italicized page numbers locate tables and illustrations.

About the Authors

Sharon Graham Niederhaus understands well the dynamics involved in living in extended family situations. She completed her master's thesis at Stanford University on multigenerational living arrangements. Sharon holds a Master of Liberal Arts degree from Stanford and a Bachelors degree in Sociology/Anthropology from Mills College. A credentialed teacher and former director of partnerships in education, she has written numerous articles in educational journals.

John L. Graham also has a deep understanding of multigenerational living through his work with a variety of cultures and their practices. A professor emeritus of Marketing and International Business in the Merage Business School at the University of California in Irvine and a UC Berkeley PhD, John has written for the *New York Times, Los Angeles Times, USAToday, Christian Science Monitor, Harvard Business Review*, and several other publications.